CATECHISM LESSONS
Pupil's Book

A Course of Instructions
in Luther's Small Catechism

Adolph F. Fehlauer

1981

Scripture quotations are from
the HOLY BIBLE New International Version
Copyright © 1978, New York International Bible Society
Used by permission.

Published by the Board for Parish Education, Wisconsin Ev. Lutheran Synod

Copyright 1981 by the Board for Parish Education, Wisconsin Ev. Lutheran Synod, Milwaukee, Wisconsin

ISBN 0-938272-09-8

INTRODUCTION TO CATECHISM LESSONS

Dear student of God's Word:

The lessons in this book have been prepared to help you study the Bible, the most important book in the world. God Himself speaks to us in the Bible. It is God's Word, and everything God tells us is the truth.

In the Bible God tells us very important things about Himself, about the world, and about ourselves. What He says is most important and necessary for our life on earth and for our eternal salvation.

Dr. Martin Luther believed that all people, also children, should know well what God has to say to them in His Word. In 1529 Luther published a book of questions and answers about the main teachings of the Bible. This book is called Dr. Martin Luther's Small Catechism.

Your book, *Catechism Lessons*, consists of 132 Bible study lessons based on Luther's Small Catechism. In these lessons you and your classmates will study God's Word in order to learn important truths that God has revealed to us in His Word.

The book is divided into two parts. Part One contains the text of Luther's Small Catechism and the Bible passages that you and your classmates will study. Part Two has questions and answers on the lessons that were taught you by your teacher together with Bible passages used in the lessons. Your teacher will make assignments from this section of your book.

It is our prayer that God the Holy Spirit will bless your study of God's Word. May He bless you with a better and fuller understanding of God's Word, with a growing faith in Jesus Christ your Savior, with greater assurance of eternal life in heaven, and with a sincere desire to serve Him in your daily living.

Adolph Fehlauer

CONTENTS

                                                                    Page No.

Introduction to *Catechism Lessons*   3

PART ONE

Catechism Text and Bible Passages   9

PART TWO
Course One

Introduction

  1. The Holy Bible 59
  2. The Two Great Teachings of the Bible 61
  3. Luther's Catechism 63

The Ten Commandments

  4. Our Fear of God 65
  5. Our Love of God 67
  6. Our Trust in God 69
  7. God's Name 70
  8. Misuse of God's Name 72
  9. Misuse of God's Name 74
10. Right Use of God's Name 75
11. The Sabbath Day 77
12. God's Word 79
13. God's Word 81
14. Review and Study Guide for Lessons 1 - 13 83
15. God's Representatives 85
16. Dishonoring God's Representatives 87
17. Honoring God's Representatives 89
18. Our Neighbor 91
19. Our and Our Neighbor's Life 92
20. Our Neighbor's Welfare 94
21. Marriage 95
22. Sins of Adultery 97
23. A Pure and Decent Life 99
24. Property and Business 101
25. Stealing Money and Goods 103
26. Helping Our Neighbor 105

27.	False Witness	107
28.	Harming Our Neighbor's Name and Reputation	108
29.	Helping Our Neighbor Keep His Good Name and Reputation	110
30.	Sinful Desires of the Heart	112
31.	God-Pleasing Desires of the Heart	114
32.	Review and Study Guide for Lessons 15 - 31	116
33.	God's Warning	118
34.	God's Promise	120
35.	The Three Uses of the Law	122

The Apostles' Creed

36.	God the Creator	124
37.	The Goodness of God	126
38.	Our Appreciation of God's Goodness	128
39.	The Person of Jesus Christ	130
40.	The Threefold Office of Christ	132
41.	The Work of Christ	134
42.	Our Redemption	136
43.	Jesus' Exaltation	138
44.	The Purpose of Our Redemption	140
45.	The Holy Spirit	143
46.	The Work of the Holy Spirit	145
47.	The Holy Christian Church	147
48.	Recognizing the True Visible Church	149
49.	The Forgiveness of Sins	151
50.	Good Works	153
51.	The Resurrection of the Body and Life Everlasting	155
52.	Review and Study Guide for Lessons 33 - 51	157

The Sacrament of Holy Baptism

53.	The Nature of Baptism	160
54.	The Blessings of Baptism	162
55.	The Power of Baptism	164
56.	The Meaning of Baptism	166

The Use of the Keys and Confession

57.	The Keys of the Kingdom of Heaven	169
58.	The Uses of the Keys of the Kingdom of Heaven	171
59.	The Called Ministers of the Gospel	173
60.	Confession	176

The Sacrament of Holy Communion and the Means of Grace

61.	The Meaning of the Sacrament of Holy Communion	179

62.	The Blessings of Holy Communion	181
63.	The Power of Holy Communion	183
64.	Preparation for Holy Communion	185
65.	The Means of Grace	187
66.	Review and Study Guide for Lessons 53 - 65	189

Course Two

1.	The Bible and the Catechism	195

The First Article of the Creed

2.	The Only True God	197
3.	The Knowledge of God	199
4.	Faith in God	201
5.	God the Father Almighty	203
6.	The Creation	205
7.	The Creation of Man	207
8.	God, the Preserver	209
9.	God's Goodness and Mercy	211
10.	Our Appreciation of God's Goodness and Mercy	213
11.	Review and Study Guide for Lessons 1 - 10	215

The Second Article of the Creed

12.	Jesus Christ, True God	217
13.	Jesus Christ, True Man	219
14.	The Two Natures of Christ	221
15.	Jesus Christ, Our High Priest	223
16.	Jesus Christ, Our Prophet	225
17.	Jesus Christ, Our King	227
18.	Lost and Condemned Sinners	229
19.	Christ, Our Redeemer	232
20.	The Cost of Our Redemption	234
21.	The Resurrection of Jesus	236
22.	Christ's Ascension and Rule	238
23.	The Second Coming of Christ	240
24.	Review and Study Guide for Lessons 12 - 23	242

The Third Article of the Creed

25.	The Person of the Holy Spirit	244
26.	The Call of the Holy Spirit	246
27.	Enlightening by the Holy Spirit	248
28.	The Gift of Forgiveness	250
29.	Sanctification by the Holy Spirit	252

30.	Preservation in the Faith	254
31.	The Communion of Saints	256
32.	The True Visible Church	259
33.	Review and Study Guide for Lessons 25 - 32	261

The Ten Commandments

34.	Law and Gospel	263
35.	The Lord Your God	265
36.	The Name of Your God	267
37.	The Sabbath of Your God	269
38.	The Representatives of Your God	271
39.	The Kindness Your God Demands	273
40.	The Purity Your God Demands	275
41.	The Gift of Your God	277
42.	The Truth of Your God	279
43.	The Holy Heart Your God Demands	281
44.	The Zeal of Your God	283
45.	Review and Study Guide for Lessons 34 - 44	285

The Lord's Prayer

46.	The Meaning of Prayer	287
47.	The Reasons for Prayer	289
48.	The Place and Time for Prayer	290
49.	God-Pleasing Prayer	293
50.	The Name of God	295
51.	The First Petition	296
52.	The Kingdom of God	298
53.	The Second Petition	300
54.	The Will of God	302
55.	The Third Petition	304
56.	Review and Study Guide for Lessons 46 - 55	307
57.	Our Daily Bread	309
58.	The Fourth Petition	311
59.	Our Trespasses	313
60.	The Fifth Petition	315
61.	Our Temptations	317
62.	The Sixth Petition	319
63.	Evils of this World	321
64.	The Seventh Petition	323
65.	The Doxology	325
66.	Review and Study Guide for Lessons 57 - 65	327

Symbols of the Church 329

Biography of Martin Luther 333

PART ONE

INTRODUCTION

(Lessons 1, 2, 3 of COURSE ONE and lessons 1 and 34 of COURSE TWO)

Leviticus
1) 19:2 — Be holy because I, the Lord your God, am holy.

Deuteronomy
2) 6:4 — The Lord our God, the Lord is one.

Psalms
3) 19:1 — The heavens declare the glory of God; the skies proclaim the work of his hands.
4) 90:2 — Before the mountains were born or you brought forth the earth and the world, from everlasting to everlasting you are God.
5) 96:5 — All the gods of the nations are idols, but the Lord made the heavens.

Matthew
6) 22:37,39 — Love the Lord your God with all your heart and with all your soul and with all your mind. Love your neighbor as yourself.
7) 28:19 — Go and make disciples of all nations, baptizing them in the name of the Father and of the Son and of the Holy Spirit.

Luke
8) 2:10,11 — The angel said to them, "Do not be afraid. I bring you good news of great joy that will be for all the people. Today in the town of David a Savior has been born to you; he is Christ the Lord."
9) 11:28 — Blessed . . . are those who hear the word of God and obey it.

John
10) 1:17 — The law was given through Moses; grace and truth came through Jesus Christ.
11) 3:16 — God so loved the world that he gave his one and only Son, that whoever believes in him shall not perish but have eternal life.

12) 5:39 — You diligently study the Scriptures because you think that by them you possess eternal life. These are the Scriptures that testify about me.
13) 17:3 — This is eternal life: that they may know you, the only true God, and Jesus Christ, whom you have sent.
14) 17:17 — Sanctify them by the truth; your word is truth.
15) 20:31 — These are written that you may believe that Jesus is the **Christ, the Son of God.**

Ephesians
16) 6:4 — Fathers, do not exasperate your children; instead, bring them up in the training and instruction of the Lord.

Colossians
17) 3:16 — Let the word of Christ dwell in you richly.
18) 3:16 — Let the word of Christ dwell in you richly as you teach and admonish one another with all wisdom, and as you sing psalms, hymns and spiritual songs with gratitude in your hearts to God.

2 Timothy
19) 3:15 — From infancy you have known the holy Scriptures, which are able to make you wise for salvation through faith in Christ Jesus.
20) 3:16 — All Scripture is God-breathed.
21) 3:16 — All Scripture is God-breathed and is useful for teaching, rebuking, correcting and training in righteousness.

Hebrews
22) 3:4 — Every house is built by someone, but God is the builder of everything.

1 Peter
23) 2:2 — Like newborn babies, crave pure spiritual milk, so that by it you may grow up in your salvation.

2 Peter
24) 1:21 — Men spoke from God as they were carried along by the Holy Spirit.

1 John
25) 3:4 — Everyone who sins breaks the law; in fact, sin is lawlessness.
26) 5:3 — This is love for God: to obey his commands. And his commands are not burdensome.

THE TEN COMMANDMENTS

(Lessons 4 - 13 of COURSE ONE and lessons 35 - 37 of COURSE TWO)

THE FIRST COMMANDMENT
You shall have no other gods.

What does this mean?
We should fear, love and trust in God above all things.

WORD MEANING
To fear — to respect
To love — to hold dear
To trust — to believe in and to depend on

THE SECOND COMMANDMENT
You shall not misuse the name of the Lord your God.

What does this mean?
We should fear and love God that we do not use his name to curse, swear, lie or deceive, or use it superstitiously, but call upon God's name in every trouble, pray, praise and give thanks.

WORD MEANING
To deceive by God's name — to pretend to be a Christian, to be a hypocrite
To lie by God's name — to teach false doctrines and then to tell people that those doctrines are correct according to the Bible
To misuse — to use carelessly
To swear — to take an oath
To use God's name superstitiously — to put our trust in things that remind us of God or His Word

THE THIRD COMMANDMENT
Remember the Sabbath day by keeping it holy.

What does this mean?
We should fear and love God that we do not despise preach-

ing and his Word, but regard it as holy, and gladly hear and learn it.

WORD MEANING
To despise — to regard as worthless
To regard as holy — to accept as the holy Word of God
Sabbath — rest

BIBLE PASSAGES
Genesis
27) 39:9 — How then could I do such a wicked thing and sin against God?

Exodus
28) 20:7 — The Lord will not hold anyone guiltless who misuses his name.
29) 20:24 — Wherever I cause my name to be honored, I will come to you and bless you.

Leviticus
30) 19:12 — Do not swear falsely by my name.

Psalms
31) 33:8 — Let all the earth fear the Lord; let all the people of the world revere him.
32) 37:5 — Commit your way to the Lord; trust in him and he will do this.
33) 50:15 — Call upon me in the day of trouble; I will deliver you, and you will honor me.
34) 103:13 — As a father has compassion on his children, so the Lord has compassion on those who fear him.
35) 118:1 — Give thanks to the Lord, for he is good; his love endures forever.
36) 118:8 — It is better to take refuge in the Lord than to trust in man.
37) 122:1 — I rejoiced with those who said to me, "Let us go to the house of the Lord."

Proverbs
38) 3:5 — Trust in the Lord with all your heart and lean not on your own understanding.
39) 23:26 — My son, give me your heart and let your eyes keep to my ways.

Ecclesiastes
40) 5:1 — Guard your steps when you go to the house of God. Go near to listen rather than to offer the sacrifice of fools.
41) 12:1 — Remember your Creator in the days of your youth.

Isaiah
42) 42:8 — I am the Lord; that is my name! I will not give my glory to another or my praise to idols.
43) 43:21 — The people I formed for myself that they may proclaim my praise.

Matthew
44) 1:21 — She will give birth to a son, and you are to give him the name Jesus, because he will save his people from their sins.
45) 4:10 — Worship the Lord your God, and serve him only.
46) 5:37 — Simply let your 'Yes' be 'Yes,' and your 'No,' 'No'; anything beyond this comes from the evil one.
47) 7:15 — Watch out for false prophets.
48) 10:37 — Anyone who loves his father or mother more than me is not worthy of me; anyone who loves his son or daughter more than me is not worthy of me.
49) 11:28 — Come to me, all you who are weary and burdened, and I will give you rest.
50) 12:8 — The Son of Man is Lord of the Sabbath.
51) 15:8 — These people honor me with their lips, but their hearts are far from me.
52) 15:9 — They worship me in vain; their teachings are but rules taught by men.
53) 22:37 — Love the Lord your God with all your heart and with all your soul and with all your mind.

Luke
54) 10:16 — He who listens to you listens to me; he who rejects you rejects me; but he who rejects me rejects him who sent me.
55) 11:28 — Blessed . . . are those who hear the word of God and obey it.

John
56) 8:47 — He who belongs to God hears what God says. The reason you do not hear is that you do not belong to God.

Colossians
57) 2:16,17 — Do not let anyone judge you by what you eat or drink, or with regard to a religious festival, a New Moon celebration or a Sabbath day. These are a shadow of the things that were to come; the reality, however, is found in Christ.
58) 3:16 — Let the word of Christ dwell in you richly.

1 Thessalonians
59) 2:13 — When you received the word of God, which you heard from us, you accepted it not as the word of men, but as it actually is, the word of God.
60) 5:17 — Pray continually.

James
61) 1:17 — Every good and perfect gift is from above, coming down from the Father of the heavenly lights.
62) 1:22 — Do not merely listen to the word, and so deceive yourselves. Do what it says.
63) 3:10 — Out of the same mouth come praise and cursing. My brothers, this should not be.

1 John
64) 2:15 — Do not love the world or anything in the world. If anyone loves the world, the love of the Father is not in him.
65) 4:19 — We love because he first loved us.

(Lessons 15 - 23 of COURSE I and lessons 38 - 40 of COURSE II)

THE FOURTH COMMANDMENT

Honor your father and mother, that it may go well with you, and that you may enjoy long life on the earth.

What does this mean?

We should fear and love God that we do not dishonor or anger our parents and others in authority, but honor, serve and obey them, and give them love and respect.

WORD MEANING

Honor — to look up to and respect, to recognize a person's authority
Dishonor — to disrespect
People in authority — those whom God has placed over us
Serve — do all we can for them

THE FIFTH COMMANDMENT
You shall not murder.

What does this mean?
We should fear and love God that we do not hurt or harm our neighbor in his body, but help and be a friend to him in every bodily need.

WORD MEANING

Be a friend — to be kind, helpful, and friendly
Bodily need — anything needed for the neighbor's health and safety

THE SIXTH COMMANDMENT
You shall not commit adultery.

What does this mean?
We should fear and love God that we lead a pure and decent life in words and actions, and that husband and wife love and honor each other.

WORD MEANING

Adultery — unfaithfulness in marriage
Decent — clean and proper

BIBLE PASSAGES
Genesis
66) 9:6 — Whoever sheds the blood of man, by man shall his blood be shed.

Psalms
67) 31:15 — My times are in your hands.
68) 51:10 — Create in me a pure heart, O God, and renew a steadfast spirit within me.
69) 90:3 — You turn men back to dust, saying, "Return to dust, O sons of men."
70) 119:73 — Your hands made me and formed me.
71) 119:105 — Your word is a lamp to my feet and a light for my path.

Proverbs
72) 30:17 — The eye that mocks a father, that scorns obedience to a mother, will be pecked out by the ravens of the valley, will be eaten by the vultures.

Isaiah
73) 58:7 — Share your food with the hungry and ... provide the poor wanderer with shelter — when you see the naked ... clothe him.

Malachi
74) 2:10 — Have we not all one Father? Did not one God create us?

Matthew
75) 5:8 — Blessed are the pure in heart, for they will see God.
76) 5:28 — Anyone who looks at a woman lustfully has already committed adultery with her in his heart.
77) 5:44 — Love your enemies and pray for those who persecute you.
78) 19:6 — What God has joined together, let man not separate.
79) 22:39 — Love your neighbor as yourself.
80) 26:41 — Watch and pray so that you will not fall into temptation.

Mark
81) 10:6-8 — At the beginning of creation God made them male and female. For this reason a man will leave his father and mother and be united to his wife, and the two will become one flesh.

Acts
82) 5:29 — We must obey God rather than men!
83) 17:26 — From one man he made every nation of men, that they should inhabit the whole earth.

Romans
84) 12:20 — If your enemy is hungry, feed him; if he is thirsty, give him something to drink.
85) 13:1 — Everyone must submit himself to the governing authorities, for there is no authority except that which God has established.
86) 13:2 — He who rebels against the authority is rebelling against what God has instituted, and those who do so will bring judgment on themselves.
87) 13:4 — He is God's servant to do you good.

Galatians
88) 5:16 — Live by the Spirit, and you will not gratify the desires of the sinful nature.
89) 6:10 — As we have opportunity, let us do good to all people, especially to those who belong to the family of believers.

Ephesians
- 90) 4:29 — Do not let any unwholesome talk come out of your mouths.
- 91) 5:12 — It is shameful even to mention what the disobedient do in secret.
- 92) 5:22 — Wives, submit to your husbands as to the Lord.
- 93) 5:25 — Husbands, love your wives, just as Christ loved the church and gave himself up for her.
- 94) 6:1 — Children, obey your parents in the Lord, for this is right.
- 95) 6:2,3 — Honor your father and mother — which is the first commandment with a promise — that it may go well with you and that you may enjoy long life on the earth.

Colossians
- 96) 3:20 — Children, obey your parents in everything, for this pleases the Lord.

1 Thessalonians
- 97) 5:12,13 — Now we ask you, brothers, to respect those who work hard among you, who are over you in the Lord and who admonish you. Hold them in the highest regard in love because of their work.

1 Timothy
- 98) 5:4 — Children or grandchildren . . . should learn first of all to put their religion into practice by caring for their own family and so repaying their parents and grandparents.

2 Timothy
- 99) 2:22 — Flee the evil desires of youth.

Hebrews
- 100) 13:4 — Marriage should be honored by all, and the marriage bed kept pure, for God will judge the adulterer and all the sexually immoral.
- 101) 13:16 — Do not forget to do good and to share with others, for with such sacrifices God is pleased.

1 John
- 102) 3:15 — Anyone who hates his brother is a murderer.

(Lessons 24 - 35 of COURSE I and lessons 41 - 44 of COURSE II)

THE SEVENTH COMMANDMENT
You shall not steal.

What does this mean?
We should fear and love God that we do not take our neighbor's money or property or get it by dishonest dealing, but help him to improve and protect his property and business.

WORD MEANING

Business — the means by which someone makes a living
Dishonest dealing — dishonest buying, selling or trading
Property — that which rightfully belongs to someone

THE EIGHTH COMMANDMENT
You shall not give false testimony against your neighbor.

What does this mean?
We should fear and love God that we do not tell lies about our neighbor, betray him or give him a bad name, but defend him, speak well of him and take his words and actions in the kindest possible way.

WORD MEANING

False — deceitful, evil
Testimony — anything spoken or written
To betray — to reveal secrets and confidential things

THE NINTH COMMANDMENT
You shall not covet your neighbor's house.

What does this mean?
We should fear and love God that we do not scheme to get our neighbor's inheritance or house or obtain it by false claims, but do all we can to help him keep it.

WORD MEANING

To covet — in the Ninth and Tenth Commandments it means a sinful desire for something God does not want us to have

Inheritance — property and goods received upon the death of a relative or someone else

To obtain by false claims — to get something in a way which seems right but isn't right

THE TENTH COMMANDMENT

You shall not covet your neighbor's wife or his workers or his animals or anything that belongs to your neighbor.

What does this mean?

We should fear and love God that we do not force or entice away from our neighbor his wife, workers or animals, but urge them to stay and do their duty.

WORD MEANING

To entice — to turn someone against another person or to win someone away from another person

THE CONCLUSION

What does God say about all these commandments?

He says, "I, the Lord your God, am a jealous God punishing the children for the sin of the fathers to the third and fourth generation of those who hate me, but showing love to thousands who love me and keep my commandments."

What does this mean?

God threatens to punish all who transgress these commandments. Therefore we should fear his anger and not disobey what he commands. But he promises grace and every blessing to all who keep these commandments. Therefore we should love and trust in him, and gladly obey what he commands.

WORD MEANING

Generation — lifetime of people born in the same period of time
Grace — free and undeserved gifts of love from God
Jealous — God demands complete obedience and all glory for himself
Keep — obey
Transgress — to break the law
Unto thousands — untold number

BIBLE PASSAGES
Genesis
103) 8:21 — Every inclination of his [man's] heart is evil from childhood.
104) 32:10 — I am unworthy of all the kindness and faithfulness you have shown your servant.

Leviticus
105) 19:35 — Do not use dishonest standards when measuring length, weight or quantity.

Deuteronomy
106) 7:11 — Take care to follow the commands, decrees and laws I give you today.
107) 27:26 — Cursed is the man who does not uphold the words of this law by carrying them out.

Psalms
108) 37:4 — Delight yourself in the Lord.
109) 37:21 — The wicked borrow and do not repay.
110) 40:8 — To do your will, O my God, is my desire.
111) 112:1 — Blessed is the man who fears the Lord, who finds great delight in his commands.
112) 119:120 — My flesh trembles in fear of you; I stand in awe of your laws.

Proverbs
113) 11:13 — A gossip betrays a confidence, but a trustworthy man keeps a secret.
114) 19:5 — A false witness will not go unpunished, and he who pours out lies will not go free.
115) 19:17 — He who is kind to the poor lends to the Lord.
116) 31:8 — Speak up for those who cannot speak for themselves, for the rights of all who are destitute.
117) 31:8,9 — Speak up for those who cannot speak for themselves, for the rights of all who are destitute. Speak up and judge fairly; defend the rights of the poor and needy.
118) 31:9 — Speak up and judge fairly; defend the rights of the poor and needy.

Isaiah
119) 5:8 — Woe to you who add house to house and join field to field till no space is left.

Matthew
120) 5:42 — Give to the one who asks you, and do not turn away from the one who wants to borrow from you.
121) 5:48 — Be perfect . . . as your heavenly Father is perfect.
122) 15:19 — Out of the heart come evil thoughts, murder, adultery, sexual immorality, theft, false testimony, slander.

Mark
123) 12:38-40 — Teachers of the law . . . like to . . . have the most important seats in the synagogues. . . . They devour widows' houses and for a show make lengthy prayers. Such men will be punished most severely.

Luke
124) 1:50 — His mercy extends to those who fear him, from generation to generation.

Romans
125) 3:20 — Through the law we become conscious of sin.
126) 3:23 — All have sinned and fall short of the glory of God.
127) 6:23 — The wages of sin is death.
128) 7:7 — I would not have known what sin was except through the law. For I would not have known what it was to covet if the law had not said, "Do not covet."

1 Corinthians
129) 13:4,5 — Love . . . is not self-seeking.

Galatians
130) 3:24 — The law was put in charge to lead us to Christ that we might be justified by faith.
131) 5:13 — Serve one another in love.
132) 6:6 — Anyone who receives instruction in the word must share all good things with his instructor.

Ephesians
133) 4:28 — He who has been stealing must steal no longer, but must work, doing something useful with his own hands.

Philippians
134) 2:4 — Each of you should look not only to your own interests, but also to the interests of others.

1 Timothy
135) 5:8 — If anyone does not provide for his relatives, and especially for his immediate family, he has denied the faith and is worse than an unbeliever.

James
136) 1:14,15 — Each one is tempted when, by his own evil desire, he is dragged away and enticed. Then, after desire has conceived, it gives birth to sin; and sin, when it is full-grown, gives birth to death.
137) 1:17 — Every good and perfect gift is from above, coming down from the Father of the heavenly lights.
138) 4:11 — Do not slander one another.
139) 4:12 — There is only one Lawgiver and Judge, the one who is able to save and destroy.

1 Peter
140) 4:8 — Love covers over a multitude of sins.

1 John
141) 3:17 — If anyone has material possessions and sees his brother in need but has no pity on him, how can the love of God be in him?
142) 5:3 — This is love for God: to obey his commands.

THE CREED
(Lessons 36 - 38 of COURSE I and lessons 2 - 10 of COURSE II)

THE FIRST ARTICLE
(Of Creation)

I believe in God the Father Almighty, Maker of heaven and earth.

What does this mean?

I believe that God made me and every creature and that he gave me my body and soul, eyes, ears and all my members, my mind and all my abilities.

And I believe that God still preserves me by richly and daily providing clothing and shoes, food and drink, house and home, wife and children, land, cattle and all I own, and all that I need to keep my body and life, and by defending me against all danger and guarding and protecting me from all evil.

All this God does only because he is my good and merciful Father in heaven, and not because I have earned or deserved it.

For all this I ought to thank and praise, to serve and obey him.

This is most certainly true.

WORD MEANING
Creature — any created being
Preserve — to keep alive

BIBLE PASSAGES
Genesis
143) 1:1 — In the beginning God created the heavens and the earth.
144) 1:31 — God saw all that he had made, and it was very good. And there was evening, and there was morning — the sixth day.
145) 32:10 — I am unworthy of all the kindness and faithfulness you have shown your servant.
146) 45:5 — It was to save lives that God sent me ahead of you.

Exodus
147) 34:6 — The Lord [is] the compassionate and gracious God.

Psalms
148) 2:7 — You are my Son; today I have become your Father.
149) 14:1 — The fool says in his heart, "There is no God."
150) 31:14 — I trust in you, O Lord; I say, "You are my God."
151) 33:4 — The word of the Lord is right and true; he is faithful in all he does.
152) 33:9 — He spoke, and it came to be.
153) 90:2 — Before the mountains were born or you brought forth the earth and the world, from everlasting to everlasting you are God.
154) 91:10 — No harm will befall you, no disaster will come near your tent.
155) 91:11 — He will command his angels concerning you to guard you in all your ways.
156) 100:2 — Serve the Lord with gladness; come before him with joyful songs.
157) 103:2 — Praise the Lord, O my soul, and forget not all his benefits.
158) 103:13 — As a father has compassion on his children, so the Lord

has compassion on those who fear him.
159) 104:14 — He makes grass grow for the cattle, and plants for man to cultivate — bringing forth food from the earth.
160) 112:1 — Blessed is the man who fears the Lord, who finds great delight in his commands.
161) 115:3 — Our God is in heaven; he does whatever pleases him.
162) 116:12 — How can I repay the Lord for all his goodness to me?
163) 118:1 — Give thanks to the Lord, for he is good; his love endures forever.
164) 124:8 — Our help is in the name of the Lord, the Maker of heaven and earth.
165) 127:1 — Unless the Lord builds the house, its builders labor in vain.
166) 136:1 — Give thanks to the Lord, for he is good. His love endures forever.
167) 139:1,2 — O Lord, you have searched me and you know me. You know when I sit and when I rise; you perceive my thoughts from afar.
168) 139:14 — I praise you because I am fearfully and wonderfully made.
169) 145:9 — The Lord is good to all; he has compassion on all he has made.
170) 145:15 — The eyes of all look to you, and you give them their food at the proper time.
171) 145:16 — You open your hand and satisfy the desires of every living thing.

Isaiah
172) 6:3 — Holy, holy, holy is the Lord Almighty.

Jeremiah
173) 23:24 — "Can anyone hide in secret places so that I cannot see him?" declares the Lord. "Do not I fill heaven and earth?" declares the Lord.

Matthew
174) 3:17 — This is my Son, whom I love; with him I am well pleased.
175) 28:19 — Go and make disciples of all nations, baptizing them in the name of the Father and of the Son and of the Holy Spirit.

Luke
176) 1:37 — Nothing is impossible with God.

John
177) 4:24 — God is spirit.
178) 5:23 — All may honor the Son just as they honor the Father.
179) 17:3 — This is eternal life: that they may know you, the only true God, and Jesus Christ, whom you have sent.
180) 17:17 — Your word is truth.
181) 20:17 — I am returning to my Father.

Romans
182) 8:28 — We know that in all things God works for the good of those who love him.
183) 10:17 — Faith comes from hearing the message, and the message is heard through the word of Christ.

1 Corinthians
184) 6:20 — You were bought at a price. Therefore honor God with your body.
185) 8:4 — There is no God but one.

2 Corinthians
186) 5:17 — If anyone is in Christ, he is a new creation.

Galatians
187) 3:26 — You are all sons of God through faith in Christ Jesus.
188) 4:4,5 — When the time had fully come, God sent his Son, born of a woman, born under law, to redeem those under law, that we might receive the full rights of sons.
189) 6:10 — As we have opportunity, let us do good to all people, especially those who belong to the family of believers.

Ephesians
190) 2:3 — We were by nature objects of wrath.
191) 4:22-24 — Put on the new self, created to be like God in true righteousness and holiness.

Colossians
192) 1:16 — By him all things were created: things in heaven and on earth, visible and invisible.
193) 3:9,10 — You have ... put on the new self, which is being renewed in knowledge in the image of its Creator.

2 Timothy
194) 3:16 — All Scripture is God-breathed and is useful for teaching, rebuking, correcting and training in righteousness.

Hebrews
195) 11:3 — By faith we understand that the universe was formed at God's command.

1 Peter
196) 5:7 — Cast all your anxiety on him because he cares for you.

(Lessons 39 - 44 of COURSE I and lessons 12 - 23 of COURSE TWO)

THE SECOND ARTICLE
(Of Redemption)

I believe in Jesus Christ, his only Son, our Lord; who was conceived by the Holy Ghost; born of the Virgin Mary; suffered under Pontius Pilate; was crucified, dead and buried; he descended into hell; the third day he rose again from the dead; he ascended into heaven, and is sitting at the right hand of God the Father Almighty; from thence he shall come to judge the living and the dead.

What does this mean?

I believe that Jesus Christ, true God, begotten of the Father from eternity, and also true man, born of the Virgin Mary, is my Lord.

He has redeemed me, a lost and condemned creature, purchased and won me from all sins, from death and from the power of the devil, not with gold or silver, but with his holy, precious blood and with his innocent suffering and death.

All this he did that I should be his own, and live under him in his kingdom, and serve him in everlasting righteousness, innocence and blessedness, just as he has risen from death and lives and rules eternally.

This is most certainly true.

WORD MEANING
Ascended — went up to heaven
Begotten from eternity — coming from the Father before time
Conceived — became human
Condemned — guilty and sentenced to be punished
Crucified — hung on the cross

Descended — went down
From thence — from that place
Innocent — free from the guilt of sin
Redeemed — paid the price to set all people free
Sitting at the right hand of God the Father — has almighty power
Virgin — a maiden, an unmarried woman

BIBLE PASSAGES

Genesis
197) 3:15 — I will put enmity between you and the woman, and between your offspring and hers; he will crush your head, and you will strike his heel.

Leviticus
198) 19:2 — Be holy because I, the Lord your God, am holy.

Deuteronomy
199) 18:15 — The Lord your God will raise up for you a prophet like me from among your own brothers. You must listen to him.

Psalms
200) 51:5 — Surely I have been a sinner from birth.
201) 73:24 — You guide me with your counsel, and afterward you will take me into glory.

Ecclesiastes
202) 7:20 — There is not a righteous man on earth who does what is right and never sins.

Isaiah
203) 53:3 — He was despised and rejected by men, a man of sorrows, and familiar with suffering
204) 53:5 — He was pierced for our transgressions, he was crushed for our iniquities.
205) 53:6 — We all, like sheep, have gone astray, each of us has turned to his own way.
206) 53:6 — The Lord has laid on him the iniquity of us all.

Jeremiah
207) 23:6 — This is the name by which he will be called: The Lord Our Righteousness.

Ezekiel
208) 18:20 — The soul who sins is the one who will die.

Matthew
209) 5:48 — Be perfect . . . as your heavenly Father is perfect.
210) 9:6 — The Son of Man has authority on earth to forgive sins.
211) 15:19 — Out of the heart come evil thoughts, murder, adultery, sexual immorality, theft, false testimony, slander.
212) 28:18 — All authority in heaven and on earth has been given to me.
213) 28:19 — Go and make disciples of all nations.
214) 28:20 — Surely I will be with you always, to the very end of the age.

Mark
215) 10:45 — The Son of Man did not come to be served, but to serve, and to give his life as a ransom for many.
216) 16:15 — Go into all the world and preach the good news to all creation.
217) 16:16 — Whoever believes and is baptized will be saved, but whoever does not believe will be condemned.

Luke
218) 2:11 — Today in the town of David a Savior has been born to you; he is Christ the Lord.
219) 2:52 — Jesus grew in wisdom and stature, and in favor with God and men.
220) 10:16 — He who listens to you listens to me; he who rejects you rejects me; but he who rejects me rejects him who sent me.
221) 19:10 — The Son of Man came to seek and to save what was lost.

John
222) 1:29 — Look, the Lamb of God, who takes away the sin of the world!
223) 2:19 — Destroy this temple, and I will raise it again in three days.
224) 3:16 — God so loved the world that he gave his one and only Son, that whoever believes in him shall not perish but have eternal life.
225) 5:23 — All may honor the Son just as they honor the Father.
226) 11:25 — I am the resurrection and the life.
227) 11:25,26 — I am the resurrection and the life. He who believes in me will live, even though he dies; and whoever lives and believes in me will never die.
228) 12:48 — That very word which I spoke will condemn him at the last day.
229) 14:2,3 — In my Father's house are many rooms; if it were not so,

I would have told you. I am going there to prepare a place for you. And if I go and prepare a place for you, I will come back and take you to be with me that you also may be where I am.
230) 14:19 — Because I live, you also will live.
231) 17:24 — Father, I want those you have given me to be with me where I am, and to see my glory.
232) 21:17 — Lord, you know all things.

Acts
233) 1:11 — This same Jesus, who has been taken from you into heaven, will come back in the same way you have seen him go into heaven.
234) 2:32 — God has raised this Jesus to life, and we are all witnesses of the fact.
235) 10:42 — He [Jesus of Nazareth] ... is the one whom God appointed as judge of the living and the dead.
236) 20:28 — Be shepherds of the church of God, which he bought with his own blood.

Romans
237) 1:4 — [Jesus] ... was declared with power to be the Son of God by his resurrection from the dead.
238) 3:23 — All have sinned and fall short of the glory of God.
239) 4:25 — He [Jesus our Lord] was delivered over to death for our sins and was raised to life for our justification.
240) 5:12 — Death came to all men, because all sinned.
241) 5:19 — Through the obedience of the one man the many will be made righteous.
242) 6:23 — The wages of sin is death.

1 Corinthians
243) 6:19,20 — You are not your own; you were bought at a price.
244) 15:3 — Christ died for our sins according to the Scriptures.
245) 15:4 — He [Christ] was raised on the third day according to the Scriptures.
246) 15:17 — If Christ has not been raised, your faith is futile; you are still in your sins.

Galatians
247) 3:13 — Christ redeemed us from the curse of the law by becoming a curse for us.
248) 4:4,5 — When the time had fully come, God sent his Son, born of a woman, born under law, to redeem those under law, that we might receive the full rights of sons.

Ephesians
249) 5:2 — Christ loved us and gave himself up for us as a fragrant offering and sacrifice to God.

1 Timothy
250) 2:5 — There is one God and one mediator between God and men, the man Christ Jesus.

2 Timothy
251) 1:10 — Our Savior, Christ Jesus, . . . has destroyed death and has brought life and immortality to light through the gospel.
252) 4:18 — The Lord will rescue me from every evil attack and will bring me safely to his heavenly kingdom. To him be glory for ever and ever.

Titus
253) 2:13 — We wait for the blessed hope — the glorious appearing of our great God and Savior, Jesus Christ.

Hebrews
254) 7:26,27 — Such a high priest meets our need — one who is holy, blameless, pure, set apart from sinners, exalted above the heavens. Unlike the other high priests, he does not need to offer sacrifices day after day, first for his own sins, and then for the sins of the people. He sacrificed for their sins once for all when he offered himself.
255) 13:8 — Jesus Christ is the same yesterday and today and forever.

1 Peter
256) 2:24 — He [Christ] himself bore our sins in his body on the tree, so that we might die to sins and live for righteousness.
257) 3:18,19 — He [Christ] was put to death in the body but made alive by the Spirit, through whom also he went and preached to the spirits in prison.

1 John
258) 1:7 — The blood of Jesus, his Son, purifies us from every sin.
259) 2:1 — If anybody does sin, we have one who speaks to the Father in our defense — Jesus Christ, the Righteous One.
260) 3:8 — The reason the Son of God appeared was to destroy the devil's work.

Revelation
261) 5:9 — You were slain, and with your blood you purchased men for God.

(Lessons 45 - 51 of COURSE I and lessons 25 - 32 of COURSE II)

THE THIRD ARTICLE
(Of Sanctification)

I believe in the Holy Ghost; the holy Christian church, the communion of saints; the forgiveness of sins; the resurrection of the body; and the life everlasting. Amen.

What does this mean?

I believe that I cannot by my own thinking or choosing believe in Jesus Christ, my Lord, or come to him.

But the Holy Ghost has called me by the gospel, enlightened me with his gifts, sanctified and kept me in the true faith. In the same way he calls, gathers, enlightens and sanctifies the whole Christian church on earth, and keeps it with Jesus Christ in the one true faith.

In this Christian church he daily and fully forgives all sins to me and all believers.

On the Last Day he will raise me and all the dead;

And he will give eternal life to me and all believers in Christ.

This is most certainly true.

WORD MEANING

Called me — invited and moved me to become a believer in Christ

Come to him — become a believer in Jesus

Enlightened me with his gifts — has given me power to understand and receive the gifts of faith, comfort, and joy in Christ

Sanctified me — made me holy through faith and gave me strength to do good works

The holy Christian church, the communion of saints — all people who believe in Jesus Christ as their Savior

BIBLE PASSAGES

Psalms

262) 16:11 — You will fill me with joy in your presence, with eternal pleasures at your right hand.
263) 33:6 — By the word of the Lord were the heavens made, their starry host by the breath of his mouth.
264) 51:5 — Surely I have been a sinner from birth.

Ecclesiastes
265) 7:20 — There is not a righteous man on earth who does what is right and never sins.

Isaiah
266) 6:3 — Holy, holy, holy is the Lord Almighty; the whole earth is full of his glory.
267) 59:2 — Your iniquities have separated you from your God.

Ezekiel
268) 18:20 — The soul who sins is the one who will die.

Matthew
269) 11:28 — Come to me, all you who are weary and burdened, and I will give you rest.
270) 15:9 — They worship me in vain; their teachings are but rules taught by men.
271) 16:18 — You are Peter, and on this rock I will build my church, and the gates of Hades [hell] will not overcome it.
272) 28:19 — Go and make disciples of all nations, baptizing them in the name of the Father and of the Son and of the Holy Spirit.
273) 28:19,20 — Go and make disciples of all nations, baptizing them in the name of the Father and of the Son and of the Holy Spirit, and teaching them to obey everything I have commanded you.

Mark
274) 16:16 — Whoever believes and is baptized will be saved, but whoever does not believe will be condemned.

John
275) 1:29 — Look, the Lamb of God, who takes away the sin of the world!
276) 3:16 — God so loved the world that he gave his one and only Son, that whoever believes is him shall not perish but have eternal life.
277) 3:36 — Whoever believes in the Son has eternal life.
278) 5:28,29 — Do not be amazed at this, for a time is coming when all who are in their graves will hear his voice and come out.
279) 8:31,32 — To the Jews who had believed him, Jesus said, "If you hold to my teaching, you are really my disciples. Then you will know the truth, and the truth will set you free."

280) 10:27,28 — My sheep listen to my voice; I know them, and they follow me. I give them eternal life.
281) 14:15 — If you love me, you will obey what I command.
282) 15:5 — I am the vine; you are the branches. If a man remains in me and I in him, he will bear much fruit; apart from me you can do nothing.

Acts
283) 5:3,4 — Peter said, "Ananias, how is it that Satan has so filled your heart that you have lied to the Holy Spirit? . . . You have not lied to men but to God."

Romans
284) 1:16 — I am not ashamed of the gospel, because it is the power of God for the salvation of everyone who believes.
285) 3:23 — All have sinned and fall short of the glory of God.
286) 6:23 — The wages of sin is death.
287) 8:1 — There is . . . no condemnation for those who are in Christ Jesus.

1 Corinthians
288) 2:10 — The Spirit searches all things, even the deep things of God.
289) 2:14 — The man without the Spirit does not accept the things that come from the Spirit of God, for they are foolishness to him.
290) 3:16 — Don't you know that you yourselves are God's temple and that God's Spirit lives in you?
291) 6:11 — You were sanctified, you were justified in the name of the Lord Jesus Christ and by the Spirit of our God.
292) 12:3 — No one can say, "Jesus is Lord," except by the Holy Spirit.

2 Corinthians
293) 4:6 — [God] made his light shine in our hearts to give us the light of the knowledge of the glory of God in the face of Christ.
294) 5:17 — If anyone is in Christ, he is a new creation.
295) 5:21 — God made him [Jesus] who had no sin to be sin for us, so that in him we might become the righteousness of God.

Galatians
296) 5:22,23 — The fruit of the Spirit is love, joy, peace, patience, kindness, goodness, faithfulness, gentleness and self-control.

Ephesians
297) 1:7 — In him [Jesus] we have redemption through his blood, the forgiveness of sins.
298) 2:1 — You were dead in your transgressions and sins.
299) 2:8 — By grace you have been saved, through faith — and this not from yourselves, it is the gift of God.
300) 2:19 — You are . . . fellow citizens with God's people and members of God's household.
301) 5:8 — You were once darkness, but now you are light in the Lord.

Philippians
302) 1:6 — Being confident of this, that he who began a good work in you will carry it on to completion until the day of Christ Jesus.

2 Timothy
303) 2:19 — The Lord knows those who are his.

1 Peter
304) 1:5 — Through faith [you] are shielded by God's power until the coming of the salvation.
305) 2:9 — God . . . called you out of darkness into his wonderful light.

1 John
306) 4:1 — Do not believe every spirit, but test the spirits to see whether they are from God, because many false prophets have gone out into the world.

THE LORD'S PRAYER
(Lessons 46 - 65 of COURSE II)

THE ADDRESS
Our Father who art in heaven.

What does this mean?

With these words God tenderly invites us to believe that he is our true Father and that we are his true children, so that we may pray to him as boldly and confidently as dear children ask their dear father.

WORD MEANING
  Boldly — with courage and certainty
  Confidently — trustingly
  Our Father — the heavenly Father of all believers in Jesus as their Savior
  Tenderly — in a loving way
  The Lord's Prayer — the prayer our Lord Jesus taught us to pray

THE FIRST PETITION
Hallowed be thy name.

What does this mean?
God's name is certainly holy by itself, but we pray in this petition that we too may keep it holy.

How is God's name kept holy?
God's name is kept holy when his Word is taught in its truth and purity, and we as children of God lead holy lives according to it. Help us to do this, dear Father in heaven! But whoever teaches and lives contrary to God's Word dishonors God's name among us. Keep us from doing this, dear Father in heaven!

WORD MEANING
  In its truth and purity — just as stated in the Bible, without error
  Keep holy — to teach and accept by us as holy
  Petition — a prayer of request
  The name of God — all that is known of God in his Word
  To hallow — to keep holy

THE SECOND PETITION
Thy kingdom come.

What does this mean?
God's kingdom certainly comes by itself even without our prayer, but we pray in this petition that it may come to us and to many others.

How does God's kingdom come?
God's kingdom comes when our heavenly Father gives his Holy Spirit, so that by his grace we believe his Holy Word and lead a godly life now on earth and forever in heaven.

WORD MEANING
A godly life — a God-pleasing life, according to God's commandments
By his grace — by God's blessings which we do not deserve
The kingdom of God — God's rule over his believers, the kingdom of grace

THE THIRD PETITION
Thy will be done on earth as it is in heaven.

What does this mean?
God's good and gracious will certainly is done without our prayer, but we pray in this petition that it may be done among us also.

How is God's will done?
God's will is done when he breaks and defeats every evil plan and purpose of the devil, the world and our sinful flesh, which try to prevent us from keeping God's name holy and letting his kingdom come. And God's will is done when he strengthens and keeps us firm in his Word and in the faith as long as we live. This is his good and gracious will.

WORD MEANING
Be done among us — be done in and through us by the power of the Holy Spirit
Evil plan and purpose — anything that opposes God's good and gracious will
God's good and gracious will — God's will to save us, who do not deserve God's mercy
God's will — God's plan or purpose
Our flesh — our sinful desires
To keep firm — to keep faithful to God's Word

BIBLE PASSAGES

Psalms
307) 50:15 — Call upon me in the day of trouble.
308) 50:15 — Call upon me in the day of trouble; I will deliver you, and you will honor me.
309) 95:6 — Come, let us bow down in worship, let us kneel before the Lord our Maker.
310) 103:13 — As a father has compassion on his children, so the Lord has compassion on those who fear him.

311) 106:1 — Give thanks to the Lord, for he is good; his love endures forever.

Ecclesiastes
312) 12:1 — Remember your Creator in the days of your youth.

Jeremiah
313) 23:28 — Let the one who has my word speak it faithfully.

Malachi
314) 1:11 — My name will be great among the nations, from the rising to the setting of the sun.

Matthew
315) 1:21 — She will give birth to a son, and you are to give him the name Jesus, because he will save his people from their sins.
316) 5:16 — Let your light shine before men, that they may see your good deeds and praise your Father in heaven.
317) 7:7 — Ask and it will be given to you; seek and you will find; knock and the door will be opened to you.
318) 7:11 — If you, then, though you are evil, know how to give good gifts to your children, how much more will your Father in heaven give good gifts to those who ask him!
319) 9:38 — Ask the Lord of the harvest . . . to send out workers into his harvest field.
320) 25:34 — The King will say to those on his right, "Come, you who are blessed by my Father; take your inheritance, the kingdom prepared for you since the creation of the world."
321) 28:19 — Go and make disciples of all nations, baptizing them in the name of the Father and of the Son and of the Holy Spirit.

Mark
322) 1:15 — The kingdom of God is near. Repent and believe the good news!

John
323) 6:40 — My Father's will is that everyone who looks to the Son and believes in him shall have eternal life, and I will raise him up at the last day.

Romans
324) 8:7,8 — The sinful mind is hostile to God. . . . Those controlled by the sinful nature cannot please God.

325) 8:28 — We know that in all things God works for the good of those who love him.

1 Corinthians
326) 12:3 — No one can say, "Jesus is Lord," except by the Holy Spirit.

Galatians
327) 3:26 — You are all sons of God through faith in Christ Jesus.
328) 5:22,23 — The fruit of the Spirit is love, joy, peace, patience, kindness, goodness, faithfulness, gentleness and self-control.

Colossians
329) 2:6 — As you received Christ Jesus as Lord, continue to live in him.

1 Thessalonians
330) 4:3 — It is God's will that you should be holy.
331) 5:17 — Pray continually.

1 Timothy
332) 2:3,4 — God our Savior . . . wants all men to be saved and to come to a knowledge of the truth.
333) 2:8 — I want men everywhere to lift up holy hands in prayer.

2 Timothy
334) 4:18 — The Lord will rescue me from every evil attack and will bring me safely to his heavenly kingdom.

Titus
335) 2:13,14 — Our great God and Savior, Jesus Christ, . . . gave himself for us to redeem us from all wickedness and to purify for himself a people that are his very own, eager to do what is good.

Hebrews
336) 4:16 — Let us then approach the throne of grace with confidence, so that we may receive mercy and find grace to help us in our time of need.

James
337) 5:16 — Pray for each other.

1 Peter
338) 1:5 — Through faith [you] are shielded by God's power until the coming of the salvation.

339) 5:8 — Be self-controlled and alert. Your enemy the devil prowls around like a roaring lion looking for someone to devour.

1 John

340) 2:15 — Do not love the world or anything in the world. If anyone loves the world, the love of the Father is not in him.
341) 3:1 — How great is the love the Father has lavished on us, that we should be called children of God!
342) 3:8 — The reason the Son of God appeared was to destroy the devil's work.

(Lessons 57 - 65 of **COURSE II**)

THE FOURTH PETITION

Give us this day our daily bread.

What does this mean?

God surely gives daily bread without our asking, even to all the wicked, but we pray in this petition that he would lead us to realize this and to receive our daily bread with thanksgiving.

What then is meant by daily bread?

Daily bread includes everything that we need for our bodily welfare, such as food and drink, clothing and shoes, house and home, fields and flocks, money and goods, a godly family, good workers, good government, honest leaders, good citizens, good weather, peace and order, health, a good name, loyal friends and good neighbors.

WORD MEANING
Bodily welfare — to keep our body well
Daily bread — all bodily needs
Good name — good reputation
This day — today

THE FIFTH PETITION

And forgive us our trespasses as we forgive those who trespass against us.

What does this mean?

We pray in this petition that our Father in heaven would

not look upon our sins or because of them deny our prayers; for we are worthy of none of the things for which we ask, neither have we deserved them, but we ask that he would give them all to us by grace; for we daily sin much and surely deserve nothing but punishment.
So we too will forgive from the heart and gladly do good to those who sin against us.

WORD MEANING
By grace — undeserved blessings given for Jesus' sake
From the heart — gladly and sincerely
Not look upon — not consider, not hold against us
To deny — to refuse
Tresspasses — sins against God's commandments
Worthy — deserving

THE SIXTH PETITION
And lead us not into temptation.

What does this mean?
God surely tempts no one to sin, but we pray in this petition that God would guard and keep us, so that the devil, the world and our flesh may not deceive us or lead us into false belief, despair and other great and shameful sins; and though we are tempted by them, we pray that we may overcome and win the victory.

WORD MEANING
Despair — without any hope
False belief — untruth
To deceive — to mislead someone by making him believe what is untrue or do what is sinful
To lead into temptation — to try to make someone sin
To win the victory — to overcome the enemies of our soul and remain faithful to God to the end of our lives

THE SEVENTH PETITION
But deliver us from evil.

What does this mean?
In conclusion we pray in this petition that our Father in heaven would deliver us from every evil that threatens body and soul, property and reputation, and finally when

our last hour comes, grant us a blessed end and graciously take us from this world of sorrow to himself in heaven.

WORD MEANING

Blessed end — a death in which God will bless us by taking our souls to heaven
Evil — sin and all the results of sin
Last hour — time of death
To deliver — to free

THE DOXOLOGY

For thine is the kingdom and the power and the glory forever and ever. Amen.

What does this mean?

We can be sure that these petitions are acceptable to our Father in heaven and are heard by him, for he himself has commanded us so to pray and has promised to hear us. Therefore we say, "Amen," yes, it shall be so.

WORD MEANING

Acceptable — pleasing
For — the reason we pray boldly and with confidence
Heard — listened to and answered

BIBLE PASSAGES

Genesis

343) 1:31 — God saw all that he had made, and it was very good.
344) 32:10 — I am unworthy of all the kindness and faithfulness you have shown your servant.

Psalms

345) 34:8 — Taste and see that the Lord is good.
346) 37:25 — I was young and now I am old, yet I have never seen the righteous forsaken or their children begging bread.
347) 46:7 — The Lord Almighty is with us; the God of Jacob is our fortress.
348) 79:9 — Help us, O God our Savior, for the glory of your name.
349) 91:10 — No harm will befall you, no disaster will come near your tent.
350) 106:1 — Give thanks to the Lord, for he is good; his love endures forever.
351) 121:2 — My help comes from the Lord, the Maker of heaven and earth.

Proverbs
352) 1:10 — My son, if sinners entice you, do not give in to them.

Matthew
353) 6:14,15 — If you forgive men when they sin against you, your heavenly Father will also forgive you. But if you do not forgive men their sins, your Father will not forgive your sins.
354) 6:34 — Do not worry about tomorrow, for tomorrow will worry about itself. Each day has enough trouble of its own.
355) 9:4 — Knowing their thoughts, Jesus said, "Why do you entertain evil thoughts in your hearts?"
356) 15:19 — Out of the heart come evil thoughts.
357) 15:19 — Out of the heart come evil thoughts, murder, adultery, sexual immorality, theft, false testimony, slander.

Luke
358) 18:13 — God, have mercy on me, a sinner.

Acts
359) 14:22 — We must go through many hardships to enter the kingdom of God.

Romans
360) 7:18 — I know that nothing good lives in me, that is, in my sinful nature.
361) 8:28 — We know that in all things God works for the good of those who love him.
362) 8:32 — He who did not spare his own Son, but gave him up for us all — how will he not also, along with him, graciously give us all things?

1 Corinthians
363) 10:13 — God is faithful; he will not let you be tempted beyond what you can bear. But when you are tempted, he will also provide a way out so that you can stand up under it.

Galatians
364) 5:17 — The sinful nature desires what is contrary to the Spirit.

Ephesians
365) 6:13 — Put on the full armor of God, so that when the day of evil comes, you may be able to stand your ground.

366) 6:17 — Take the helmet of salvation and the sword of the Spirit, which is the word of God.

2 Thessalonians
367) 3:3 — The Lord is faithful, and he will strengthen and protect you from the evil one.

2 Timothy
368) 4:18 — The Lord will rescue me from every evil attack and will bring me safely to his heavenly kingdom.

James
369) 1:14 — Each one is tempted when, by his own evil desire, he is dragged away and enticed.
370) 1:17 — Every good and perfect gift is from above, coming down from the Father of the heavenly lights.

1 Peter
371) 3:10 — Whoever would love life and see good days must keep his tongue from evil and his lips from deceitful speech.
372) 5:8,9 — Be self-controlled and alert. Your enemy the devil prowls around like a roaring lion looking for someone to devour. Resist him, standing firm in the faith.

1 John
373) 5:19 — The whole world is under the control of the evil one.

Revelation
374) 21:4 — He will wipe every tear from their eyes. There will be no more death or mourning or crying or pain, for the old order of things has passed away.

THE SACRAMENT OF HOLY BAPTISM
(Lessons 53 - 56 of COURSE I)

First: What is baptism?
Baptism is not just plain water, but it is water used by God's command and connected with God's Word.

Which is that Word of God?
Christ our Lord says in the last chapter of Matthew, "Go

and make disciples of all nations, baptizing them in the name of the Father and of the Son and of the Holy Spirit!"

Second: What does baptism do for us?

Baptism works forgiveness of sin, delivers from death and the devil and gives eternal salvation to all who believe this, as the words and promises of God declare.

What is God's promise?

Christ our Lord says in the last chapter of Mark, "Whoever believes and is baptized will be saved, but whoever does not believe will be condemned."

Third: How can water do such great things?

It is certainly not the water that does such things, but God's Word which is in and with the water, and faith which trusts this Word used with the water.

For without God's Word the water is just plain water and not baptism. But with this Word it is baptism. God's Word makes it a washing through which God graciously forgives our sin and grants us rebirth and a new life through the Holy Spirit.

Where is this written?

St. Paul says in Titus, chapter 3, "God saved us through the washing of rebirth and renewal by the Holy Spirit, whom he poured out on us generously through Jesus Christ our Savior, so that, having been justified by his grace, we might become heirs having the hope of eternal life. This is a trustworthy saying."

Fourth: What does baptizing with water mean?

It means that our old Adam with his evil deeds and desires should be drowned by daily contrition and repentance, and die, and that day by day a new man should arise, as from the dead, to live in the presence of God in righteousness and purity now and forever.

Where is this written?

St. Paul says in Romans, chapter 6, "We were buried with Christ through baptism into death in order that, just as Christ was raised from the dead through the glory of the Father, we too may live a new life."

WORD MEANING
A new life — a life pleasing to God
Arise — grow and improve in holiness
Baptism — a sacramental washing by sprinkling or pouring
Buried with Christ — as though we had been buried with Christ in his burial
Connected with God's Word — used together with God's Word
Contrition — Godly sorrow over sin
Generously — in great plenty, not sparingly
Great things — forgiveness of sins, deliverance from death and the devil, and eternal life
Heirs of eternal life — people who inherit eternal life
New man — new spiritual person created by Baptism
Old Adam — our sinful nature that moves us to think and do evil
Sacrament — a holy act or rite instituted by God to give grace and salvation
Should be drowned — should be resisted and overcome

BIBLE PASSAGES

Numbers
375) 6:27 — They will put my name on the Israelites, and I will bless them.

Matthew
376) 28:19 — Go and make disciples of all nations, baptizing them in the name of the Father and of the Son and of the Holy Spirit.

Mark
377) 16:16 — Whoever believes and is baptized will be saved, but whoever does not believe will be condemned.

Acts
378) 2:38 — Repent and be baptized, every one of you, in the name of Jesus Christ so that your sins may be forgiven.

Romans
379) 6:4 — We were . . . buried with him [Christ] through baptism into death.
380) 6:23 — The wages of sin is death.

Galatians
381) 3:27 — All of you who were baptized into Christ have been clothed with Christ.

Ephesians
382) 4:24 — Put on the new self, created to be like God in true righteousness and holiness.
383) 5:25,26 — Christ loved the church and gave himself up for her to make her holy, cleansing her by the washing with water through the word.

Colossians
384) 3:9 — You have taken off your old self with its practices.

THE USE OF THE KEYS AND CONFESSION
(Lessons 57 - 60 of COURSE I)

I. THE KEYS

First: What is the use of the keys?
The use of the keys is that special power and right which Christ gave to his church on earth, to forgive the sins of penitent sinners, but to refuse forgiveness to the impenitent as long as they do not repent.

Where is this written?
The holy Evangelist John writes in chapter 20, "Jesus breathed on his disciples and said, 'Receive the Holy Spirit. If you forgive anyone his sins, they are forgiven; if you do not forgive them, they are not forgiven.'"

Second: How does a Christian congregation use the keys?
A Christian congregation with its called pastor uses the keys in accordance with Christ's command, by forgiving those who repent of their sin and are willing to amend, and by excluding from the congregation those who are plainly impenitent that they may repent. I believe that when it does so this is as valid and certain in heaven also, as if Christ, our dear Lord, dealt with us himself.

Where is this written?
Jesus says in Matthew, chapter 18, "Whatever you bind on earth will be bound in heaven, and whatever you loose on earth will be loosed in heaven."

WORD MEANING

Breathed on his disciples — gave them the Holy Spirit and the Keys of the Kingdom of Heaven

Called pastor — man chosen and called by the congregation to serve it with the gospel

Exclude plainly impenitent sinners — publicly put out of a congregation those who continue in their openly sinful life by refusing to repent

Forgive those who repent — publicly announce that they have forgiveness and are again members of the congregation

Keys — that which locks and unlocks the door to heaven, the gospel in the Word of God and in the Sacraments

Penitent sinners — sinners who repent of their sins, believe in the Savior, and are willing to lead godly lives

Special power and right of the church — the spiritual power Christ gave the church, that is, all believers in him

To amend — to improve

Valid — true, sure

II. CONFESSION

First: What is confession?

Confession has two parts. The one is that we confess our sins; the other, that we receive absolution or forgiveness from the pastor as from God himself, not doubting but firmly believing that our sins are thus forgiven before God in heaven.

Second: What sins should we confess?

Before God we should plead guilty of all sins, even those we are not aware of, as we do in the Lord's Prayer.

But before the pastor we should confess only those sins which we know and feel in our hearts.

Third: How can we recognize these sins?

Consider your place in life according to the Ten Commandments. Are you a father, mother, son, daughter, employer, or employee? Have you been disobedient, unfaithful or lazy? Have you hurt anyone by word or deed? Have you been dishonest, careless, wasteful or done other wrong?

49

Fourth: How will the pastor assure a penitent sinner of his forgiveness?

He will say, "According to the command of our Lord Jesus Christ, I forgive you your sins in the name of the Father and of the Son and of the Holy Spirit. Amen."

WORD MEANING

Absolution — forgiveness of sins
Confess — acknowledge, admit

BIBLE PASSAGES

Psalms
385) 19:12 — Who can discern his errors? Forgive my hidden faults.

Proverbs
386) 13:13 — He who scorns instruction will pay for it.

Matthew
387) 16:19 — I will give you the keys of the kingdom of heaven.
388) 18:18 — Whatever you bind on earth will be bound in heaven, and whatever you loose on earth will be loosed in heaven.
389) 28:18 — All authority in heaven and on earth has been given to me.
390) 28:19 — Go and make disciples of all nations, baptizing them in the name of the Father and of the Son and of the Holy Spirit.

Mark
391) 16:16 — Whoever believes and is baptized will be saved.

Luke
392) 24:47 — Repentance and forgiveness of sins will be preached in his name to all nations.

John
393) 3:36 — Whoever believes in the Son has eternal life.
394) 20:23 — If you forgive anyone his sins, they are forgiven.
395) 20:23 — If you do not forgive them, they are not forgiven.

Romans
396) 3:23 — All have sinned and fall short of the glory of God.

1 Corinthians
397) 4:1 — Men ought to regard us as servants of Christ and as those entrusted with the secret things of God.
398) 5:13 — Expel the wicked man from among you.
399) 14:40 — Everything should be done in a fitting and orderly way.

2 Timothy
400) 1:10 — Our Savior, Christ Jesus, . . . has destroyed death and has brought life and immortality to light through the gospel.

James
401) 5:16 — Confess your sins to each other.

THE SACRAMENT OF HOLY COMMUNION AND THE MEANS OF GRACE

(Lessons 61 - 65 of COURSE I)

First: What is the sacrament of Holy Communion?
It is the true body and blood of our Lord Jesus Christ together with the bread and wine, instituted by Christ for us Christians to eat and to drink.

Where is this written?
The holy Evangelists Matthew, Mark, Luke and the Apostle Paul tell us: The Lord Jesus, on the night he was betrayed, took bread; and when he had given thanks, he broke it, gave it to his disciples and said, "Take and eat. This is my body, which is given for you. Do this in remembrance of me."

In the same way after supper he took the cup, gave thanks, gave it to them and said, "Drink from it, all of you. This cup is the new convenant in my blood, which is poured out for you for the forgiveness of sins. Do this, whenever you drink it, in remembrance of me."

Second: What blessing do we receive through this eating and drinking?
That is shown us by these words, "Given and poured out for you for the forgiveness of sins."

Through these words we receive forgiveness of sins, life and salvation in this sacrament.

For where there is forgiveness of sins, there is also life and salvation.

Third: How can eating and drinking do such great things?

It is certainly not the eating and drinking that does such things, but the words, "Given and poured out for you for the forgiveness of sins."

These words are the main thing in this sacrament, along with the eating and drinking.

And whoever believes these words has what they plainly say, the forgiveness of sins.

Fourth: Who then is properly prepared to receive this sacrament?

Fasting and other outward preparations may serve a good purpose, but he is properly prepared who believes these words, "Given and poured out for you for the forgiveness of sins."

But whoever does not believe these words or doubts them is not prepared, because the words "for you" require nothing but hearts that believe.

WORD MEANING

Cup — wine
Evangelists — writers of the life of Christ
To fast — to eat very little or not at all
New Testament in my blood — new promise of redemption through Jesus' blood
Preparation — act of getting ready
Require — demand

BIBLE PASSAGES

Psalms

402) 119:32 — I run in the path of your commands, for you have set my heart free.

John

403) 3:16 — God so loved the world that he gave his one and only Son, that whoever believes in him shall not perish but have eternal life.

Acts

404) 2:38,39 — Repent and be baptized, every one of you, in the name of Jesus Christ so that your sins may be forgiven. . . . The promise is for you and your children and for all who are far off.

Romans

405) 1:16 — I am not ashamed of the gospel, because it is the power of God for the salvation of everyone who believes.
406) 6:22 — Now that you have been set free from sin and have become slaves to God, the benefit you reap leads to holiness, and the result is eternal life.
407) 10:17 — Faith comes from hearing the message, and the message is heard through the word of Christ.

1 Corinthians

408) 11:27 — Whoever eats the bread or drinks the cup of the Lord in an unworthy manner will be guilty of sinning against the body and blood of the Lord.

Ephesians

409) 1:7 — In him we have redemption through his blood, the forgiveness of sins.

1 John

410) 1:7 — The blood of Jesus, his Son, purifies us from every sin.

DAILY PRAYERS

MORNING PRAYER

In the name of the Father, Son and Holy Spirit. Amen.

My heavenly Father, I thank you through Jesus Christ, your dear Son, for keeping me through the night from all harm and danger. Keep me through this day also from sin and every evil that all my doings and life may please you. I commend my body and soul and all things into your hands. Let your holy angel be with me, so that the devil may have no power over me. Amen.

EVENING PRAYER

In the name of the Father, Son and Holy Spirit. Amen.

My heavenly Father, I thank you through Jesus Christ, your dear Son, for graciously keeping me through this day. Forgive me all the sins that I have done against you, and graciously keep me through this night. I commend my body and soul and all things into your hands. Let your holy angel be with me, so that the devil may have no power over me. Amen.

TO ASK A BLESSING

The eyes of all look to you, O Lord, and you give them their food at the proper time. You open your hand and satisfy the desires of every living thing. Amen.

Lord God, heavenly Father, bless us through these gifts which we receive from your bountiful goodness, through Jesus Christ, our Lord. Amen.

TO SAY GRACE

Give thanks to the Lord, for he is good; his love endures forever. Amen.

Lord God, heavenly Father, we thank you for all your gifts, through Jesus Christ, our Lord. Amen.

TABLE OF DUTIES

PASTORS

A pastor must be above reproach, the husband of but one wife, temperate, self-controlled, respectable, hospitable, able to teach, not given to much wine, not violent but gentle, not quarrelsome, not a lover of money. He must manage his own family well and see that his children obey him with proper respect. He must not be a recent convert. He must hold firmly to the trustworthy message as it has been taught, so that he can encourage others by sound doctrine and refute those who oppose it. (See 1 Timothy 3:2,3,4,6; Titus 1:9.)

WHAT WE OWE TO OUR PASTORS AND TEACHERS

Anyone who receives instruction in the word must share all good things with his instructor. (See Galatians 6:6.)

In the same way, the Lord has commanded that those who preach the gospel should receive their living from the gospel. (See 1 Corinthians 9:14.)

The elders who direct the affairs of the church well are worthy of double honor, especially those whose work is preaching and teaching. For the Scripture says, "The worker deserves his wages." (See 1 Timothy 5:17,18.)

Obey your leaders and submit to their authority. They keep watch over you as men who must give an account. Obey them so that their work will be a joy, not a burden, for that would be of no advantage to you. (See Hebrews 13:17.)

GOVERNMENT

Everyone must submit himself to the governing authorities, for there is no authority except that which God has established. The authorities that exist have been established by God. Consequently, he who rebels against the authority is rebelling against what God has instituted, and those who do so will bring judgment on themselves. For he is God's servant to do you good. But if you do wrong, be afraid, for he does not bear the sword for nothing. He is God's servant, an agent of wrath to bring punishment on the wrongdoer. (See Romans 13:1,2,4.)

HUSBANDS

Husbands, be considerate as you live with your wives, and treat them with respect as the weaker partner and as heirs with you of the gracious gift of life, so that nothing will hinder your prayers. Husbands, love your wives and do not be harsh with them. (See 1 Peter 3:7; Colossians 3:19.)

WIVES

Wives, submit to your husbands as to the Lord, like Sarah, who obeyed Abraham and called him her master. You are her daughters if you do what is right and do not give way to fear. (See Ephesians 5:22; 1 Peter 3:6.)

PARENTS

Fathers, do not exasperate your children; instead, bring them up in the training and instruction of the Lord. Fathers, do not embitter your children, or they will become discouraged. (See Ephesians 6:4; Colossians 3:21.)

CHILDREN

Children, obey your parents in the Lord, for this is right. "Honor your father and mother" — which is the first commandment with a promise — "that it may go well with you and that you may enjoy long life on the earth." (See Ephesians 6:1-3.)

EMPLOYEES

Obey your earthly masters with respect and fear, and with sincerity of heart, just as you would obey Christ. Obey them not only to win their favor when their eye is on you, but like slaves of Christ, doing the will of God from your heart. Serve wholeheartedly, as if you were serving the Lord, not men, because you know that the Lord will reward everyone for whatever good he does. (See Ephesians 6:5-8.)

EMPLOYERS

Treat your employees in the same way. Do not threaten them, since you know that he who is both their Master and yours is in heaven, and there is no favoritism with him. (See Ephesians 6:9.)

YOUNG PEOPLE

Young men, be submissive to those who are older. Clothe yourselves with humility toward one another, because "God opposes the proud but gives grace to the humble." Humble yourselves, therefore, under God's mighty hand, that he may lift you up in due time. (See 1 Peter 5:5,6.)

WIDOWS

The widow who is really in need and left all alone puts her hope in God and continues night and day to pray and to ask God for help. But the widow who lives for pleasure is dead even while she lives. (See 1 Timothy 5:5,6.)

A WORD FOR ALL

Love your neighbor as yourself. This is the sum of all the commandments. (See Romans 13:8-10; Galatians 5:14.) And continue praying for everyone. (See 1 Timothy 2:1.)

> Let each his lesson learn with care,
> And all the household well shall fare.

PART TWO

Catechism Lessons
Course One

I. THE HOLY BIBLE

For Me to Learn
Why the Bible is the most important Book

For Me to Remember
Who wrote the Bible? (A. Men of God)
2 Peter 1:21. *Men spoke from God as they were carried along by the Holy Spirit.*
This work of the Holy Spirit is called inspiration.

Who told or inspired men what to write?
2 Timothy 3:16. *All Scripture is God-breathed.*

How can we describe the Bible? (A. As true and holy)
John 17:17. *Sanctify them by the truth: your word is truth.*

Why, then, is the Bible the most important book?

THE BIBLE IS GOD'S HOLY WORD.

What can we learn from nature? (A. That there is a God who made everything)
Psalm 19:1. *The heavens declare the glory of God; the skies proclaim the work of his hands.*

What does nature not tell us about God? (A. What He is like and what He has done for us)
Where can we find that information?
What does the Bible tell us about God? (A. That He is everlasting)
Psalm 90:2. *Before the mountains were born or you brought forth*

the earth and the world, from everlasting to everlasting you are God.

The Bible tells us that the true God is the Father, Son, and Holy Spirit.
Matthew 28:19. *Go and make disciples of all nations, baptizing them in the name of the Father and of the Son and of the Holy Spirit.*

The Bible tells us that there is one God.
Deuteronomy 6:4. *The Lord our God, the Lord is one.*

Why, then, is the Bible the most important Book?

THE BIBLE TELLS US WHO THE TRUE GOD IS.

Why did God give us the Bible? (A. That we may learn to know Jesus as our Savior and believe in Him)
John 20:31. *These are written that you may believe that Jesus is the Christ, the Son of God.*

What can we learn from the Bible? (A. That we are saved through faith in Jesus Christ.)
2 Timothy 3:15. *From infancy you have known the holy Scriptures, which are able to make you wise for salvation through faith in Christ Jesus.*

Why, then, is the Bible the most important book?

THE BIBLE TELLS US HOW WE ARE SAVED.

Summary
Why, then, is the Bible the most important book?

THE BIBLE IS GOD'S HOLY WORD THAT TELLS US HOW WE ARE SAVED.

What This Means to Me
I will always want to remember that the Bible is not an ordinary book. It is the most important book. It is God's Word in which He tells me about Himself and how I am saved. I will want to read it often and listen very attentively when my parents, teachers, and pastor read from it, for I know that God Himself is speaking to me. I pray that God will help me respect and love His Word, the Bible.

For Me to Do
Learn to pronounce correctly the names of the books of the Bible. Have a classmate name a book of the Bible. Then tell him whether

the book named is in the Old Testament or the New Testament.

For Me to Prepare for the Next Lesson
Read the Bible story "The Giving of the Law" in your Bible history book.
    Who went up the mountain to receive the Law of God?
    What did God give to Moses as He spoke to him?
    On what did God write the commandments?

Read the Bible story "The Pharisee and the Tax Collector" (Luke 18:9-14) in your Bible history book.
    Of what did the Pharisee boast?
    What did the tax collector confess?
    What did Jesus say of the tax collector?

2. THE TWO GREAT TEACHINGS OF THE BIBLE

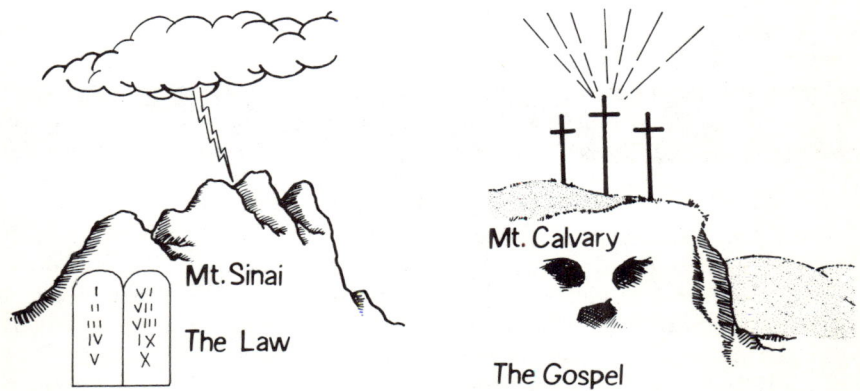

For Me to Learn
What the two great teachings of the Bible are

For Me to Remember
What does God demand of all people?
Leviticus 19:2. **Be holy because I, the Lord your God, am holy.**
Where did God first write His law? (A. Into man's heart)
What made God's law unclear? (A. The fall into sin) Because man no longer knows God's law perfectly, God wrote it again.
Where does God tell us what we should and should not do? (A. In the Ten Commandments) The Ten Commandments are a summary of God's Law.

What is one of the great teachings of the Bible? What does it tell us?

THE LAW TELLS US WHAT WE SHOULD AND SHOULD NOT DO.

What did God do in His great love for all sinners?
John 3:16. *God so loved the world that he gave his one and only Son, that whoever believes in him shall not perish but have eternal life.*
What did Jesus do for us? (A. He kept the Law and suffered and died for the sins of all people.)
What does God in His grace now do? (A. He forgives our sins for Jesus' sake.)
The good news that Jesus kept the Law for us and suffered and died for our sins is called the Gospel.

What is the other great teaching of the Bible? What does it tell us?

THE GOSPEL TELLS US WHAT GOD HAS DONE FOR US.

Summary
What, then, are the two great doctrines of the Bible?

THE TWO GREAT TEACHINGS OF THE BIBLE ARE THE LAW AND GOSPEL.

What God's Law and Gospel Mean to Me
God's Law tells me that I must be sinless, that I must love God with my whole being and my neighbor as myself. I know I have not done this. I realize I am guilty of breaking God's commandments. I know there is no way I can save myself. God's Law tells me I am a sinner. But then I read of God's wonderful love for me and all sinners. The Gospel tells me that Jesus kept the Law for me and saved me when He suffered and died for my sins. I shall want to thank, praise, serve, and obey my Lord and Savior all my life.

For Me to Memorize
Assigned Bible passages
Assigned books of the Bible

For Me to Do
On a sheet of paper print the title, LAW. Then print the first three commandments without the explanations. On another sheet print the title, LAW. Then print the remaining seven commandments without explanations. On the top of a third sheet of paper print the title,

GOSPEL. Then draw a large cross below the title. On the lower part of the paper print the Bible passage found in John 3:16.

For Me to Prepare for the Next Lesson
Read the short biography of Luther beginning on page 333.
Your teacher may want you to read *The Life and Faith of Martin Luther* which is a longer and more interesting biography of Luther. It was written by Adolph Fehlauer and is published by the Northwestern Publishing House of Milwaukee, Wisconsin.

3. LUTHER'S CATECHISM

For Me to Learn
How the catechism helps us study the Bible

For Me to Remember
What should we study early in our childhood?
2 Timothy 3:15. *From infancy you have known the holy Scriptures, which are able to make you wise for salvation through faith in Christ Jesus.*
Colossians 3:16. *Let the word of Christ dwell in you richly.*

What kind of book is Luther's Catechism? (A. A book of instructions in God's Word)
What teachings of the Bible are found in the Catechism? (A. The chief or most important doctrines and teachings)
John 17:3. *This is eternal life: that they may know you, the only true God, and Jesus Christ, whom you have sent.*
1 John 5:3. *This is love for God: to obey his commands.*
From where did Luther take the teachings that are in his Catechism?

How can the Catechism help us study God's Word?

THE CATECHISM HELPS US STUDY THE SIX CHIEF PARTS OF CHRISTIAN DOCTRINE.

What This Means to Me
Luther's Small Catechism is a helpful guide in studying God's Word. It contains the most necessary and important teachings of the Bible. It is simply and clearly written. The six chief teachings of the Bible are explained by means of questions and answers. It is my prayer that God will bless my study of the Catechism so that I may learn to know well the most important teachings of the Bible.

For Me to Memorize
   Continue to memorize the names of the books of the Bible. Memorize the assigned Bible passages.

For Me to Do
   Luther also wrote a Large Catechism. Ask your teacher to show you a copy. Examine it to see how it differs from the Small Catechism.

For Me to Prepare for the Next Lesson
   Read the Bible story "Joseph's Purity" (Genesis 39:1-9).
   What did Joseph say when Potiphar's wife wanted him to sin?
   Against whom did Joseph not want to sin?

THE TEN COMMANDMENTS
4. FEAR OF GOD

THE FIRST COMMANDMENT
You shall have no other gods.

What does this mean?
We should fear, love and trust in God above all things.

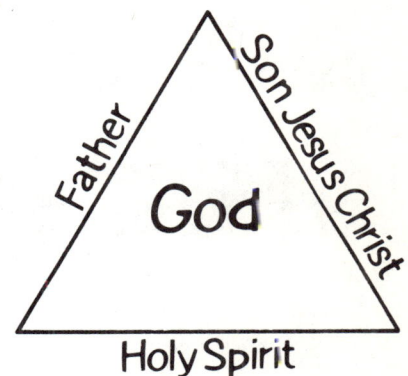

For Me to Learn
What it means to fear God above all things

For Me to Remember
Who is the true God? (A. Father, Son, and Holy Spirit)
How did Daniel show that he feared God? (A. He obeyed Him)
Proverbs 23:26. *My son, give me your heart and let your eyes keep to my ways.*

How did the Children of Israel show that they did not fear the true God? (A. They worshiped a false god.)
Matthew 4:10. *Worship the Lord your God, and serve him only.*
What sin did they commit? (A. Idolatry)

What does it mean to fear God above all things?

TO FEAR GOD MEANS TO WORSHIP AND OBEY HIM ABOVE ALL THINGS.

Whom was Joseph afraid to grieve when he was tempted? What did he say?
Genesis 39:9. *How then could I do such a wicked thing and sin against God?*
Why did Joseph fear to sin against God? (A. He respected God and did not want to disobey Him.)

What does it mean to fear God above all things?

TO FEAR GOD MEANS TO RESPECT HIM ABOVE ALL THINGS.

Summary

To fear God means to worship God above all things. To fear God means to obey God above all things. To fear God means to respect Him above all things.

What, then, does it mean to fear God above all things?

TO FEAR GOD ABOVE ALL THINGS MEANS TO OBEY, WORSHIP, AND RESPECT HIM ABOVE ALL THINGS.

What This Means to Me

I believe in the Triune God, Father, Son, and Holy Spirit. By worshiping Him I give Him greater honor than anything or anyone else. The true God of the Bible is a great and loving God. He has made the world; He has made me; He has given me all that I need. He sent His Son to die for me, and when I die, He will take me to heaven. I will want to obey Him. I fear to sin against God, because I do not want to be unthankful for what He has done and still is doing for me. I have not always feared God as I should. I pray that God will forgive my sins for Jesus' sake and make me strong when I am tempted to sin.

For Me to Memorize

Assigned passages
Continue to memorize the names of the books of the Bible.

For Me to Do (Optional)

Read Daniel 6:7-10. How did Daniel show that he feared to disobey God more than he feared being killed by the lions?
Read Proverbs 8:13. What will we do if we fear the Lord?

Practice finding the books of the Bible. Have a classmate name a book of the Bible, such as Joshua, and then open your Bible to that book. Do this whenever you have time and until you can quickly locate any book in the Bible.

For Me to Prepare for the Next Lesson

Read the Bible story "Abraham and Isaac" (Genesis 22:1-13).
   What did God ask Abraham to do?
   How did Abraham show that he was ready to obey God?

Whom did Abraham love more than his son?

Read the Bible story "The Rich Young Ruler" (Mark 10:17-22).
What question did the rich ruler ask Jesus?
What did Jesus tell the man to do with all his money and property?
Why did the rich ruler not do what Jesus asked him to do?

5. LOVE OF GOD

THE FIRST COMMANDMENT
You shall have no other gods.

What does this mean?
We should fear, *love* and trust in *God above all things.*

For Me to Learn
What it means to love God above all things

For Me to Remember
What strange and hard thing did God ask Abraham to do? How did Abraham show that he loved God more dearly than his only son? (A. He obeyed God and was willing to sacrifice his son.) How much should we love God?

Matthew 22:37. *Love the Lord your God with all your heart and with all your soul and with all your mind.*

How did God show His greatest love for us? (A. By giving us His Son to be our Savior.) Why should we love Him?

1 John 4:19. *We love because he first loved us.*

Whom does God not want us to love more than Him?

Matthew 10:37. *Anyone who loves his father or mother more than me is not worthy of me; anyone who loves his son or daughter more than me is not worthy of me.*

How much should we love God?

WE SHOULD LOVE GOD MORE THAN ANY PERSON.

Why did the rich young man go away sad?
What did he love more than God?

1 John 2:15. *Do not love the world or anything in the world. If anyone loves the world, the love of the Father is not in him.*

How much should we love God?

WE SHOULD LOVE GOD MORE THAN ANYTHING ELSE.

Summary

What, then, does it mean to love God above all things?

TO LOVE GOD ABOVE ALL THINGS MEANS TO LOVE HIM MORE THAN ANY PERSON OR THING.

What This Means to Me

There is no one in heaven or on earth who loves me more than my God. He made me, gives me what I need every day, forgives my sins for Jesus' sake, and will at the end of my life take me to heaven. He is my dearest and best Friend. He is my Lord and Savior. I thank Him for all His goodness.

Psalm 100:2. *Serve the Lord with gladness; come before him with joyful songs.*

I pray that with God's help I will always love Him more than anyone or anything, and that I will gladly serve Him every day of my life. I know that I have not always loved God as I should. I pray that He will forgive me for Jesus' sake.

For Me to Memorize

Assigned Bible passages
Continue memorizing the names of the books of the Bible.

For Me to Do

List some ways by which we may sometimes show that we love things of this world more than God.
Read the Bible story of the "Rich Fool" in Luke 12:15-21.
What did he love more than God? Why was he a fool?

For Me to Prepare for the Next Lesson

Read the Bible story "Noah and the Flood" (Genesis 6:5 - 8:22).
   What did God say He would do?
   Who only believed God?
   How did he show he believed God?

Read the Bible story "David and Goliath" (1 Samuel 17).
   What did David say to King Saul?
   What did David say to the giant?

6. TRUST IN GOD

THE FIRST COMMANDMENT
You shall have no other gods.

What does this mean?
We should fear, love and *trust in* God *above all things.*

For Me to Learn
What it means to trust in God above all things

For Me to Remember
Whom did most of the people not believe in at Noah's time?
How did Noah show that he believed in God?
Proverbs 3:5. *Trust in the Lord with all your heart and lean not on your own understanding.*

What does it mean to trust in God above all things?

TO TRUST IN GOD MEANS TO BELIEVE IN HIM ABOVE ALL THINGS.

In whom did Goliath foolishly trust?
Psalm 118:8. *It is better to take refuge in the Lord than to trust in man.*
In whom did David put his trust to defeat Goliath?
Psalm 37:5. *Commit your way to the Lord; trust in him and he will do this.*
On whom did David depend to defeat the giant?
Psalm 50:15. *Call upon me in the day of trouble; I will deliver you, and you will honor me.*

What does it mean to trust in God above all things?

TO TRUST IN GOD MEANS TO DEPEND ON HIM ABOVE ALL THINGS.

Summary
What two things, then, are meant when we say we trust in God above all things?

> **TO TRUST IN GOD ABOVE ALL THINGS MEANS TO BELIEVE IN HIM AND DEPEND ON HIM.**

What This Means to Me
I know from the Bible that God is willing and able to help me. Therefore I should not worry but believe in the Lord. He is good and He is almighty. People who want to help me often can't, and some who could help me are not willing to do so. God can and will help. I can depend on Him. I thank Him for helping me and taking care of me. He does this through my parents, my friends, my pastor, my teacher, my doctor, and others. I ask God to forgive me for not always trusting in Him above all things.

For Me to Memorize
Assigned Bible passages
First Commandment

For Me to Do
Read Hymn 428. The poet mentions many things for which we can trust (depend on) Jesus. List them on a sheet of paper.

7. GOD'S NAME

THE SECOND COMMANDMENT
You shall not misuse the name of the Lord your God.

For Me to Learn
What is meant by God's name?

For Me to Remember
God has given Himself many names.
Matthew 28:19. *Go and make disciples of all nations, baptizing them in the name of the Father and of the Son and of the Holy Spirit.*
What are some other names by which God is known to us? (A. Creator, Savior, Almighty God, Jesus Christ)

What is meant with God's name?

GOD'S NAME MEANS EVERY WORD THAT STANDS FOR GOD.

How are God's names different from the names of people? (A. God's names tell us what God is like and what He has done.)

Ecclesiastes 12:1. *Remember your Creator in the days of your youth.*

Matthew 1:21. *She will give birth to a son, and you are to give him the name Jesus, because he will save his people from their sins.*

Where does God make His name (Himself) known to us? (A. In the Bible)

Through whom did God the Father make His name (Himself) known? (A. Through His Son)

What should we think of when we think of using God's name? (A. Of what God has told us about Himself)

What, then, is meant with God's name?

GOD'S NAME MEANS ALL WORDS THAT STAND FOR GOD AND EVERYTHING GOD TELLS US ABOUT HIMSELF.

Summary

What, then, does God's name mean?

GOD'S NAME MEANS ALL WORDS THAT STAND FOR GOD AND EVERYTHING GOD TELLS US ABOUT HIMSELF.

What This Means to Me

God has made His name known to me in the Bible. From His name I know what He is like, what He has done, what He still does, and what He will do. Since God's name and all He has told me about Himself are holy, God wants me to show great respect for His name and for what He has done for me and all people. I know that I have not always done this. I pray that God will forgive me for Jesus' sake.

For Me to Memorize

Assigned Bible passages

For Me to Do

List all the names given to God in the Three Articles of the Apostles' Creed.

For Me to Prepare for the Next Lesson
Read the Bible story "Peter's Denial" (Matthew 26:69-74).
Of what was Peter accused?
What did he deny?
What did he do to convince his accusers that he was telling the truth?

Read Genesis 24:2-4.
What did Abraham want his servant to do for Isaac?
What did he make him swear?
By whose name did he swear?

Read Matthew 14:6-9.
What pleased Herod?
What did he promise with an oath?
What did the daughter ask for?
How did Herod feel?

8. MISUSE OF GOD'S NAME

THE SECOND COMMANDMENT
You shall not misuse the name of the Lord your God.

What does this mean?
We should fear and love God that we do not use his name to curse, swear, lie or deceive, or use it superstitiously, but call upon God's name in every trouble, pray, praise and give thanks.

For Me to Learn
What it means to curse and swear by God's name

For Me to Remember
What did Peter do when he denied knowing Jesus? (A. He cursed.)
James 3:10. *Out of the same mouth come praise and cursing. My brothers, this should not be.*
What did he thereby ask God to do if he were not telling the truth? (A. To punish him)

What does it mean to curse by God's name?

TO CURSE BY GOD'S NAME MEANS TO CALL ON GOD TO SEND EVIL.

Give an example of swearing that is not sinful. Swearing that is for the good of our neighbor is not wrong.

Why was Peter's swearing sinful? (A. He swore falsely.)
Leviticus 19:12. *Do not swear falsely by my name.*

Why was Herod's swearing sinful? (A. He swore thoughtlessly.)
Matthew 5:37. *Simply let your 'Yes' be 'Yes,' and your 'No,' 'No'; anything beyond this comes from the evil one.*

On whom do people call when they swear to prove that they are telling the truth? What are they asking God to do? (A. To be their witness that they are speaking the truth)

What, then, does it mean to swear by God's name?

TO SWEAR BY GOD'S NAME MEANS TO CALL ON GOD AS A WITNESS.

Summary
What, then, does it mean to curse and swear by God's name?

TO CURSE BY GOD'S NAME MEANS TO CALL ON GOD TO SEND EVIL. TO SWEAR BY GOD'S NAME MEANS TO CALL ON GOD AS A WITNESS.

What This Means to Me
From God's Word I have learned that it is a great sin to use God's name in vain by cursing and by false, thoughtless, and needless swearing. I pray God to guard me and help me so that I will not use curse words or swear falsely or thoughtlessly. I pray that God will always make me realize when I have sinfully used His name and lead me to repent and ask for forgiveness for Jesus' sake.

For Me to Memorize
Assigned Bible passages

For Me to Prepare for the Next Lesson
Read the Bible story "The Ark of the Covenant Is Taken" in your Bible (1 Samuel 4:1-11).
  Who defeated the Israelites?
  What did the elders think would save the Israelites?
  What did they have some men bring to the battlefield?
  What did the Philistines do?

Read the Bible story "Ananias and Sapphira" in your Bible (Acts 5:1-11) or in your Bible history book.
  What lie did Ananias and Sapphira tell?
  Who knew they were lying?

9. MISUSE OF GOD'S NAME

THE SECOND COMMANDMENT
You shall not misuse the name of the Lord your God.

What does this mean?
We should fear and love God that we do not use his name to curse, swear, *lie or deceive, or use it superstitiously,* but call upon God's name in every trouble, pray, praise and give thanks.

For Me to Learn
How God's name is misused

For Me to Remember
What did the elders of Israel believe would give them victory?
In what did they put their trust?
What kind of trust was that? (A. False or superstitious)
What had they done with God's name? (A. They misused it.)
Exodus 20:7. *The Lord will not hold anyone guiltless who misuses his name.*
How did Israel misuse God's name? (A. Israel used it superstitiously.)

How is God's name misused?

GOD'S NAME IS MISUSED WHEN PEOPLE USE IT SUPERSTITIOUSLY.

What did the Scribes and Pharisees teach and believe? (A. In teachings of men)
As what did they teach them? (A. As God's Word)
What were they therefore doing? (A. Lying and deceiving by God's name)
Matthew 7:15. *Watch out for false prophets.*

What did Ananias and Sapphira try to make the Apostles believe?
What were Ananias and Sapphira doing? (A. Lying and deceiving)
Matthew 15:8. *These people honor me with their lips, but their hearts are far from me.*

How is God's name misused?

GOD'S NAME IS MISUSED WHEN PEOPLE LIE AND DECEIVE BY HIS NAME.

Summary
How, then, is God's name misused?

> **GOD'S NAME IS MISUSED WHEN PEOPLE USE IT SUPERSTITIOUSLY AND LIE AND DECEIVE BY GOD'S NAME.**

What This Means to Me
I am thankful that God has given me the opportunity to hear, read and study God's Word in all its truth and purity. It should be my desire to study God's Word diligently so that I will understand it correctly and so I can defend it and my faith against any false teachings and teachers. I pray God to guard and direct me so that I do not become deceived by false teachings. Daily I must also be reminded to ask God to guard me against hypocrisy. My thoughts, words, and actions cannot please God unless they come from a heart that fears, loves, and trusts in Him above all things. I pray God to forgive my sins for Jesus' sake and to give me strength to overcome any temptations to lie or deceive by His name.

For Me to Memorize
Assigned Bible passages

For Me to Do
Name some ways in which some people use God's name superstitiously.

For Me to Prepare for the Next Lesson
Read the Bible story "The Ten Lepers" in your Bible (Luke 17:11-19) or Bible history book.
  On whom did the lepers call for help?
  What did Jesus do?
  What did one leper do?

10. THE RIGHT USE OF GOD'S NAME

THE SECOND COMMANDMENT
You shall not misuse the name of the Lord your God.

What does this mean?
We should fear and love God that we do not use his name to curse, swear, lie or deceive, or use it superstitiously, but *call upon God's name in every trouble, pray, praise and give thanks.*

For Me to Learn
How we should use God's name

For Me to Remember
On whom did the ten lepers call for help in their trouble?
℞ Psalm 50:15. *Call upon me in the day of trouble; I will deliver you, and you will honor me.*

How should we use God's name?

WE SHOULD USE GOD'S NAME TO CALL UPON HIM IN EVERY TROUBLE.

To whom did the lepers and Daniel pray?
N✗ 1 Thessalonians 5:17. *Pray continually.*

How should we use God's name?

WE SHOULD USE GOD'S NAME TO PRAY TO HIM AT ALL TIMES.

What did one leper do after he was healed?
℞ Psalm 118:1. *Give thanks to the Lord, for he is good; his love endures forever.*
What does God expect that His people will do? (A. Praise Him)
N Isaiah 43:21. *The people I formed for myself that they may proclaim my praise.*

How should we use God's name?

WE SHOULD USE GOD'S NAME TO THANK AND PRAISE HIM.

Summary
The lepers *called upon Jesus* in their trouble.
They *prayed to Jesus* to help them.
One leper *praised and thanked God* for healing him.

How, then, should we use God's name?

WE SHOULD USE GOD'S NAME TO CALL UPON HIM IN EVERY TROUBLE, TO PRAY, PRAISE, AND GIVE THANKS.

What This Means to Me
God wants me to use His name in the right way so He can bless me.

Exodus 20:24. *Wherever I cause my name to be honored, I will come to you and bless you.*

Whenever I am in need or have trouble, my first thought should be to go to God in prayer, talk to Him, and ask Him to help me. I know He wants me to do that, and I know that He hears every prayer. This is a great comfort to me. Not only when I am in need of help will I pray, but I will want to do so regularly for the many blessings I receive daily from my Lord and Savior, both bodily and spiritual blessings. Never should I forget to thank and praise Him every day and especially when He has helped me in my troubles. I must not forget that my prayers and praises should not be said only for myself but for all people, especially for my loved ones and my fellow Christians.

For Me to Memorize
Assigned Bible passages
The Second Commandment

For Me to Do
Write a prayer in which you ask God for His blessings and also thank Him for His goodness.
Find a psalm in which we praise or glorify God.

II. THE SABBATH DAY

THE THIRD COMMANDMENT
Remember the Sabbath day by keeping it holy.

For Me to Learn
What the Sabbath means

For Me to Remember
What were the Old Testament believers not permitted to do on the Sabbath day? (A. To work)
How did they worship God and find rest for their souls? (A. They offered sacrifices.)

Of whom were their worship services a shadow?

What did the Sabbath mean to the Old Testament believers?

THE SABBATH MEANT REST FOR THE BODIES AND SOULS OF THE OLD TESTAMENT BELIEVERS.

According to what are New Testament believers not judged?

N Colossians 2:16,17. *Do not let anyone judge you by what you eat or drink, or with regard to a religious festival, a New Moon celebration or a Sabbath day. These are a shadow of the things that were to come; the reality, however, is found in Christ.*

Of what were the Old Testament worship rules and regulations to remind the Jews? (A. Of the promises about the coming Savior)
Of whom were they a shadow?
Since when is that shadow no longer needed? (A. Since Jesus came)

Whose coming abolished the Old Testament Sabbath rules and requirements? (A. Jesus' coming)

NX Matthew 12:8. *The Son of Man is Lord of the Sabbath.*

What did the promised Savior do for us? (A. Saved us from our sin)

What do we receive through Jesus Christ? (A. Forgiveness of sins)

NX Matthew 11:28. *Come to me, all you who are weary and burdened, and I will give you rest.*

What does the Sabbath mean to us?

THE SABBATH MEANS REST FOR OUR SOULS THROUGH JESUS.

Summary
What, then, does the Sabbath mean today?

TODAY THE SABBATH MEANS REST FOR THE SOUL.

What This Means to Me

Through sleep my body is refreshed. My soul also needs to be refreshed. When I stop to think of what I have thought, said, and done, I realize that I have not always thought, said, and done those things that please my Savior. I must admit that I have sinned many times against God's commandments. This troubles me and makes me restless, because God says that I must keep His commandments and that I must love Him with my whole being and my neighbor as myself. Where can I find peace and rest for my soul? I can go to Jesus who says to me, "Come to me, . . . and I will give you rest." God forgives my sins through Jesus' blood and righteousness. I thank my God for giving rest to my soul by assuring me of the forgiveness of my sins for Jesus' sake.

For Me to Memorize
Assigned Bible passages

For Me to Do
The church year is divided into seasons. The seasons and names of the Sundays in each season are given in the front of the hymnal. List the names of the seasons on a sheet of paper.

The hymnal also mentions the church festivals. List them on a sheet of paper.

For Me to Prepare for the Next Lesson
Read the Bible story "The Parable of the Great Supper" in your Bible (Luke 14:16-24), or in your Bible history book.
  What did the good man prepare?
  What did his servant say to many people?
  What did they all refuse to do?
  Who later accepted the invitation in their place?

12. GOD'S WORD

THE THIRD COMMANDMENT

Remember the Sabbath day by keeping it holy.

What does this mean?
We should fear and love God that we do not despise preaching and his Word, but regard it as holy, and gladly hear and learn it.

For Me to Learn
What God forbids in the Third Commandment

For Me to Remember
What do people do who do not listen to God's Word? (A. They despise it.)

Luke 10:16. *He who listens to you listens to me; he who rejects you rejects me; but he who rejects me rejects him who sent me.*

What do people do who do not believe God's Word? (A. They despise it.)

John 8:47. *He who belongs to God hears what God says. The reason you do not hear is that you do not belong to God.*

What does God forbid in the Third Commandment?

GOD FORBIDS US TO DESPISE THE PREACHING OF HIS WORD.

What do people do when they do not study and learn God's Word? (A. They despise God's Word.)

Colossians 3:16. *Let the Word of Christ dwell in you richly.*

Ecclesiastes 5:1. *Guard your steps when you go to the house of God. Go near to listen rather than to offer the sacrifice of fools.*

What does God forbid in the Third Commandment?

GOD FORBIDS US TO DESPISE THE LEARNING OF HIS WORD.

Summary

What, then, does God forbid in the Third Commandment?

GOD FORBIDS US TO DESPISE THE PREACHING AND LEARNING OF HIS WORD.

What This Means to Me

God's Word is very precious. It is very important that I hear and learn it whenever I have the opportunity to do so. I thank God that He has given me a church where I can hear His Word read and preached and a school where I can learn more from God's Word every school day. I pray that I may never despise the preaching and learning of God's Word.

For Me to Memorize

Assigned Bible passages

For Me to Do

Do you have family devotions in your home? If you do not, talk with your parents about having daily devotions. Ask your teacher to suggest devotion books.

Write a prayer that you can pray silently after you have entered the church. In your prayer ask God to help you to be attentive and to bless His Word that you are about to hear.

For Me to Prepare for the Next Lesson
Read the Bible story "The Twelve-year Old Jesus" in your Bible (Luke 2:41-52), or in your Bible history book.
Where did Jesus remain after His parents left Jerusalem?
What did He do there?

Read the Bible story "Mary and Martha" in your Bible (Luke 10:38-42), or in your Bible history book.
To whom did Mary listen?
What did Martha want her to do?
Who made the right choice?

13. GOD'S WORD

THE THIRD COMMANDMENT
Remember the Sabbath day by keeping it holy.

What does this mean?
We should fear and love God that we do not despise preaching and his Word, but *regard it as holy, and gladly hear and learn it.*

For Me to Learn
What God commands in the Third Commandment

For Me to Remember
Whose Word did Jesus speak?
How did Mary regard God's Word?
As what did the Christians regard the Word which Paul preached to them? (A. As God's Word)
That means they held it sacred.
1 Thessalonians 2:13. *When you received the word of God, which you heard from us, you accepted it not as the word of men, but as it actually is, the word of God.*

What does God command us to do with His Word?

GOD COMMANDS US TO HOLD HIS WORD SACRED.

What should we gladly do? (A. Attend church services)
Psalm 122:1. *I rejoiced with those who said to me, "Let us go to the hourse of the Lord."* Why should we gladly go to the house of God?

(A. Because God's Word is preached there) Why should we learn and remember God's Word? (A. God promises to bless us through His Word.)

R✓ Luke 11:28. *Blessed . . . are those who hear the Word of God and obey it.*
Not only should we hear God's Word. What should we also do? (A. Believe and obey it)

R✓ James 1:22. *Do not merely listen to the word, and so deceive yourselves. Do what it says.*

What does God command us to do gladly?

GOD COMMANDS US TO HEAR AND LEARN HIS WORD GLADLY.

Summary

How does God command us to hold His Word? What are we to do gladly?

What, then, does God command us to do with His Word?

GOD COMMANDS US TO HOLD HIS WORD SACRED AND TO HEAR AND LEARN IT GLADLY.

What This Means to Me

When I hear or read God's Word, I know that God is speaking to me. His Word is holy or sacred. Everything He tells me is true. What He has to tell me is precious and very important. God has given me many opportunities to hear, read, and learn His Word. I am glad that I can go to church and school to hear and learn God's Word. But I know that I have not always regarded God's Word as I should and that I have not always made full use of the many opportunities to hear and learn God's Word. I pray God to forgive me my sins for Jesus' sake and to help me keep the Third Commandment.

For Me to Memorize

Assigned Bible passages
The First, Second and Third Commandments

For Me to Prepare for the Next Lesson

Use the Review and Study Guide (Number 14) to prepare for the next lesson. Write the answers on a sheet of paper and study them. The review is on lessons 1 - 13.

14. REVIEW AND STUDY GUIDE

(Lessons 1 - 13)

I. *Answer*

Answer these questions.

1. Why is the Bible the most important book?
2. Who wrote the Bible?
3. What can we learn from nature?
4. What can we not learn from nature?
5. What are the two great teachings of the Bible?
6. What does the Law teach us? The Gospel?
7. Who wrote our Catechism?
8. From which book were the teachings of the Catechism taken?
9. What is the purpose of the Catechism?
10. How many chief parts of Christian teachings does the Catechism contain?

II. *Complete*

Complete these sentences.

1. To fear God means to .... and .... Him above all things.
2. Some names for God are ...., ..., ...
3. To love God means to .... and .... Him above all things.
4. To trust in God means to .... in God and to .... upon Him for everything.
5. God's name means every .... that stands for God.
6. God's name means .... that God tells us about Himself.
7. People .... by God's name when they ask God to send evil on someone or something.
8. When people swear by God's name they call on God as a ....
9. .... swearing is sinful.
10. People who teach false teachings .... and .... by God's name.

III. *Match*

Match column A with column B.

A	B
............1. The right use of God's name	a. Saturday
............2. The Old Testament Sabbath Day	b. rest for our souls
............3. Our Sabbath	c. despise it
............4. Right use of God's Word	d. holy
............5. Sacred	e. hold it sacred, gladly hear and learn it.
............6. Refuse to hear or learn God's Word	f. pray, praise, give thanks

IV. *Choose*

Choose the correct commandment. Which commandment

1. forbids the use of curse words?
2. commands us to respect God more than anyone else?
3. forbids us to neglect the hearing and learning of God's Word?
4. commands us to depend upon God more than anyone else?
5. commands us gladly to go to church and hear God's Word?
6. commands us to love God more than anyone or anything else?
7. forbids us to listen to false teachers?
8. commands us to pray to God in time of trouble?
9. tells us that to trust someone more than God is idolatry?
10. forbids false swearing?

For Me to Prepare for the Next Lesson

Read the Bible story "Joseph Makes Himself Known to His Brothers" in your Bible history book.

Over what country was Joseph ruler?

Who made him ruler?

What did Joseph tell his brothers?

15. GOD'S REPRESENTATIVES

THE FOURTH COMMANDMENT

Honor your father and mother, that it may go well with you, and that you may enjoy long life on the earth.

What does this mean?
We should fear and love God that we do not dishonor or anger our parents and others in authority, but honor, serve and obey them, and give them love and respect.

For Me to Learn
How God rules over us

For Me to Remember
Through whom did God rule Egypt?
From whom did he receive his power to rule? (A. From God)
Romans 13:1. *Everyone must submit himself to the governing authorities, for there is no authority except that which God has established.*

From whom did Jacob receive his power to rule over his sons? (A. From God)
Ephesians 6:1. *Children, obey your parents in the Lord, for this is right.*

In whose place did Joseph and Jacob rule? (A. In God's place)
Whose representatives were they? (A. God's representatives)
Whom did God choose as His representative to rule the Children of Israel and lead them out of Egypt? (A. Moses)
Whom did God choose to rule over us?

How does God rule over us?

GOD RULES OVER US THROUGH HIS REPRESENTATIVES.

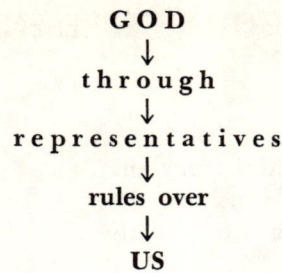

What This Means to Me

God chooses various representatives through whom He rules on earth. He has given parents the right and responsibility to rule their children. Superiors, such as the president of a country, the governor of a state, the mayor of a city, the policeman of a city, the pastor of a church, the teacher of a school, and others are God's representatives. I am to be subject to them just as Jesus was subject to God's representatives. I sin when I do not regard them as God's representatives. I ask God to forgive my sins for the sake of Jesus, who always regarded His parents and others as God's representatives. May I always realize that God has given me parents and superiors for my good. I thank God for my parents and superiors.

For Me to Memorize

Assigned Bible passages

For Me to Do

Make a list of people who are God's representatives in your home, your school, your church, your federal government, your state government, your city government.

Read Psalm 47. Copy the lines which tell us that God rules the world and its people.

For Me to Prepare for the Next Lesson

Read the Bible story "Absalom's Rebellion" in your Bible (2 Samuel 15:1-14).

    Against whom did Absalom turn the people?

    In whose place did Absalom want to rule?

Read in your Bible the story "Elisha Is Jeered" (2 Kings 2:23,24).

    What did some youths say to the prophet Elisha?

    How did God punish them?

16. DISHONORING GOD'S REPRESENTATIVES

THE FOURTH COMMANDMENT

Honor your father and mother, that it may go well with you, and that you may enjoy long life on the earth.

What does this mean?
We should fear and love God that we do not dishonor or anger our parents and others in authority, but honor, serve and obey them, and give them love and respect.

For Me to Learn
How we dishonor God's representatives

For Me to Remember
Whose representative was David? (A. God's)
How did Absalom show that he did not honor his father David?
How did he dishonor his father and his king? (A. He despised them.)

How do we dishonor God's representatives?

WE DISHONOR GOD'S REPRESENTATIVES WHEN WE DESPISE THEM.

Romans 13:2. *He who rebels against the authority is rebelling against what God has instituted, and those who do so will bring judgment on themselves.*

Colossians 3:20. *Children, obey your parents in everything, for this pleases the Lord.*

Whose representative was Elisha?
How did the children show that they did not honor Elisha?
How did they dishonor him? (A. They made him angry.)

How do we dishonor God's representatives?

WE DISHONOR GOD'S REPRESENTATIVES WHEN WE ANGER THEM.

What will God do to those who despise God's representatives or anger them? (A. Punish them)

Proverbs 30:17. *The eye that mocks a father, that scorns obedience to a mother, will be pecked out by the ravens of the valley, will be eaten by the vultures.*

Summary
How, then, do we dishonor God's representatives?

WE DISHONOR GOD'S REPRESENTATIVES WHEN WE DESPISE THEM AND ANGER THEM.

What This Means to Me
I despise my parents and superiors when I do not regard them as God's representatives. I sin when I have disrespectful and despising thoughts about my parents and superiors. Such disrespectful, despising thoughts toward my parents and superiors may show themselves in what I say or do. Despising words and actions cause parents and others in authority much sorrow and grief and cause them to become angry. Many parents and other people have been grieved by the disobedience of children, their backtalk, their resentful attitude, and their constant bickering and quarreling. When my parents and others in authority are provoked to anger, they must correct me so that I will change my evil ways.

It is seldom that I am not with my parents or others whom God has placed over me. I, therefore, ask God to keep me from having disrespectful thoughts in my heart toward them and from speaking and doing things that could anger them. When I have been guilty of sinning against God's representatives, I should go to them, confess my sin, and ask for their forgiveness. And I will also go to my heavenly Father, confess my sin, and ask him to forgive me for the sake of Jesus, who was never guilty of being disrespectful to His parents and others in authority.

For Me to Memorize
Assigned Bible passages

For Me to Do
Read Exodus 16:1-3. How did the Children of Israel show that they dishonored Moses?
Read 1 Peter 2:18. Does God demand that we should be obedient also to harsh superiors?

For Me to Prepare for the Next Lesson
Read the Bible story "Jacob in Egypt" (Genesis 46:26-30) in your Bible or Bible history book.
    What did Joseph do when he heard that his father was coming to Egypt?
    What did he do when he met his father?
    To whom did Joseph introduce his father? Read Genesis 47:7.

Read the Bible story "Ruth" in your Bible history book.
Who was Ruth's mother-in-law?
Why did she want to return to Canaan?
What did she tell Ruth and Orpah to do?
What did Ruth say to her mother-in-law?
What did Ruth do?

17. HONORING GOD'S REPRESENTATIVES

THE FOURTH COMMANDMENT

Honor your father and mother, that it may go well with you, and that you may enjoy long life on the earth.

What does this mean?

We should fear and love God that we do not dishonor or anger our parents and others in authority, but honor, serve and obey them, and give them love and respect.

For Me to Learn

How we honor God's representatives

For Me to Remember

Whom has God placed over us in the home, school, church, and state? (A. Parents and others in authority)

How do we honor them? (A. By regarding them as God's representatives)

Ephesians 6:2,3. *Honor your father and mother — which is the first commandment with a promise — that it may go well with you and that you may enjoy long life on the earth.*

How do we honor God's representatives with our actions? (A. By serving and obeying them)

1 Timothy 5:4. *Children or grandchildren . . . should learn first of all to put their religion into practice by caring for their own family and so repaying their parents and grandparents.*

Romans 13:1. *Everyone must submit himself to the governing authorities, for there is no authority except that which God has established.*

How do we honor God's representatives with our thoughts or in our hearts? (A. By loving and respecting them)

1 Thessalonians 5:12,13. *Now we ask you, brothers, to respect those who work hard among you, who are over you in the Lord and who admonish you. Hold them in the highest regard in love because of their work.*

How, then, do we honor God's representatives?

> **WE HONOR GOD'S REPRESENTATIVES BY SERVING AND OBEYING THEM AND BY LOVING AND RESPECTING THEM.**

What This Means to Me

My loving God has given me His representatives in the home, church, school, and government. Out of love for God and for the many blessings I receive through these representatives, especially through my parents, I will want to honor them, to obey them gladly, to find various ways to help them, and to love them dearly. I will be with my parents for only a few years. Therefore, I will especially want to take every opportunity to show my love for them in what I say and do. I know that I have often sinned by not honoring my parents and others whom God has placed over me. I ask God to forgive me for Jesus' sake and to help me keep this commandment.

For Me to Memorize

Assigned passages
The Fourth Commandment

For Me to Do

Read Hymn 287 (TLH), stanza 5. How can we show our love for our parents? Write a short prayer in which you thank God for giving you parents to take care of you. Include in your prayer some of the things your parents are doing for you.

For Me to Prepare for the Next Lesson

Read the Bible story "The Good Samaritan" (Luke 10:25-37) in your Bible or Bible history book.
   Why was the man in need of help?
   How did the Samaritan help him?

18. OUR NEIGHBOR

For Me to Learn
Who our neighbors are

For Me to Remember
What was the wounded man in need of?
In what way was the Samaritan a neighbor to him?
How do we show that we are neighbors to our enemies?
Matthew 22:39. *Love your neighbor as yourself.*
Matthew 5:44. *Love your enemies and pray for those who persecute you.*

Which people are our closest neighbors? (A. Our fellow believers)
Galatians 6:10. *As we have opportunity, let us do good to all people, especially to those who belong to the family of believers.*

Who made all people?
Acts 17:26. *From one man he made every nation of men, that they should inhabit the whole earth.*
Malachi 2:10. *Have we not all one Father? Did not one God create us?*

Who, then, are our neighbors?

ALL PEOPLE ARE OUR NEIGHBORS.

What This Means to Me
God has created many people. They live in many different parts of the world. A few of them I shall learn to know, but most of them I shall never see or learn to know. Yet they are all my neighbors. Those of my faith and my relatives are my closest neighbors, but even my

enemies are my neighbors. I pray that I will always be a good neighbor to all people whenever I have the opportunity to be kind and helpful. May God give me the strength and willingness to follow the example of Jesus, who always was a good neighbor to everyone.

For Me to Memorize
Assigned Bible passages

For Me to Do
Read Genesis 13:5-11. How was Abraham a neighbor to Lot?

For Me to Prepare for the Next Lesson
Read the Bible story "Cain and Abel" (Genesis 4:1-12) in your Bible or Bible history book.
 How did Cain feel toward his brother?
 What did he do?

Read the Bible story "Judas' Despair" (Matthew 27:3-7) in your Bible or Bible history book.
 For what had Judas betrayed Jesus?
 What did he do in his despair?

Read the Bible story "Joseph Sold by His Brothers" (Genesis 37:31-35) in your Bible or Bible history book.
 Whom did the brothers hate?
 What did they do that caused their father great grief?

19. OUR AND OUR NEIGHBOR'S LIFE

THE FIFTH COMMANDMENT
You shall not murder.

What does this mean?

We should fear and love God that we do not hurt or harm our neighbor in his body, but help and be a friend to him in every bodily need.

For Me to Learn
What God forbids in the Fifth Commandment

For Me to Remember
Who made us and all people?
Psalm 119:73. *Your hands made me and formed me.*

Who only has the right to end or shorten the lives of people?
Psalm 90:3. *You turn men back to dust, saying, "Return to dust, O sons of men."*

Who took Abel's life? Who took the life of Judas?
Genesis 9:6. *Whoever sheds the blood of man, by man shall his blood be shed.*

Taking a life is a terrible sin. Whom did God give the duty to punish the murderer? (A. The government)

What does God forbid?

GOD FORBIDS US TO TAKE OUR AND OUR NEIGHBOR'S LIFE.

How did the brothers hurt Joseph?
1 John 3:15. *Anyone who hates his brother is a murderer.*
What is hatred in God's sight?
How did the brothers hurt their father?
How did the thieves harm the man on the road to Jericho?

What does God forbid?

GOD FORBIDS US TO HATE, HURT OR HARM OUR NEIGHBOR.

Summary

God forbids us to shorten our own or our neighbor's life. We should not do or say anything that will shorten or embitter the life of anyone; and we should not have anger or hatred in our hearts against our neighbor.

What words in the explanation of the Fifth Commandment tell us what God forbids?

What, then, does God forbid in the Fifth Commandment?

GOD FORBIDS US TO MURDER, HATE, HURT OR HARM OUR NEIGHBOR.

What This Means to Me

God has created me and all people. The lives of all people are in His hands. Only He may end their time on earth. But God has given the government the power, the right, and the duty to punish, even with death. God has also given the government the right to call on its citizens to defend their country. When a soldier, therefore, kills an enemy, he has not committed murder.

In this commandment God forbids me to think, say or do anything that may hurt or harm my neighbor, endanger him or make him unhappy. Even hatred and anger in my heart against my neighbor are sins of murder. I must confess that I have hurt or harmed my parents, teachers, brothers, sisters, playmates, and others many times. I pray that God will forgive me for the sake of Jesus, who helped His neighbors in times of need.

For Me to Memorize
Assigned Bible passages

For Me to Do
Read 2 Samuel 11:14-17. How did David sin against the Fifth Commandment?

20. OUR NEIGHBOR'S WELFARE

THE FIFTH COMMANDMENT
You shall not murder.

What does this mean?
We should fear and love God that we do not hurt or harm our neighbor in his body, but *help and be a friend to him in every bodily need.*

For Me to Learn
What God commands in the Fifth Commandment

For Me to Remember
How did the Samaritan help the man in need?
Romans 12:20. *If your enemy is hungry, feed him; if he is thirsty, give him something to drink.*

With what is God pleased?
Hebrews 13:16. *Do not forget to do good and to share with others, for with such sacrifices God is pleased.*

How can we be a friend to people?
Isaiah 58:7. *Share your food with the hungry and . . . provide the poor wanderer with shelter — when you see the naked, . . . clothe him.*

Whom did Jonathan befriend at the risk of his life?
What words in the explanation of the Fifth Commandment tell us what God commands?

What, then, does God command us to do in the Fifth Commandment?

GOD COMMANDS US TO HELP AND BE A FRIEND TO OUR NEIGHBOR.

What This Means to Me

My gracious God is good to me. He gives me all I have and He helps me in my need. Jesus is my best Friend. He gave His life so that I may live with Him forever. Out of love for my Lord and Savior I will want to be a friend to my neighbor, especially those who are in need of my help. I have not always been kind and helpful. I pray God to forgive me for the sake of Jesus, who kept the Fifth Commandment perfectly. I also pray that God will give me a loving heart that is eager to help and be a friend to my neighbor whenever I can.

For Me to Memorize

Assigned Bible passages

For Me to Do

How can you help some needy people in your community?
What institutions are in your area that help people in need? Do they have volunteers who go there to help the needy? How do they help those in need?

For Me to Prepare for the Next Lesson

Read Genesis 2:18-24.
How did God make woman?
To whom did He bring the woman?
What did Adam call the woman?

21. MARRIAGE

THE SIXTH COMMANDMENT

You shall not commit adultery.

What does this mean?

We should fear and love God that we lead a pure and decent life in words and actions, and *that husband and wife love and honor each other.*

For Me to Learn
What marriage is

For Me to Remember
Who instituted marriage? When? Between whom can a marriage take place? (A. Between one man and one woman)

Mark 10:6-8. At the beginning of creation God made them male and female. For this reason a man will leave his father and mother and be united to his wife, and the two will become one flesh.

Who joins a man and a woman in marriage? (A. God) When already does the union between man and woman take place before God? (A. When they become engaged) How long should a marriage last?

What cannot be done? (A. This marriage union cannot be broken.)

Matthew 19:6. What God has joined together, let man not separate.

What, then, is marriage?

MARRIAGE IS A LIFELONG UNION BETWEEN ONE MAN AND ONE WOMAN.

What This Means to Me
It is pleasing to God when men and women who keep company give much serious thought to the meaning of their marriage in their lives and the lives of their loved ones. A Christian man and woman will always keep in mind that marriage means establishing a home — a Christian home where the whole family can worship together. They will keep in mind that love based on physical attractions is not the most important. It is more important that their love for each other is based on their love for Christ. They will always take the matter of their possible marriage to the Lord in prayer and throughout their life rely on Him to guide and bless them in their marriage.

For Me to Memorize
Assigned Bible passages

For Me to Prepare for the Next Lesson
Read the Bible story "Joseph's Purity" (Genesis 39:4-12) in your Bible or Bible history book.

Whom did Potiphar's wife want to lead into sin?
What did she want Joseph to be to her?

22. SINS OF ADULTERY

THE SIXTH COMMANDMENT
You shall not commit adultery.

What does this mean?
We should fear and love God that we lead a pure and decent life in words and actions, and that husband and wife love and honor each other.

For Me to Learn
How sins of adultery are committed

For Me to Remember
About whom did Potiphar's wife have sinful thoughts? What were those sinful thoughts? (A. The desire to have Joseph as her husband) What sin did she commit?
Matthew 5:28. *Anyone who looks at a woman lustfully has already committed adultery with her in his heart.*

How are sins of adultery committed?

SINS OF ADULTERY ARE COMMITTED WITH THOUGHTS.

What kind of talk should not come from us? (A. Unwholesome or filthy)
Ephesians 4:29. *Do not let any unwholesome talk come out of your mouths.*

How are sins of adultery committed?

SINS OF ADULTERY ARE COMMITTED WITH WORDS.

How would Potiphar's wife have broken her marriage bond? (A. Joseph would have been like a husband to her.)
What should not be broken?
What sin is committed when the marriage bond is broken? (A. Adultery)
Matthew 19:6. *What God has joined together, let man not separate.*

What deeds are often committed in secret? (A. Shameful)

97

Ephesians 5:12. *It is shameful even to mention what the disobedient do in secret.*

How are sins of adultery committed?

SINS OF ADULTERY ARE COMMITTED WITH DEEDS.

Summary

In what ways are sins of adultery committed?

SINS OF ADULTERY ARE COMMITTED WITH THOUGHTS, WORDS, AND DEEDS.

What This Means to Me

Hebrews 13:4. *Marriage should be honored by all, and the marriage bed kept pure, for God will judge the adulterer and all the sexually immoral.*
God blesses rightful marriages, but punishes all those who live in adultery.

I am thankful that there are many happy Christian homes where father and mother respect and love each other and where children receive Christian guidance. I am grateful for the guidance I receive from my parents, teachers, pastor, and Christian friends. I know that I am surrounded now and will always be surrounded by many temptations in this world. I pray that God through His word will guide me so that I do not become guilty of committing adultery in what I think, say, or do. Only with His power can I overcome and remain a faithful child of God. May I always remember God's warning: "Flee the evil desires of youth" (2 Timothy 2:22).

For Me to Memorize

Bible passage assignments

For Me to Do

Discuss with your parents the harm that can come from watching certain TV programs and movies.
Discuss with your parents, friends, and teacher various types of unwholesome and sinful entertainment.

23. A PURE AND DECENT LIFE

THE SIXTH COMMANDMENT
You shall not commit adultery.

What does this mean?
We should fear and love God that we lead a pure and decent life in words and actions, and that husband and wife love and honor each other.

For Me to Learn
What God commands in the Sixth Commandment

For Me to Remember
Whom did Joseph want to please?
What does the Bible call people who have a pure heart?
Matthew 5:8. *Blessed are the pure in heart, for they will see God.*

Who alone can give us a pure heart?
Psalm 51:10. *Create in me a pure heart, O God, and renew a steadfast spirit within me.*
What kind of life will those lead who have a pure heart? (A. A pure and decent life)

What does God command in the Sixth Commandment?

GOD COMMANDS US TO LEAD A PURE AND DECENT LIFE.

For whom does God have special instructions in this commandment? (A. For husbands and wives)
How will a husband show his love for his wife? (A. He will love her, support her, and be kind to her.)
Ephesians 5:25. *Husbands, love your wives, just as Christ loved the church and gave himself up for her.*
How will the wife show that she honors and loves her husband? (A. She will love him, be his helper, and serve him.)
Ephesians 5:22. *Wives, submit to your husbands as to the Lord.*

What does God command in the Sixth Commandment?

GOD COMMANDS HUSBANDS AND WIVES TO HONOR AND LOVE EACH OTHER.

Summary
What words in the explanation of the Sixth Commandment tell us what God commands?

> **GOD COMMANDS THAT WE SHOULD LEAD A PURE AND DECENT LIFE AND THAT HUSBANDS AND WIVES LOVE AND HONOR EACH OTHER.**

What This Means to Me
I pray that I will always remember that I am God's child for whom Jesus suffered and died to cleanse me from all my sins. I want to thank Him for His goodness and love. I pray that He will bless me with a pure heart that wants to please Him in all I think, say, or do.

Galatians 5:16. *Live by the Spirit, and you will not gratify the desires of the sinful nature.*

May I seek and find pleasure and enjoyment in those things and with those people who help me grow in Christian knowledge and grace of God.

Psalm 119:105. *Your word is a lamp to my feet and a light for my path.*

When I am tempted, may God give me the strength to say, "How can I do that great wickedness and sin against my loving God!"

Matthew 26:41. *Watch and pray so that you will not fall into temptation.*

For Me to Memorize
Assigned Bible passages
The Sixth Commandment

For Me to Do
Discuss with your parents TV programs that are wholesome for Christian family viewing.

Discuss with your parents and teachers entertainment, books, and magazines that are wholesome for Christians.

For Me to Prepare for the Next Lesson
Read Genesis 42:1-3 in your Bible.
  Why did Jacob send his sons to Egypt?

Read the Bible story "Zacchaeus" (Luke 19:1-10).
  What did Zacchaeus promise to do?

Read the Bible story of the "Widow's Offering" (Mark 12:41-44).
  How much did she put into the church treasury?

24. PROPERTY AND BUSINESS

THE SEVENTH
COMMANDMENT
You shall not steal.

What does this mean?
We should fear and love God that we do not take our neighbor's money or property or get it by dishonest dealing, but *help him to improve and protect his property and business.*

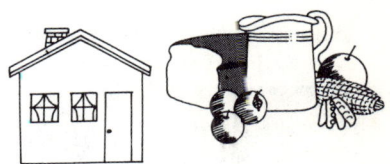

For Me to Learn
How God wants us to use our property and business

For Me to Remember
How did Jacob provide for his family?
What do people deny who do not provide for their families? (A. Their faith)
1 Timothy 5:8. *If anyone does not provide for his relatives, and especially for his immediate family, he has denied the faith and is worse than an unbeliever.*

Whom did Zacchaeus help?
Whom do people not love when they have no compassion for the needy? (A. God)
1 John 3:17. *If anyone has material possessions and sees his brother in need but has no pity on him, how can the love of God be in him?*

How, then, does God want us to use our property and business?

GOD WANTS US TO USE OUR PROPERTY AND BUSINESS TO PROVIDE FOR OUR FAMILIES AND TO HELP THE NEEDY.

How did the poor widow help support the work of the church?
What should we also be willing to support so that God's Word is preached and taught? (A. The work of the church)
Galatians 6:6. *Anyone who receives instruction in the word must share all good things with his instructor.*

How should we support our government?
Matthew 22:21. *Give to Caesar what is Caesar's.*

How, then, does God want us to use our property and business?

GOD WANTS US TO USE OUR PROPERTY AND BUSINESS TO SUPPORT OUR CHURCH AND OUR GOVERNMENT.

Summary
We have learned several ways in which God wants us to use our property and business. What are they?

GOD WANTS US TO USE OUR PROPERTY AND BUSINESS TO PROVIDE FOR OUR FAMILIES, TO HELP THE NEEDY, AND TO SUPPORT OUR CHURCH AND OUR GOVERNMENT.

What This Means to Me
Everything I have is a gift from God — whatever wealth I may have, my parents, my health, my ability to learn and work, my school, my church, my country, and many more things. The greatest gift that God has given me is my faith that trusts in Jesus as my Savior. Many of these things I can and should share with others. As I grow older, God will give me even more with which to help others. It is my prayer that I shall always have many opportunities to show my love for my Savior by using the gifts God has given me to help others.

For Me to Memorize
Assigned Bible passages

For Me to Do
Read Genesis 13:7-9. How did Abraham show his unselfishness?

For Me to Prepare for the Next Lesson
Read the Bible story "Achan's Sin" (Joshua 7).
  What did Joshua command the people?
  What did Achan do?
  Who lost the battle of Ai?
  How was Achan punished?

25. STEALING MONEY AND GOODS

THE SEVENTH COMMANDMENT
You shall not steal.

What does this mean?
We should fear and love God that we do not take our neighbor's money or property or get it by dishonest dealing, but help him to improve and protect his property and business.

For Me to Learn
What God forbids in the Seventh Commandment

For Me to Remember
How did the man on the road to Jericho lose his possessions?
How did Achan sin?
Of what were the robbers and Achan guilty? (A. Stealing)
What does God forbid?
Ephesians 4:28. *He who has been stealing must steal no longer, but must work, doing something useful with his own hands.*

What does God forbid in the Seventh Commandment?

GOD FORBIDS US TO STEAL OUR NEIGHBOR'S MONEY AND GOODS.

Dishonest people sin when they sell things that they have priced above their true value.
What does the Seventh Commandment call that sin? (A. Dishonest dealing)
What do people do who cheat their neighbor in buying and selling?
Leviticus 19:35. *Do not use dishonest standards when measuring length, weight or quantity.*

What does God forbid in the Seventh Commandment?

GOD FORBIDS US TO TAKE OUR NEIGHBOR'S MONEY OR GOODS BY DISHONEST DEALING.

Summary
What words of the explanation of the Seventh Commandment tell us what God forbids?

What, then, does God forbid in the Seventh Commandment?

GOD FORBIDS US TO TAKE OUR NEIGHBOR'S POSSESSIONS OR TO GET THEM BY DISHONEST DEALING.

What This Means to Me

God gives people all their possessions. They may be big and expensive possessions, such as a home, an auto, a farm, a large sum of money; or they may be small, inexpensive possessions, such as a book, a coat, a pair of skates. God gives all people what He pleases and as much as He knows is best for them. They are to use and enjoy their possessions in a God-pleasing way. They may sell these possessions or give them away, but God forbids me to take them from my neighbor by force or to steal them secretly. God also forbids me to cheat my neighbor when I sell him something or trade something with him. Even the thought of wanting to steal or to cheat is a sin.

I confess that I have been guilty of sinning against the Seventh Commandment and I pray God to forgive my sins for Jesus' sake and to give me strength to resist every temptation to steal from my neighbor.

For Me to Memorize

Assigned Bible passages

For Me to Do

Read Matthew 15:19. Where does the sin of stealing begin?

For Me to Prepare for the Next Lesson

Read the Bible story "The Separation of Abraham and Lot" (Genesis 13:5-11).
   Why was it necessary for Abraham and Lot to separate?
   What did Abraham permit Lot to do?

Read the Bible story "Abraham Rescues Lot" (Genesis 14:14-24).
   Whom did Kedorlaomer and the kings capture?
   What did Abraham do when he heard this?

26. HELPING OUR NEIGHBOR

THE SEVENTH COMMANDMENT
You shall not steal.

What does this mean?
We should fear and love God that we do not take our neighbor's money or property or get it by dishonest dealing, but *help him to improve and protect his property and business.*

For Me to Learn
What God commands in the Seventh Commandment

For Me to Remember
How did Abraham help Lot improve his property and business?
About whose property and business does God want us to be concerned?
Philippians 2:4. *Each of you should look not only to your own interests, but also to the interests of others.*
In what ways can we help people?
Matthew 5:42. *Give to the one who asks you, and do not turn away from the one who wants to borrow from you.*
On whom does the Lord want us to have pity?
Proverbs 19:17. *He who is kind to the poor lends to the Lord.*

What does God command us to do in the Seventh Commandment?

GOD COMMANDS US TO HELP OUR NEIGHBOR IMPROVE HIS PROPERTY AND BUSINESS.

How did Abraham protect Lot's property?
What should move us to help our neighbor protect his property and business? (A. Love)
1 Corinthians 13:4,5. *Love . . . is not self-seeking.*

What does God command us to do in the Seventh Commandment?

GOD COMMANDS US TO HELP OUR NEIGHBOR PROTECT HIS PROPERTY AND BUSINESS.

Summary
What words of the explanation of the Seventh Commandment tell us what God commands?

What, then, does God command in the Seventh Commandment?

GOD COMMANDS US TO HELP OUR NEIGHBOR IMPROVE AND PROTECT HIS PROPERTY AND BUSINESS.

What This Means to Me

I love God who has been kind and good to me. In return I will also want to love my neighbor. The Bible says: "He has given us this command: Whoever loves God must also love his brother" (1 John 4:21). May God fill my heart with love for all children and grown-ups with whom I come into contact and make me eager and willing to help them improve and protect what God has given them. I ask the Lord to give me an unselfish heart, so that I will be happy to help others, especially the poor and needy. I must confess that I have sinned many times because I have not always been kind and helpful to my parents, older people, teachers, pastors, children, and others. I ask God to forgive me for the sake of Jesus, who kept this and all commandments perfectly in my place.

For Me to Memorize

Assigned Bible passages
The Seventh Commandment

For Me to Do

Read hymn number 442 (TLH), stanzas 2 and 4.
What do we ask God to do with our hearts?
What is blessed?
What do we see all around us?
What opportunities do we have?

For Me to Prepare for the Next Lesson

Read the Bible story "Ahab's Outrage Against Naboth" (1 Kings 21:8-11).
What did Naboth not want to sell to Ahab?
What did Ahab's wife have the two scoundrels do?
What lies did they tell about Naboth?
What was done to Naboth?

Read the Bible story "Jesus Before Caiaphas" (Matthew 26:59-61).
Who tried to find false witnesses against Jesus?
What did two false witnesses say about Jesus?

27. FALSE TESTIMONY

THE EIGHTH COMMANDMENT

You shall not give false testimony against your neighbor.

For Me to Learn
What false testimony is

For Me to Remember
About whom did John give testimony? (A. About Jesus)
What kind of testimony or witness is sinful?
Proverbs 19:5. *A false witness will not go unpunished, and he who pours out lies will not go free.*
Who brought false testimony before Caiaphas? (A. Jesus' enemies)
Where does the sin of false testimony begin?
Matthew 15:19. *Out of the heart come evil thoughts, murder, adultery, sexual immorality, theft, false testimony, slander.*
Whom did the Jews intend to harm with their false testimony? (A. Jesus)

What is false testimony?

FALSE TESTIMONY IS ANYTHING SPOKEN TO HARM OUR NEIGHBOR.

What This Means to Me
God tells me to love my neighbor as myself. If I love my neighbor as myself, I will not want to hurt or harm him in any way. I will not even want to have harmful thoughts about anyone in my mind. I will not want to say anything about other children and about grown-ups that is untruthful and that will harm their reputation. I confess that sometimes I have been guilty of sinning by saying harmful things

and by thinking sinful thoughts about others. I pray God to be merciful to me and to forgive my sins of false witness. I pray that I will always keep in mind His great love for me, so that I will want to show my love for all people also in what I say and think about them.

For Me to Memorize
Assigned Bible passages

For Me to Do
Read stanza three of hymn number 395 (**TLH**). Write the thoughts of that stanza in your own words. Write them as a prayer. Begin with these words: Dear God. . . .

For Me to Prepare for the Next Lesson
Read the Bible story "Absalom's Treachery" (2 Samuel 15:1-6).
   To whom did Absalom speak?
   What did he tell the people about David?
Read the Bible story "Judas' Betrayal" (Matthew 26:14-16, 47-50).
   What did Judas offer to do?
   What secret did Judas reveal?

28. HARMING OUR NEIGHBOR'S NAME AND REPUTATION

THE EIGHTH COMMANDMENT
You shall not give false testimony against your neighbor.

What does this mean?
We should fear and love God that we do not tell lies about our neighbor, betray him or give him a bad name, but *defend him, speak well of him and take his words and actions in the kindest possible way.*

For Me to Learn
What God forbids in the Eighth Commandment

For Me to Remember
How did Potiphar's wife lie about Joseph?
What will God do to those who lie?
Proverbs 19:5. *A false witness will not go unpunished, and he who pours out lies will not go free.*

To whom did Judas *betray* Jesus?
How was his heart? (A. Deceitful)
What do we reveal when we betray someone?
Proverbs 11:13. *A gossip betrays a confidence, but a trustworthy man keeps a secret.*

How did Absalom slander David?
What did this do to David's name and reputation? (A. It gave him a bad name and reputation.)
James 4:11. *Do not slander one another.*

What is all talk that betrays, slanders, defames or lies about our neighbor? (A. Sinful)
What words in the explanation of the Eighth Commandment tell us what God forbids?

What does God forbid in the Eighth Commandment?

GOD FORBIDS US TO LIE ABOUT OUR NEIGHBOR, BETRAY HIM OR GIVE HIM A BAD NAME.

What This Means to Me
Jesus tells me that the devil is a liar and the father of lies. If I tell a lie, I do the work of the devil. But I am a child of God. I fear and love God and I love my neighbor. I will want to show my love toward God and my neighbor also by what I say. I can hurt my neighbor's good name by telling lies about him and by telling others things about my neighbor that they have no right to know. I also sin against this commandment when I tell untruths about others. I pray my Savior to strengthen the love for all people in my heart, so that I will say only those things to them and about them that will help them, not hurt them.

For Me to Memorize
Assigned Bible passages

For Me to Do
Be ready to read to the class James 3:7-10 and to give the thoughts of the reading in your own words.

For Me to Prepare for the Next Lesson
Read the Bible story "Jonathan Defends David" (1 Samuel 20:30-32).
  What did Saul want Jonathan to do?
  What questions did Jonathan ask Saul?
Read the Bible story "Jesus Heals the Centurion's Servant" (Luke 7:1-5).

What did the centurion want Jesus to do?
Why did the elders of the Jews want Jesus to help the centurion?

29. HELPING OUR NEIGHBOR KEEP HIS GOOD NAME AND REPUTATION

THE EIGHTH COMMANDMENT

You shall not give false testimony against your neighbor.

What does this mean?

We should fear and love God that we do not tell lies about our neighbor, betray him or give him a bad name, but *defend him, speak well of him and take his words and actions in the kindest possible way.*

For Me to Learn
What God commands in the Eighth Commandment

For Me to Remember
What did Jonathan do when Saul said that he wanted to kill David? (A. He defended David.)
What does God want us to do when we hear evil talk about a person?
Proverbs 31:8,9. *Speak up for those who cannot speak for themselves, for the rights of all who are destitute. Speak up and judge fairly; defend the rights of the poor and needy.*
What does this passage call those who are not able to defend themselves?

What does God command us to do in the Eighth Commandment?

GOD COMMANDS US TO DEFEND OUR NEIGHBOR.

Why did Jonathan speak for David? (A. Because Jonathan feared and loved God.)
What did he tell King Saul? (A. Good things about David)
How does God want us to speak about a person who is slandered? (A. He wants us to defend him and speak well about him.)
Proverbs 31:9. *Speak up and judge fairly; defend the rights of the poor and needy.*

What does God command in the Eighth Commandment?

GOD COMMANDS US TO SPEAK WELL OF OUR NEIGHBOR.

What did the Jews think the Roman soldier's reason was for building their synagogue? (A. Love for their nation)
How did they explain his actions? (A. In the best way)
What should make us explain the actions of people in the kindest way? (A. Love)
1 Peter 4:8. *Love covers over a multitude of sins.*

What does God command us to do in the Eighth Commandment?

GOD COMMANDS US TO TAKE OUR NEIGHBOR'S WORDS AND ACTIONS IN THE KINDEST POSSIBLE WAY.

Summary

In what three ways are we to help our neighbor keep his good name and reputation?
What words in the explanation of the Eighth Commandment tell us what God commands?

What does God command in the Eighth Commandment?

> **GOD COMMANDS US TO DEFEND OUR NEIGHBOR, TO SPEAK WELL OF HIM, AND TO TAKE HIS WORDS AND ACTIONS IN THE KINDEST POSSIBLE WAY.**

What This Means to Me

In the Eighth Commandment God commands me not to listen to untruths or to believe lies that are told about someone but to defend such a person and say good things about him. I should do that especially when that person is absent and can't defend himself. God also commands me to try to explain things said and done by others in the kindest possible way. I am always to believe the best about my neighbor.

When I think of what I have and have not said about others, I must confess that I have often sinned against this commandment. I know I deserve God's punishment. I pray that God will not punish me for my sins but forgive them for the sake of Jesus, who kept this commandment perfectly in my place. May God give me strength always to use my mouth for the good of my neighbor.

For Me to Memorize

Bible passage assignments
The Eighth Commandment

For Me to Do

Tell about a real or imaginary incident in which someone 1) defended his neighbor, 2) spoke well of his neighbor, 3) explained the words or the actions of someone in the kindest way. Select one of the three. Do not use the actual names of people.

For Me to Prepare for the Next Lesson
Read the Bible story "Jezebel Schemes to Get Naboth's Vineyard" (1 Kings 21:1-16).
    What did Ahab want very much?
    Why did Naboth not want to give it up?
    How did Jezebel arrange to have Naboth killed?
    What could Ahab then do?

Read the Bible story "Absalom's Rebellion" (2 Samuel 15:1-6).
    What did Absalom urge the people to do?
    About whom did he tell untruths?
    Against whom did he turn the people?

30. SINFUL DESIRES OF OUR HEARTS

THE NINTH COMMANDMENT
You shall not covet your neighbor's house.

What does this mean?
We should fear and love God that we do not scheme to get our neighbor's inheritance or house or obtain it by false claims, but do all we can to help him keep it.

THE TENTH COMMANDMENT
You shall not covet your neighbor's wife or his workers or his animals or anything that belongs to your neighbor.

What does this mean?
We should fear and love God that we do not force or entice away from our neighbor his wife, workers or animals, but urge them to stay and do their duty.

For Me to Learn
What God forbids in the Ninth and Tenth Commandments

For Me to Remember
    What did Ahab covet?
    Of what was Naboth falsely convicted? (A. Blasphemy)
    How did Ahab gain possession of Naboth's inheritance? (A. By false

testimony or claims)
What did the teachers of the law covet?
What is coveting in the sight of God? (A. Sin)
Mark 12:38-40. *Teachers of the law ... like to ... have the most important seats in the synagogues. ... They devour widows' houses and for a show make lengthy prayers. Such men will be punished most severely.*

What does God forbid in the Ninth Commandment?

GOD FORBIDS US TO COVET OUR NEIGHBOR'S PROPERTY.

What did Absalom covet?
What did he do to turn the people against David?
What is this called? (A. Enticing away)
What is another word for covet? (A. Lust)
Romans 7:7. *I would not have known what sin was except through the law. For I would not have known what it was to covet if the law had not said, "Do not covet."*
For what do some people covet or lust according to the Tenth Commandment?

What does God forbid in the Tenth Commandment?

GOD FORBIDS US TO COVET OUR NEIGHBOR'S WIFE, WORKERS, AND ANIMALS.

What may coveting or sinful desires lead to?
James 1:14,15. *Each one is tempted when, by his own evil desire, he is dragged away and enticed. Then, after desire has conceived, it gives birth to sin; and sin, when it is full-grown, gives birth to death.*

Summary

What does God forbid in the Ninth and Tenth Commandments?

GOD FORBIDS US TO HAVE SINFUL DESIRES IN OUR HEARTS.

What This Means to Me

In the Ninth and Tenth Commandments God teaches me that I sin when I envy my neighbor or wish in a sinful way to get what someone has. It is not wrong for me to wish to get what others have in a right or lawful way, but if my neighbor cannot or does not want to part with what I desire, I must no longer desire it in my heart.

God also tells me to be content with what I have. When I am discontented and envious of others, I am dissatisfied with God's will for my life. This is the sin of coveting. It may happen that I covet clothes, a better home, or a new bike that I know I cannot have for some reason. My coveting can lead me to commit sinful deeds, such as cruelty, dishonesty, stealing, cheating, trickery.

I must confess that I have coveted by having sinful desires. I pray God to forgive me my sins for Jesus' sake and to give me a heart that does not lust for anything that is not mine.

For Me to Memorize
Assigned Bible passages

For Me to Do
Read Genesis 3:6. What did Eve covet?
Read Genesis 39:7. Whom did Potiphar's wife covet?

For Me to Prepare for the Next Lesson
Read Genesis 1:26,27. In whose image were Adam and Eve created?
Read the Bible story "The Fall into Sin" (Genesis 3:1-7).
What did Satan tempt Eve to do?
What did Eve tempt Adam to do?
Whom did they disobey?

31. GOD-PLEASING DESIRES OF THE HEART

THE NINTH COMMANDMENT
You shall not covet your neighbor's house.

What does this mean?
We should fear and love God that we do not scheme to get our neighbor's inheritance or house or obtain it by false claims, but *do all we can to help him keep it.*

THE TENTH COMMANDMENT
You shall not covet your neighbor's wife or his workers or his animals or anything that belongs to your neighbor.

What does this mean?
We should fear and love God that we do not force or entice away from our neighbor his wife, workers or animals, but *urge them to stay and do their duty.*

For Me to Learn
   What kind of hearts God wants us to have

For Me to Remember
   How were the first people, Adam and Eve? (A. Holy)
   What were they able to do? (A. Please God with perfect obedience)
   How are all people since man's fall into sin?
   Genesis 8:21. *Every inclination of his heart is evil from childhood.*
   How does God want us to be?
   Matthew 5:48. *Be perfect . . . as your heavenly Father is perfect.*

What kind of hearts does God want us to have?

GOD WANTS US TO HAVE PERFECT HEARTS.

   How did Abraham show that he was concerned about Lot?
   About whose welfare will an unselfish heart be concerned?
   Philippians 2:4. *Each of you should look not only to your own interests, but also to the interests of others.*

   What will cause us to be helpful and kind to others?
   Galatians 5:13. *Serve one another in love.*
   What will be our great desire? (A. To delight in serving the Lord)
   Psalm 37:4. *Delight yourself in the Lord.*

What kind of hearts does God want us to have?

GOD WANTS US TO HAVE HEARTS THAT DELIGHT IN KEEPING HIS COMMANDMENTS.

Summary
   God wants us to have hearts that are holy (perfect).
   God wants us to have hearts that take pleasure (delight) in pleasing Him.

What kind of hearts does God want us to have?

GOD WANTS US TO HAVE PERFECT HEARTS THAT DELIGHT IN KEEPING HIS COMMANDMENTS.

What This Means to Me
   God tells me, "Serve one another in love" (Galatians 5:13). If I truly love my parents, brothers and sisters, grandparents, schoolmates, and all people, I will be happy when God gives them good things. I will want to let them know how happy I am for them. I will also

offer to help them take care of their belongings and to protect them as if they were my own.

But I know that sinful desires want to arise in my heart. I know that I am not always satisfied with what I have and that I sometimes become envious and jealous of those who have what I would like to have. I pray that God will take such sinful thoughts out of my heart and make me eager to keep His commandments. This should be my great delight. Create a clean heart within me, dear Savior, and forgive my sins of coveteousness!

For Me to Memorize
Assigned Bible passages
The Ninth and Tenth Commandments

For Me to Do
Discuss: Is it wrong for me to admire a classmate's new bicycle? Is it always wrong to want one like the one he has? How can this admiration for the bike become sinful?

For Me to Prepare for the Next Lesson
Use the Review and Study Guide (Number 32) to prepare for the next lesson. Write the answers on a sheet of paper and study them. The review is on lessons 15 - 31.

32. REVIEW AND STUDY GUIDE

(Lessons 15 - 31)

I. *Answer*

Answer these questions.

1. What do we call people whom God has placed over us?
2. Whom has God placed over us in the home? In the church? In the school? In government?
3. Whom did Absalom dishonor and despise?
4. How are God's representatives dishonored?
5. How do we honor God's representatives?
6. Whom does the Bible mean when it speaks about our neighbor?
7. Who was a good neighbor to the man who was robbed on the road to Jericho?
8. How much should we love our neighbor?

9. What does God forbid us to do to our neighbor? *to hurt or harm*
10. What does God command us to do in the Fifth Commandment? *to help and be a friend to him in his need.*

II. Complete these sentences.

1. Marriage was instituted by .... *God* .
2. Marriage is a union between .... *one* man and .... *one* woman.
3. Sins of adultery are committed with shameful and filthy .... *thoughts* , ... *words* , and .... *deeds* .
4. We must depend upon .... to keep us from sinning.
5. God commands us to lead a .... *chaste* and .... *decent* life.
6. Everything we own comes from .... *God* .
7. God wants us to use what He has given to us to help our .... *neighbor* .
8. We should especially help the .... *needy* .
9. God forbids us to steal our neighbor's .... *property* . or .... *business* . or get them by .... *dishonest* .... *dealings* .
10. .... *love* for our neighbor will make us want to help him improve and protect his property and business.

III. Match

Match column A with column B

A		B
1. Potiphar's wife	*b*	a. betrayed Jesus
2. False testimony	*f*	b. lied about Joseph
3. Jonathan	*c*	c. defended David
4. Judas	*a*	d. what people think about our neighbor
5. Reputation	*d*	e. gave David a bad name
6. Absalom	*e*	f. anything spoken to harm our neighbor

IV. Underline

Underline the correct answer(s) to these questions.

1. When does coveting take place?
   (When we desire something we should not have, when we do something we should not do, when we say something we should not say.)
2. When is a desire sinful?
   (When we wish to buy our neighbor's property that he has for sale, when we lust for things that are not ours or that we

should not have, when we scheme to get our neighbor's property in a dishonest way.)
3. About whose belongings should we be concerned?
(Only about our own, only our neighbor's, our own and our neighbor's)
4. What will we want to do if we delight in keeping God's commandments?
(Love our neighbor, rejoice when our neighbor is blessed by God, try to outdo our neighbor by gaining more and more property)
5. What kind of heart does God want us to have?
(A perfect heart, a selfish heart, an unselfish heart)

V. *Choose*

1. Which commandment forbids us to hurt or harm our own bodies and the bodies of others?
2. Which commandment requires us to respect all people whom God has placed over us?
3. Which commandment forbids us to have a sinful desire for that which belongs to our neighbor?
4. What commandment requires us to lead a pure and clean life?
5. What commandment requires us to help our neighbor so that his property will be improved?
6. Which commandment forbids us to lie about our neighbor and say things that will harm him?

33. GOD'S WARNING

THE CONCLUSION

What does God say about all these commandments?

He says, "I, the Lord your God, am a jealous God punishing the children for the sin of the fathers to the third and fourth generation of those who hate me, but showing love to thousands who love me and keep my commandments."

What does this mean?

God threatens to punish all who transgress these commandments. Therefore we should fear his anger and not disobey what he commands.

For Me to Learn

Why God threatens to punish us

For Me to Remember

What right does God have? (A. To give us the Law)
James 4:12. *There is only one Lawgiver and Judge, the one who is able to save and destroy.*

What does God expect us to do with His commandments?
Deuteronomy 7:11. *Take care to follow the commands, decrees and laws I give you today.*

How does God become when His commandments are disobeyed? (A. Angry)
What does He do in His anger? (A. He punishes.)
How did God punish the wicked people at the time of the Flood?
Deuteronomy 27:26. *Cursed is the man who does not uphold the words of this law by carrying them out.*

What does God want us to fear?

GOD WANTS US TO FEAR HIS ANGER.

With what did God threaten Adam and Eve if they ate of the tree of knowledge of good and evil? (A. Death)
Romans 6:23. *The wages of sin is death.*
With what did God threaten the wicked people at the time before the Flood?
What were God's threats supposed to stop the people from doing? (A. Sinning, or breaking His commandments)

Why does God threaten us with punishment?

GOD WANTS TO KEEP US FROM BREAKING HIS COMMANDMENTS.

Summary

What parts of the Conclusion tell about God's threat to punish transgressors of His commandments?

Why, then, does God threaten to punish us?

GOD WANTS US TO FEAR HIS ANGER AND TO KEEP FROM BREAKING HIS COMMANDMENTS.

What This Means to Me

God means it when He tells me in His commandments what I am to do and not to do. He does not overlook even the smallest disobedience. My disobedience to His commandments angers Him. I am

God's child through Baptism. I believe that Jesus is my Savior, but my sinful heart so often tries to make me say and do things that anger God. Then I remember God's threat, "The wages of sin is death." I also remember and believe that Jesus died for my sins and that it is only because of what He did for me that God will turn His anger away from me and forgive me.

For Me to Memorize
Assigned passages

For Me to Do
Read Genesis 19:24,25. How did the Lord carry out His threat against the wicked people in the two cities?
Read Matthew 25:41-46. How will God's threat, "The wages of sin is death," be carried out against the ungodly on Judgment Day?

For Me to Prepare for the Next Lesson
Read the Bible story "Jacob's Return" (Genesis 32:1-10).
   Of whom was Jacob afraid?
   How did he show his faith in God?
   Whom did he give credit for his riches?

34. GOD'S PROMISES

THE CONCLUSION

What does God say about all these commandments?

He says, "I, the Lord your God, am a jealous God punishing the children for the sin of the fathers to the third and fourth generation of those who hate me, but *showing love to thousands who love me and keep my commandments."*

What does this mean?
God threatens to punish all who transgress these commandments. Therefore we should fear his anger and not disobey what he commands. *But he promises grace and every blessing to all who keep these commandments. Therefore we should love and trust in him, and gladly obey what he commands.*

For Me to Learn
Why God promises to show us His mercy

For Me to Remember

Whom had Jacob learned to fear and love? (A. God)

How did God show His mercy to Jacob? (A. He blessed him with great riches and brought him back to his home.)

What does no one deserve?

Genesis 32:10. *I am unworthy of all the kindness and faithfulness you have shown your servant.*

To whom does God show mercy?

Luke 1:50. *His mercy extends to those who fear him, from generation to generation.*

How great is God's mercy? (A. He promises to show mercy to the children of parents that love Him and keep His commandments.)

Whom does God promise to bless?

Psalm 112:1. *Blessed is the man who fears the Lord, who finds great delight in his commands.*

What parts of the Conclusion tell us of God's mercy and goodness to those who keep His commandments?

Why does God show us His mercy and promise to bless us?

GOD WANTS US TO LOVE AND TRUST IN HIM AND GLADLY KEEP HIS COMMANDMENTS.

What This Means to Me

God is gracious and merciful to me. I know I do not deserve His kindness and mercy, because I am a sinner. Still, God promises to bless me if I fear and love Him and keep His commandments. But, even if I would keep all of His commandments perfectly, I still would have done only what is my duty to God. He doesn't owe me anything. It is only His love to me that can move me to love Him in return. Then I am eager and willing to keep His commandments. 1 John 5:3. *This is love for God: to obey his commands.*

For Me to Memorize
Bible passages assigned
The Conclusion of the Commandments

For Me to Do
Read hymn number 416 (TLH). Be prepared to answer these questions:
  What do you want God to grant you in His grace?
  How should God order your footsteps?
  In what should God assist you?
  According to what should God help you walk?

For Me to Prepare for the Next Lesson
Read Luke 10:25-28.
What question did the lawyer ask Jesus?
What does the Law of God tell him that he must do to be saved?

35. THE THREE USES OF THE LAW

For Me to Learn
What purposes the Law of God is to serve

For Me to Remember
What does the Law of God demand? (A. That we love God with all our heart, soul, strength, and mind; and that we love our neighbor as ourselves)
Who can keep the Law of God perfectly?
Romans 3:23. *All have sinned and fall short of the glory of God.*

We cannot be saved by trying to keep the Law of God. Yet, God's Law (the Ten Commandments) serves necessary purposes.
What do we see and realize when we read the commandments?
Romans 3:20. *Through the law we become conscious of sin.*

To what can the commandments be compared? (A. A mirror)
What do we realize we need when we see our sins and know we cannot save ourselves? (A. A Savior from sin)
Galatians 3:24. *The law was put in charge to lead us to Christ that we might be justified by faith.*

What is one purpose of the Law?

THE LAW IS TO SERVE AS A MIRROR TO SHOW US OUR SINS AND THE NEED OF THE SAVIOR.

What will people fear who still are conscious of right and wrong?
Psalm 119:120. *My flesh trembles in fear of you; I stand in awe of your laws.*
The conscience of people and the commandments may check or curb the evil deeds people are tempted to commit. To what can the commandments be compared? (A. A curb)

What is the second purpose of the Law?

THE LAW IS TO SERVE AS A CURB TO CHECK WICKED DEEDS.

Whose will are the commandments? (A. God's will)
Psalm 40:8. *To do your will, O my God, is my desire.*
What do the commandments tell us? (A. They tell us what we are to do to please God.) The commandments are to serve as our guide. They tell us what things please and do not please God. To what can the commandments or God's Law be compared? (A. To a rule)

What is the third purpose of the Law?

THE LAW IS TO SERVE AS A RULE TO GUIDE US IN LEADING GOD-PLEASING LIVES.

Summary
What are the three purposes of the Law of God?

THE LAW OF GOD IS TO SERVE AS A MIRROR, AS A CURB, AND AS A RULE.

What This Means to Me
"Your Word is a lamp to my feet and a light for my path" (Psalm 119:105). The Law of God is to hold the wicked desires of my sinful heart in check. The Law of God makes me aware of my sinful nature and shows me how I have sinned against God and my neighbor. It makes me realize that I am helpless to save myself and that I must rely entirely on God's mercy to save me for Jesus' sake. I am thankful to my heavenly Father that He sent His Son to keep the Law for me and to earn forgiveness for my sins. As God's believing child, I want to do all I can to please Him. The commandments tell me how I am to show my love for God who first loved me.

For Me to Memorize
Assigned Bible passages

For Me to Do
Read James 2:10. Of what would we be guilty if we committed just *one* sin?
Read Matthew 22:10-13. Why was the man not admitted to the wedding feast? (A. He had not put on a wedding garment to cover his dirty, torn garment.)
Whose righteousness must we put on to cover our sins in order to enter heaven?

For Me to Prepare for the Next Lesson
Read Genesis 1:1-27.
   What did God create on each of the six days?

THE APOSTLES' CREED
36. GOD THE CREATOR

THE FIRST ARTICLE
(Of Creation)

I believe in God the Father Almighty, Maker of heaven and earth.

What does this mean?
I believe that God made me and every creature and that he gave me my body and soul, eyes, ears and all my members, my mind and all my abilities.

For Me to Learn
What we believe about the creation of all things

For Me to Remember
What is a creed? (A. A statement of what we believe)
Into how many articles is the Apostles' Creed divided? (A. Three)
What are the three persons of the Holy Trinity? (A. God the Father, God the Son, God the Holy Spirit)

Where does God tell us about the creation of all things? (A. In Genesis chapter 1)
Genesis 1:1. *In the beginning God created the heavens and the earth.*
With what did God create heaven and earth? (A. With His almighty power)
Psalm 115:3. *Our God is in heaven; he does whatever pleases him.*

What do we believe about the creation of heaven and earth?

WE BELIEVE THAT GOD MADE HEAVEN AND EARTH WITH HIS ALMIGHTY POWER.

What did God use to make all creatures? (A. His almighty Word or power)
Colossians 1:16. *By him all things were created: things in heaven and on earth, visible and invisible.*

Which is the most important of God's creatures?

How did He make man?
In whose image did God make man?

What do we believe about the creation of all creatures?

WE BELIEVE THAT GOD MADE ALL CREATURES WITH HIS ALMIGHTY POWER.

Summary
What part of this article tells us that God is the Creator of all things?

What do we believe about the creation of all things?

WE BELIEVE THAT GOD MADE HEAVEN AND EARTH AND ALL CREATURES WITH HIS ALMIGHTY POWER.

What This Means to Me

The Bible tells me that God is the Creator of all things. That is why I confess, "I believe in God the Father Almighty, Maker of heaven and earth." I believe that God is the Father of the Lord Jesus and my Father because I believe that God's Son has redeemed me from my sins. I believe that God made heaven and earth and all creatures by the power of His Word. I believe that God made me through my parents. He gave me my body, soul, eyes, ears, my members, my reason, and my abilities.

Psalm 139:14. *I praise you because I am fearfully and wonderfully made.* When I consider God's great work of creation, I realize that He is a mighty and powerful God. No one is equal to Him. He is *all*-mighty. When I consider how wonderfully this world is made, I realize that our God is an *all*-wise God. No one can equal Him in wisdom. When I consider that God made this wonderful world as my home and that He made me and gave me senses and abilities to enjoy this world, I realize that our God is an *all*-loving God. No one can equal His great love. I thank God that He led me to believe in Him who is the Creator of heaven and earth!

For Me to Memorize
Assigned Bible passages
The first paragraph of the explanation of the First Article

For Me to Do
Make a copy of the Trinity symbol.

For Me to Prepare for the Next Lesson
Read the Bible story "Moses Rescued" (Exodus 2:1-10).

In what danger was the baby?
What did the mother do to protect the baby?
What did the sister do to guard the baby?
What did Pharaoh's daughter decide to do with the baby?

37. THE GOODNESS OF GOD

THE FIRST ARTICLE
 (Of Creation)

I believe in God the Father Almighty, Maker of heaven and earth.

What does this mean?

I believe that God made me and every creature and that he gave me my body and soul, eyes, ears and all my members, my mind and all my abilities.

And *I believe that God still preserves me by richly and daily providing clothing and shoes, food and drink, house and home, wife and children, land, cattle and all I own, and all that I need to keep my body and life, and by defending me against all danger and guarding and protecting me from all evil.*

For Me to Learn

What we believe about the goodness of God

For Me to Remember

What did God promise Noah and his descendants? (A. That He would preserve them)

What does God send regularly so that crops can be raised? (A. Seasons)

To whom do we look for all our needs?
Psalm 145:15. *The eyes of all look to you, and you give them their food at the proper time.*

Why can we depend on God to preserve us?
1 Peter 5:7. *Cast all your anxiety on him because he cares for you.*

What do we believe about the goodness of God?

WE BELIEVE THAT GOD RICHLY AND DAILY PROVIDES FOR OUR DAILY NEEDS.

Whom did God use to guard and protect the baby Moses? (A. His mother, his sister, the daughter of Pharaoh)
From what will God protect us?
Psalm 91:10. *No harm will befall you, no disaster will come near your tent.*

Sometimes God permits troubles to come to us. For what purpose are they sent to us? (A. For our good)
Romans 8:28. *We know that in all things God works for the good of those who love him.*

Whom does God often use to protect us?
Psalm 91:11. *He will command his angels concerning you to guard you in all your ways.*

What do we believe about the goodness of God?

WE BELIEVE THAT GOD DEFENDS US AGAINST DANGER AND GUARDS AND PROTECTS US FROM EVIL.

Summary

What part of the explanation of the article tells about God's goodness?

What do we believe about the goodness of God?

WE BELIEVE THAT GOD PROVIDES FOR US, DEFENDS US AND PROTECTS US.

What This Means to Me

The Bible tells me that God provides for my daily needs and that He guards and protects me day and night. That is why I confess, "I believe in God the Father Almighty, Maker of heaven and earth."

God is good. I see His goodness all around me and especially in the way He cares for me. He provides me with a home, with parents, with food and clothing, and with many more things. I have no reason to worry because I know that He cares for me. He watches over me so that nothing can harm me. I cannot always understand God's ways and the reason why certain things happen, but I trust that God in His goodness will never leave me nor forsake me and will always give me what is best for me.

For Me to Memorize
> Bible passages assigned
> The second paragraph of the explanation of the First Article

For Me to Do
> Read the Fourth Petition and Luther's explanation.
> What do we ask God to give us when we pray, "Give us this day our daily bread?"

For Me to Prepare for the Next Lesson
> Read the Bible story "The Ten Lepers" (Luke 17:11-19).
>> How many lepers returned to Jesus?
>> What did he do to show his gratitude to Jesus?
>
> Read the Bible story "The Widow's Offering" (Luke 21:1-4).
>> How much of her money did the widow give to the church?

38. OUR APPRECIATION FOR GOD'S GOODNESS

THE FIRST ARTICLE
   (Of Creation)

I believe in God the Father Almighty, Maker of heaven and earth.

What does this mean?
All this God does only because he is my good and merciful Father in heaven, and not because I have earned or deserved it.

For all this I ought to thank and praise, to serve and obey him. This is most certainly true

For Me to Learn
> What can we do to show our appreciation for God's goodness?

For Me to Remember
> How did one of the ten lepers show his appreciation to God? (A. He thanked and praised God.)
> How can we show our appreciation for God's goodness and mercy? Psalm 136:1. *Give thanks to the Lord, for he is good. His love endures forever.*

What can we do to show our appreciation for God's goodness?

WE CAN THANK AND PRAISE GOD.

How did the poor widow show her appreciation to God? (A. She gave the last of her money to the church.)
Whom did she serve? (A. God)
How will we serve God if we appreciate His goodness?
Psalm 100:2. *Serve the Lord with gladness; come before him with joyful songs.*

How are all people who fear the Lord? (A. Blessed)
What will they appreciate? (A. God's goodness)
What will they delight in doing?
Psalm 112:1. *Blessed is the man who fears the Lord, who finds great delight in his commands.*

What can we do to show our appreciation for God's goodness?

WE CAN SERVE AND OBEY GOD.

Summary

What part of the explanation of this article tells us how we can show our appreciation for God's goodness?

What, then, can we do to show our appreciation for God's goodness?

WE CAN SHOW OUR APPRECIATION TO GOD FOR HIS GOODNESS BY THANKING, PRAISING, SERVING, AND OBEYING HIM.

What This Means to Me

I know from God's Word that God the Father, the almighty Creator of heaven and earth, made me, that He preserves me and blesses me every day with all I have and need. He does this not because I deserve His blessings but only because He is my good and merciful Father in heaven. I pray that I will always truly appreciate God's goodness and that He will give me the desire to thank, praise, serve, and obey Him all my life.

For Me to Memorize

Assigned Bible passage
The entire First Article

For Me to Do
   Write a prayer of thanks to God for blessings you have received from Him.

For Me to Prepare for the Next Lesson
   Read the Bible story "The Baptism of Jesus" (Matthew 3:13-17).
      Who spoke from heaven when Jesus was baptized?
      What did He say?
   Read the Bible story "The Birth of Jesus" (Luke 2:1-7).
      How did Jesus come to earth?
      Who was His mother?

39. THE PERSON OF JESUS CHRIST

THE SECOND ARTICLE
   (Of Redemption)

I believe in Jesus Christ, his only Son, our Lord; who was conceived by the Holy Ghost; born of the Virgin Mary.

What does this mean?
I believe that Jesus Christ, true God, begotten of the Father from eternity, and also true man, born of the Virgin Mary, is my Lord.

For Me to Learn
   Who Jesus Christ is

For Me to Remember
   What did the heavenly Father call Jesus at His Baptism? (A. My beloved Son)
   From when was Jesus begotten of the Father? (A. From eternity)
   What name does Jesus have that belongs only to God?
   Jeremiah 23:6. *This is the name by which he will be called: The Lord our Righteousness.*

   How much power does Jesus Christ have?
   Matthew 28:18. *All authority in heaven and on earth has been given to me.*
   How did Jesus show His power as almighty God? (A. By doing miracles)

Who, then, is Jesus Christ?

JESUS CHRIST IS TRUE GOD.

Why does Jesus' birth prove that He is true man? (A. He was born of a woman.) In what ways was Jesus like all people? (A. He had a body and soul. He grew up and lived like the people of that time.)

Who, then, is Jesus Christ?

JESUS CHRIST IS TRUE MAN.

Summary

What words of the Second Article tell us that Jesus Christ is true God and true man?

What do we believe about the person of Jesus Christ?

JESUS CHRIST IS TRUE GOD AND TRUE MAN.

What This Means to Me

God's Word tells me very clearly that God sent His only Son Jesus Christ to earth to save me and all lost sinners. Jesus lived on earth as true God and true man. While He was on earth He kept the Law perfectly in our place. He could do so because He was the holy sinless Son of God.

Romans 5:19. *Through the obedience of the one man the many will be made righteous.*

Not only did He keep the Law perfectly, He also suffered and died for my sins and the sins of all people. He could suffer and die because He was true man.

Mark 10:45. *The Son of Man did not come to be served, but to serve, and to give his life as a ransom for many.*

The sinless Son of God had no sins for which He had to suffer and die. He paid for our guilt with His innocent suffering and death. Now I and all who believe that Jesus Christ is the Savior from sin, have eternal life. This is most certainly true.

For Me to Memorize

Sections of Second Article studied in the lesson
Assigned Bible passages

For Me to Do

What is Jesus called in these Bible passages?
    Matthew 16:16   John 20:28   Matthew 9:6

For Me to Prepare for the Next Lesson
   Read John 18:28-37.
      What question did Pilate ask Jesus?
      What kind of kingdom did Jesus not come to set up?
      What did Jesus say He was?
      What did Jesus come to teach and preach?

40. THE THREEFOLD OFFICE OF CHRIST

THE SECOND ARTICLE
   (Of Redemption)
I believe in Jesus Christ, his only Son, *our Lord.*

For Me to Learn
   What the threefold office of Christ is

For Me to Remember
   What were the Old Testament priests commanded to do? (A. They were commanded to offer sacrifices for themselves and the people, and to pray to God for them.)
   Who is our High Priest? (A. Jesus Christ)
   What did He do once for the sins of all people? (A. He sacrificed Himself.)
   What does He still do? (A. He pleads for us before the heavenly Father.)
   1 John 2:1. *If anybody does sin, we have one who speaks to the Father in our defense — Jesus Christ, the Righteous One.*

   What office does Christ have?
CHRIST IS OUR HIGH PRIEST.

   What did Old Testament prophets do? (A. Prophesied, preached, taught)

Who is our prophet? What did He do while on earth?
Deuteronomy 18:15. *The Lord your God will raise up for you a prophet like me from among your own brothers. You must listen to him.*
Through whom does Christ carry on His work as prophet today? (A. Through us, especially through ministers and teachers)
Mark 16:15. *Go into all the world and preach the good news to all creation.*

What office does Christ have?

CHRIST IS OUR PROPHET.

Over what does Christ rule in His Kingdom of Power?
Matthew 28:18. *All authority in heaven and on earth has been given to me.*
Over whom does Christ rule in His Kingdom of Grace? (A. Over those who believe in Him as their Savior)
With what does He rule in His Kingdom of Grace? (A. His Gospel)
When will the believers in Christ enter the Kingdom of Glory? (A. After this life on earth)
Psalm 73:24. *You guide me with your counsel, and afterward you will take me into glory.*

What office does Christ have?

CHRIST IS OUR KING.

Summary

As priest Christ redeemed the world from sin.
As prophet Christ made and still makes known the way to eternal salvation.
As king Christ rules the world. He rules the hearts of the believers by His Gospel and finally takes them to His heavenly kingdom.

What threefold office does Christ have?

CHRIST IS OUR PRIEST, PROPHET, AND KING.

What This Means to Me

My heart is filled with thanksgiving to Christ who is my Priest, Prophet, and King. As my Priest he sacrificed Himself for me when he suffered and died for my sins. As my Priest He asks the heavenly Father to answer my prayers and to forgive my sins. As my Prophet he lets me hear His Gospel of salvation. As my King He keeps me in faith through the Gospel, governs and protects me. Finally He will take me to live with Him forever in His Kingdom of Glory in heaven.

For Me to Memorize
Assigned Bible passages

For Me to Do
These Bible passages tell about Christ's work as Priest, Prophet, or King. Read the passages in your Bibles. Copy the passage locations on a piece of paper, then write behind each passage location Priest, Prophet, or King.
    Ephesians 5:2   Luke 1:32,33   Matthew 17:5

41. THE WORK OF CHRIST

THE SECOND ARTICLE
    (Of Redemption)

I believe in Jesus Christ, his only Son, our Lord; *who was conceived* by the Holy Ghost; born of the Virgin Mary; *suffered under Pontius Pilate; was crucified, dead and buried.*

For Me to Learn
How Christ redeemed us

For Me to Remember
    What does God demand of us? (A. That we keep His Law)
    How are all people since the Fall into sin?
    What can no one keep perfectly as God requires?
    Romans 3:23. *All have sinned and fall short of the glory of God.*

    What do we and all people deserve? (A. Eternal punishment)
    Who redeemed us? How did He redeem us?
    Galatians 3:13. *Christ redeemed us from the curse of the law by becoming a curse for us.*

What kind of life did Jesus live on earth? (A. A humble and lowly life)

Mark 10:45. *The Son of Man did not come to be served, but to serve, and to give his life as a ransom for many.*

When did Jesus endure great suffering? (A. When He was on trial before Pontius Pilate)

In whose place did He endure the suffering?

Isaiah 53:5. *He was pierced for our transgressions, he was crushed for our iniquities.*

How did Christ redeem us?

CHRIST SUFFERED FOR US.

What was Pilate's verdict at the end of the trial? (A. That Jesus should be crucified)

For whom did Jesus suffer the most cruel and shameful death?

Why did He suffer death on the cross?

John 1:29. *Look, the Lamb of God, who takes away the sin of the world!*

What did Christ do to redeem us?

CHRIST DIED FOR US.

Summary

What words in the Second Article tell us how Christ redeemed us?

How did Christ redeem us?

CHRIST SUFFERED AND DIED TO REDEEM US.

What This Means to Me

The name Jesus means Savior. I believe that Jesus is my Savior. He kept the commandments for me. He suffered under Pontius Pilate and died a cruel and shameful death on the cross. He suffered and died because He wanted to save me and all people. By His holy life and innocent suffering and death I am redeemed from all my sin and guilt. "Thousand, thousand thanks shall be, dearest Jesus, unto Thee."

For Me to Memorize

Assigned Bible passages

The section of the Second Article studied in this lesson

For Me to Do
   Read stanza 4 of Hymn number 172 (TLH) and answer these questions?
      Whose burden of sin did Jesus bear?
      What brought the great suffering on Jesus?
      What do we rightfully deserve?
      For what do we pray Jesus?

For Me to Prepare for the Next Lesson
   Read Matthew 17:1-8.
      With whom was God pleased?
   Read Matthew 28:1-6.
      Whom did the two women not find?
      What did the angel say to them?
   Read the Bible story "The Temptation of Jesus" (Matthew 4:1-11).
      How did the devil tempt Jesus to sin?
      What did Jesus say to the devil?
      What did the devil finally have to do?

42. OUR REDEMPTION

THE SECOND ARTICLE

I believe that Jesus Christ, true God, begotten of the Father from eternity, and also true man, born of the Virgin Mary, is my Lord.

He has redeemed me, a lost and condemned creature, purchased and won me from all sins, from death and from the power of the devil, not with gold or silver, but with his holy, precious blood and with his innocent suffering and death.

For Me to Learn
   From what Christ has redeemed me

For Me to Remember
   What did Christ keep perfectly in our place? (A. The Law)
   By whose obedience does God consider us obedient to Him?
   Romans 5:19. *Through the obedience of the one man the many will be made righteous.*
   What did God lay on Jesus?
   Isaiah 53:6. *The Lord has laid on him the iniquity of us all.*
   From what does Jesus' blood cleanse us?
   1 John 1:7. *The blood of Jesus, his Son, purifies us from every sin.*

From what has Christ redeemed us?

CHRIST REDEEMED US FROM SIN.

What did Christ prove by His resurrection? (A. That He has power over death)
John 11:25. *I am the resurrection and the life.*
Why need we not fear death? (A. Christ has overcome death for us.)
John 14:19. *Because I live, you also will live.*

From what has Christ redeemed us?

CHRIST REDEEMED US FROM DEATH.

What did Jesus prove when He was tempted by the devil? (A. He has power over the devil.)
Whose works did Christ destroy by His suffering and death?
1 John 3:8. *The reason the Son of God appeared was to destroy the devil's work.*

From what did Christ redeem us?

CHRIST REDEEMED US FROM THE POWER OF THE DEVIL.

Summary

Read the words of the Second Article that tell us from what Christ has redeemed us.

From what, then, has Christ redeemed us?

CHRIST REDEEMED US FROM SIN, DEATH, AND THE POWER OF THE DEVIL.

What This Means to Me

Christ has purchased me with His holy, precious blood and with His innocent suffering and death. I belong to Him. He is my Savior and my Lord. By His suffering and death He endured the punishment I should receive for my sins. By His resurrection He showed His power over death. I do not have to be afraid of death. I know that death is like a sleep from which Jesus will awaken me on the Last Day. I belong to Jesus. Satan cannot accuse me of sins because Jesus redeemed me from all of them. He will also give me strength to overcome the devil's temptations. I joyfully confess: I believe that Jesus Christ "has redeemed me, a lost and condemned creature, purchased and won me from all sins, from death and from the power of the devil, not with gold or silver, but with his holy, precious blood and with his innocent suffering and death."

For Me to Memorize
Assigned Bible passages
First two paragraphs of the explanation of this article

For Me to Do
Read Hymn 371:1-4 and answer these questions:
What will be our glorious dress on the Last Day?
From what has Christ absolved (freed) us?
Who is our Lord and God? Why?
What does Jesus do for you before the throne of God?

For Me to Prepare for the Next Lesson
Read the Bible story "The Resurrection of Jesus" (Mark 16:1-14).
What did the women see when they entered the tomb?
What did the angel say?

Read the Bible story "The Ascension of Jesus" (Acts 1:9-11).
Who saw Jesus ascend to heaven?
What did the angel tell the disciples of Jesus?

Read the Bible story "Judgment Day" (Matthew 25:31-46).
How will Jesus come on Judgment Day?
Who will be gathered before Him?
What will Jesus tell those who had accepted Him as their Savior?
What will Jesus tell those who had not accepted Him as their Savior?

43. JESUS EXALTATION

THE SECOND ARTICLE

He [Jesus] descended into hell; the third day he rose again from the dead; he ascended into heaven, and is sitting at the right hand of God the Father Almighty; from thence he shall come to judge the living and the dead.

For Me to Learn
What the Bible teaches about Jesus' exaltation

For Me to Remember

Where did Jesus go before He showed Himself alive to His disciples? (A. To hell)

Why did He descend to hell? (A. To show that He was victorious over Satan)

1 Peter 3:18,19. *He was put to death in the body but made alive by the Spirit, through whom also he went and preached to the spirits in prison.*

What does the Bible teach about the exaltation of Jesus?

THE BIBLE TEACHES THAT JESUS DESCENDED INTO HELL.

What did Jesus do on the third day after His death? (A. He arose from death.)

To whom did He show Himself alive?

1 Corinthians 15:4. *He was raised on the third day according to the Scriptures.*

Of what can we be certain? (A. That Jesus is alive)

What does the Bible teach about the exaltation of Jesus?

THE BIBLE TEACHES THAT JESUS ROSE FROM DEATH AND SHOWED HIMSELF ALIVE.

What did Jesus do 40 days after His resurrection? (A. He ascended to heaven.) His "sitting at the right hand of God the Father Almighty" means that He is equal with the Father and rules heaven and earth.

How much power has Jesus?

Matthew 28:18. *All authority in heaven and on earth has been given to me.*

Whose glory does Jesus want us to see?

John 17:24. *Father, I want those you have given me to be with me where I am, and to see my glory.*

What does the Bible teach about the exaltation of Jesus?

THE BIBLE TEACHES THAT JESUS ASCENDED TO HEAVEN AND RULES HEAVEN AND EARTH.

What do we look forward to?

Titus 2:13. *We wait for the blessed hope — the glorious appearing of our great God and Savior, Jesus Christ.*

When will Jesus return? (A. On the Last Day)
Why will Jesus return? (A. To judge all people)
How will He return? (A. Visibly and in great glory)

What does the Bible teach about the exaltation of Jesus?
THE BIBLE TEACHES THAT JESUS WILL RETURN VISIBLY AND IN GLORY TO JUDGE ALL PEOPLE.

What words in the Second Article tell about the exaltation of Jesus?

What This Means to Me
God was satisfied with Jesus' work on earth, His work of saving all people from their sins. Therefore God highly exalted Him. Now Christ makes full use of His divine power and majesty. As King of kings and Lord of lords He rules heaven and earth. On Judgment Day all people will see Him as the mighty Lord and Savior, and those who have accepted and worshiped Him as their only Savior will live with Him forever in the glories of heaven. This, I believe, is most certainly true.

For Me to Memorize
Assigned Bible passages
Second Article without explanation

For Me to Do
Make a ladder with five rungs or make five steps. On each step or rung write in correct order the five states of Christ's exaltation. The five states (not given in right order here) are Ascended, Rose, Sitting, Descended, Judge.

44. THE PURPOSE OF OUR REDEMPTION

THE SECOND ARTICLE
All this he did that I should be his own, and live under him in his kingdom, and serve him in everlasting righteousness, innocence and blessedness, just as he has risen from death and lives and rules eternally.

For Me to Learn
Why Christ redeemed us

For Me to Remember

Whom did Jesus have to overcome to redeem us? (A. The devil)
Genesis 3:15. *I will put enmity between you and the woman, and between your offspring and hers; he will crush your head, and you will strike his heel.*
What price did Jesus pay to redeem us from sin, death, and the devil?
Revelation 5:9. *You were slain, and with your blood you purchased men for God.*
To whom do we now belong? (A. To Jesus)
1 Corinthians 6:19,20. *You are not your own; you were bought at a price.*

Why did Christ redeem us?

CHRIST REDEEMED US THAT WE SHOULD BE HIS OWN.

To whom did we belong before Christ redeemed us? (A. Satan)
We were members of Satan's kingdom.
From whose evil work did Christ redeem us? (A. Satan's)
Into whose kingdom did Christ take us? (A. His kingdom)
2 Timothy 4:18. *The Lord will rescue me from every evil attack and will bring me safely to his heavenly kingdom. To him be glory for ever and ever.*
With what does He rule in His kingdom? (A. With His Word)
What do we call that kingdom? (A. The Kingdom of Grace)
We now live under him in the Kingdom of Grace.
When will Christ take us to the Kingdom of Glory? (A. When we die)

Why did Christ redeem us?

CHRIST REDEEMED US THAT WE SHOULD LIVE UNDER HIM IN HIS KINGDOM.

For whose sins did Jesus suffer in His own body?
To what should we now be dead? (A. To sin)
What kind of life should we lead? (A. A life that pleases God)
1 Peter 2:24. *He himself bore our sins in his body on the tree, so that we might die to sins and live for righteousness.*
Whom should we want to serve?

Why did Christ redeem us?

CHRIST REDEEMED US THAT WE SHOULD SERVE HIM BY OBEYING HIS COMMANDMENTS.

Summary
Read that part of the Second Article that tells why Christ redeemed us. The reasons Christ redeemed me with His holy precious blood and innocent suffering and death are:
That I should be His own.
That I should serve Him now in his Kingdom of Grace.
That I should live with Him forever in his Kingdom of Glory.
That I should serve Him in everlasting righteousness, innocence, and blessedness.

What This Means to Me
Since Christ purchased and won me with His blood, suffering, and death, I am His own. I should now live for Him and do what pleases Him. Christ should control all my thoughts, words, and deeds. Living under Him in His kingdom means to do, say, and think what is right in His sight and to avoid everything that displeases Him. I realize that I am still sinful and at times displease my Savior. Therefore I will daily ask Him to give me strength to overcome all temptations and live each day in blessed service to Him.

For Me to Memorize
Assigned Bible passages
Entire Second Article

For Me to Do
Love for our dear Savior should move us to do what pleases Him. Read Hymn 409:1 (TLH) and answer these questions:
With whom should you walk every day?
Who should be your example?
What should you flee?
Whose bidding should you want to do?
What do you promise Jesus?

For Me to Prepare for the Next Lesson
Read the Bible story "The Baptism of Jesus" (Mark 1:9-11).
Who was baptized?
Who appeared in the form of a dove?
Who spoke from heaven?

45. THE HOLY SPIRIT

THE THIRD ARTICLE
(Of Sanctification)

I believe in the Holy Ghost; the holy Christian church, the communion of saints; the forgiveness of sins; the resurrection of the body; and the life everlasting. Amen.

For Me to Learn
Who the Holy Spirit is

For Me to Remember
Jesus has redeemed us and all people, but what can we not do by ourselves? (A. Believe that He is our Savior from sin)
1 Corinthians 12:3. *No one can say, "Jesus is Lord," except by the Holy Spirit.*

In what form did the Holy Spirit show Himself at the Baptism of Jesus? (A. A dove)
Who is meant with the Holy Trinity? (A. God the Father, God the Son, and God the Holy Spirit)
Matthew 28:19. *Go and make disciples of all nations, baptizing them in the name of the Father and of the Son and of the Holy Spirit.*
Why do we say that the Holy Spirit is the third person of the Holy Trinity? (A. He is generally mentioned last when all Persons of the Trinity are given.)

Who is the Holy Spirit?

THE HOLY SPIRIT IS THE THIRD PERSON OF THE HOLY TRINITY.

To whom did Ananias lie? (A. The Holy Spirit)
What does the Bible call the Holy Spirit? (A. God)
Acts 5:3,4. *Peter said, "Ananias, how is it that Satan has so filled your heart that you have lied to the Holy Spirit? . . . You have not lied to men but to God."*
The Holy Spirit therefore is divine. He is holy. What kind of name does the Holy Spirit have? (A. The Holy Spirit has a divine name.)

How were all things created? (A. By the word of the Lord and the Breath of His mouth)

Psalm 33:6. *By the word of the Lord were the heavens made, their starry host by the breath of his mouth.*

Who is meant with the "breath of his mouth"? (A. The Holy Spirit.)
Only God can create. Creation is a divine work.
What work can the Holy Spirit do? (A. The Holy Spirit can do divine work.)
What power does the Holy Spirit have? (A. The Holy Spirit has divine power.)
Read Psalm 139:7-10.

Who is the Holy Spirit?

THE HOLY SPIRIT IS TRUE GOD.

Summary
The Holy Spirit has divine names. The Holy Spirit can do divine works.
The Holy Spirit has divine power. Who is the Holy Spirit? (A. The Holy Spirit is true God.)

Together with whom is the Holy Spirit true God?

THE HOLY SPIRIT IS TRUE GOD TOGETHER WITH THE FATHER AND THE SON.

What This Means to Me
When I say in the Third Article of the Creed, "I believe in the Holy Ghost," I confess that I believe that the Holy Spirit is true God and equal with the Father and the Son. I honor and glorify Him as a person of the Holy Trinity.

> Glory to God the Father, Son,
> And Holy Spirit, Three in one!
> To Thee, O blessed Trinity,
> Be praise now and eternally. Amen.
> (TLH 245:6)

For Me to Memorize
Assigned Bible passages

For Me to Do (Optional)
Draw a symbol that stands for the Holy Spirit.
Read these Bible passages. What names are used for the Holy Spirit in these passages? John 14:26;   1 Corinthians 6:11;   Galatians 4:6

For Me to Prepare for the Next Lesson
Read the Bible story "Pentecost" (Acts 2:1-47).
What happened as the disciples of Jesus were together in Jerusalem?
Who preached to the people?
About whom did he preach?
How many people became believers in Jesus as their Savior?

46. THE WORK OF HOLY THE SPIRIT

THE THIRD ARTICLE
I believe that I cannot by my own thinking or choosing believe in Jesus Christ, my Lord, or come to him.
But the Holy Ghost has called me by the gospel, enlightened me with his gifts, sanctified and kept me in the true faith.

For Me to Learn
What the work of the Holy Spirit is

For Me to Remember
Who came together in Jerusalem to wait for the Lord's promise to be fulfilled? (A. Jesus' disciples)
Who filled the hearts of the disciples? (A. The Holy Spirit)
What did the disciples do, especially Peter? (A. Preached God's Word)
What was the result of the preaching? (A. Many were brought to believe in Jesus as their Savior.)
Who brought them to faith? (A. The Holy Spirit)
What can we not do by our own reason and strength? (A. Believe in God's Word)
Who works faith in us through God's Word?
1 Corinthians 12:3. *No one can say, "Jesus is Lord," except by the Holy Spirit.*

What is the work of the Holy Spirit?

THE HOLY SPIRIT BRINGS US TO FAITH THROUGH GOD'S WORD AND BAPTISM.

Who constantly tries to make us sin and take away our faith in the Savior? (A. Our sinful desires, the devil, and the ungodly people)
Who alone can keep us in the true faith?

1 Peter 1:5. *Through faith [you] are shielded by God's power until the coming of the salvation.*

Through what means does the Holy Spirit keep us in the true faith? (A. God's Word and Sacraments)

What is the work of the Holy Spirit?

THE HOLY SPIRIT KEEPS US IN THE TRUE FAITH THROUGH GOD'S WORD AND THE LORD'S SUPPER.

Summary

We cannot come to faith in Jesus as our Savior nor remain in the true faith in Jesus by our own thinking or choosing. God the Holy Spirit brings us to faith through Baptism and the Word of God and keeps us in the true faith through the Word of God and the Lord's Supper.

What, then, is the work of the Holy Spirit?

THE HOLY SPIRIT BRINGS US TO FAITH AND KEEPS US IN THE TRUE FAITH THROUGH THE WORD OF GOD AND THE SACRAMENTS.

What This Means to Me

Who gives faith as a gift?

Ephesians 2:8. *By grace you have been saved, through faith — and this not from yourselves, IT IS THE GIFT OF GOD.*

God not only gave His Son to redeem me and earn salvation for me, but He also gives me the gift of faith to believe that Jesus is my Savior. The Holy Spirit invites and urges me to come to Jesus when I hear and read God's Word. Through the Gospel He also keeps me in the true faith to the end of my life. Daily I will want to pray God to make me eager to hear His Word so that the Holy Spirit can bless me with the gift of a strong faith.

For Me to Memorize

The sections of the Third Article studied in this lesson
Assigned Bible passages

For Me to Do

The Holy Spirit uses three means to do His work. Each of the passages that follow speak of one of those means. Copy the passage locations on a sheet of paper and write the name of the means behind each passage location.

Romans 10:17;   Galatians 3:27;   1 Corinthians 11:23-26.

For Me to Prepare for the Next Lesson
Read Acts 2:38-41.
What did Peter tell the people to do?
How many people believed the Word of God that Peter preached?

47. THE HOLY CHRISTIAN CHURCH

THE THIRD ARTICLE
[I believe] in the holy Christian church, the communion of saints.

What does this mean?
[I believe that the Holy Ghost] calls, gathers, enlightens and sanctifies the whole Christian church on earth, and keeps it with Jesus Christ in the one true faith.

For Me to Learn
Who the members of the holy Christian church are

For Me to Remember
What does the Holy Spirit call people to do? (A. To believe that Jesus is their Savior)
Through what does the Holy Spirit call people to believe? (A. Through the Word of God)
What does the Holy Spirit work in the hearts of people? (A. Faith)
Who are saved?
Mark 16:16. *Whoever believes and is baptized will be saved, but whoever does not believe will be condemned.*

Only who knows which people are the believers in the Savior?
2 Timothy 2:19. *The Lord knows those who are his.*
Where will believers in the Savior be found? (A. Wherever the Word of God is read, taught, or preached)
What are all the believers called? (A. The holy Christian church)
Why are they called holy? (A. They have forgiveness of sins through faith in the Savior.)

By what name are they also known? (A. The communion of saints)
Ephesians 2:19. *You are . . . fellow citizens with God's people and members of God's household.*

Summary

Read that part of the Third Article that tells about the holy Christian church.

The Holy Spirit brings people to faith and keeps them in the one true faith through the Gospel.

The Holy Spirit gathers the believers into the holy Christian church.

Who, then, are members of the holy Christian church?

ALL WHO BELIEVE IN JESUS AS THEIR SAVIOR ARE MEMBERS OF THE HOLY CHRISTIAN CHURCH.

What This Means to Me

As a believer in Jesus, my Savior, I am God's child and a member of the holy Christian church. Many boys and girls and men and women throughout the world are members of the holy Christian church because they believe that Jesus is their Savior. The devil tries to destroy the holy Christian church, but he will not succeed. There will always be faithful believers in the Savior.

Matthew 16:18. *You are Peter, and on this rock I will build my church, and the gates of Hades [hell] will not overcome it.*

I am truly grateful that the Holy Spirit has brought me to faith and made me a member of the holy Christian church. I pray that He will keep me in the one true faith all my life and that many people throughout the world will become and remain believers in Jesus as their Savior.

For Me to Memorize

Assigned Bible passages
First two paragraphs of the explanation of the Third Article

For Me to Do

The Bible gives other names to the holy Christian church. What name is given to the church in each of these passages?
    1 Peter 2:9,10;   Revelations 21:2;   Ephesians 1:22,23.

48. RECOGNIZING THE TRUE VISIBLE CHURCH

For Me to Learn
How we recognize the true visible church

For Me to Remember
Who are disciples of Jesus? (A. All people who believe in Him)
Whose Word will they teach and believe? (A. God's Word)
How will Christ's disciples teach God's Word? (A. In truth and purity)
John 8:31,32. *To the Jews who had believed him, Jesus said, "If you hold to my teaching, you are really my disciples. Then you will know the truth, and the truth will set you free."*

A congregation or any group of people who come together to worship God is called a visible church. Why is such a group of people called a visible church? (A. Because we can see who belongs to that church) Name some visible churches. (A. Lutheran, Catholic, Methodist, Baptist)
Not all churches teach all the truths of the Bible. Some add their own ideas to the teachings of God's Word. They do not teach God's Word in its truth and purity. They do not have the marks of a true visible church.

How, then, do we recognize the true visible church?

THE TRUE VISIBLE CHURCH TEACHES GOD'S WORD IN ITS TRUTH AND PURITY.

What does Christ command His believers to teach? (A. What He has commanded them)
Christ wants His Word preached and taught in all its truth and purity. What did He also command his believers to do? (A. To baptize all nations, children, and adults)
Matthew 28:19,20. *Go and make disciples of all nations, baptizing them in the name of the Father and of the Son and of the Holy Spirit, and teaching them to obey everything I have commanded you.*
What do we call Baptism? (A. A sacrament)
How are the believers to observe this sacrament? (A. As Christ commanded that it be observed when He instituted it)

What did Christ institute just before His suffering and death? (A. Holy Communion)
What do we call Holy Communion? (A. A sacrament)
How must the believers observe this sacrament? (A. As Christ commanded that it be observed when He instituted it)

How, then, do we recognize the true visible church?

THE TRUE VISIBLE CHURCH OBSERVES THE SACRAMENTS AS CHRIST INSTITUTED THEM.

Summary
The visible churches are groups of people who worship together.
There are many different churches and church bodies.
Many do not teach God's Word in its truth and purity nor observe the sacraments as Christ instituted them. They show thereby that they are false churches.

How, then, do we recognize the true visible church?

THE TRUE VISIBLE CHURCH TEACHES GOD'S WORD IN ITS TRUTH AND PURITY AND OBSERVES THE SACRAMENTS AS CHRIST INSTITUTED THEM.

What This Means to Me
John 10:27,28. *My sheep listen to my voice; I know them, and they follow me. I give them eternal life.*
It is very important that I am and remain a member of the true visible church where God's Word is taught and preached in all its truth and purity and where the sacraments are observed just as Christ instituted them. I would be sinning if I would become a member of a church that does not teach all the truths of God's Word or does not observe the sacraments as Christ commanded us to observe them. Then I would not be listening to the voice of my Savior and obeying Him. I thank God that in my catechism lessons I have the opportunity to study the teachings of the Evangelical Lutheran church. As I study them with my teachers and classmates I turn to God's Word to prove that these teachings are true and correct.
May God keep me faithful to His Word all my life, and may he grant that my church will always remain the true visible church.

For Me to Memorize
Assigned Bible passages

For Me to Do
You may need help from your teacher or pastor to answer the following questions:
What other Lutheran synods are there besides our synod?
Where does our synod train its pastors and teachers?

For Me to Prepare for the Next Lesson
Read the Bible story "The Pharisee and the Tax Collector" (Luke 18:9-14)
  About what did the Pharisee boast?
  How did the tax collector show he depended on God for help?

Read the Bible story "The Paralytic Man" (Matthew 9:1-7)
  Why was the sick man brought to Jesus?
  What did Jesus do for the man?

49. FORGIVENESS OF SINS

THE THIRD ARTICLE
[I believe in] the forgiveness of sins.

What does this mean?
[I believe that in the Christian church the Holy Ghost] daily and fully forgives all sins to me and all believers.

For Me to Learn
How we receive forgiveness of sins

For Me to Remember
With what did Jesus redeem us?
Ephesians 1:7. *In him we have redemption through his blood, the forgiveness of sins.*

What did Jesus earn for all people?

JESUS EARNED FORGIVENESS FOR ALL PEOPLE.

On whom did God put the sins of all people? (A. On Jesus)
God accepted Jesus' sacrifice for the sins of the world.
What does God do for all people? (A. He declares them righteous.)
2 Corinthians 5:21. *God made him who had no sin to be sin for us, so that in him we might become the righteousness of God.*

For whose sake does God declare all people righteous?

GOD DECLARES THAT ALL PEOPLE ARE RIGHTEOUS FOR JESUS' SAKE.

What good news did Jesus tell the paralytic man? (A. That his sins were forgiven)

What word do we use for the good news of forgiveness of sins? (A. Gospel)

What does God offer through the Gospel?

THROUGH THE GOSPEL GOD OFFERS FORGIVENESS OF SINS.

Not all people accept this free offer of forgiveness.
Why didn't the Pharisee ask for mercy and forgiveness? (A. He believed that he was just and needed no forgiveness.)
Why did the tax collector pray God to have mercy on him? (A. He knew he was a sinner and believed that God would forgive him his sins.)
Who gives us faith to believe in the forgiveness of sins?
Ephesians 2:8. *By grace you have been saved, through faith — and this not from yourselves, it is the gift of God.*
The good news of forgiveness through faith is proclaimed in the Gospel of Jesus Christ.

Who gives us faith to believe the Gospel?

THE HOLY SPIRIT GIVES US FAITH TO BELIEVE THE GOSPEL.

Summary
Jesus earned forgiveness of sins for all people.
God declares all people righteous for Jesus' sake.
Through the Gospel God offers forgiveness of sins.
The Holy Spirit gives us faith to believe the Gospel.

How do we receive forgiveness of sins?

WE RECEIVE FORGIVENESS THROUGH FAITH IN THE GOSPEL.

What This Means to Me
In the Bible God tells me that all my sins are forgiven for Jesus' sake. He is my holy and righteous Savior. God looks upon Jesus' righteous-

ness as my righteousness, and therefore He declares me just and holy (justified).

There is nothing I can do to earn my forgiveness and salvation. Jesus has done all that can be done and need be done. But in return for Jesus' love and God's mercy I will want to show my appreciation by thanking, praising, serving, and obeying my merciful Lord and Savior.

For Me to Memorize
Assigned Bible passages

For Me to Do
Read Isaiah 1:18.
What words describe our sins?
What words tell us that *all* our sins are forgiven?

For Me to Prepare for the Next Lesson
Read the Bible story "Zacchaeus" (Luke 19:1-10).
Whom did Zacchaeus want to see?
What did Jesus tell Zacchaeus that He wanted to do?
What did Zacchaeus willingly do?
What had come to the house of Zacchaeus?

50. GOOD WORKS

THE THIRD ARTICLE

[*I believe that the Holy Ghost*] calls, gathers, enlightens and *sanctifies the whole Christian church on earth,* and keeps it with Jesus Christ in the one true faith.

For Me to Learn
What good works are in the sight of God

For Me to Remember
What was the result of Jesus' talk with Zacchaeus? (A. He became a believer in Jesus as his Savior.)
How did he show his faith? (A. He gave much of his wealth to the poor and to those whom he had cheated.)
What does faith in Jesus do to a person? (A. It makes him a Christian, a new and sanctified person.)
2 Corinthians 5:17. *If anyone is in Christ, he is a new creation.*

What do we call good works? (A. Fruits of faith)
Who only can do good works? (A. Those who have faith in Jesus as their Savior)

153

John 15:5. *I am the vine; you are the branches. If a man remains in me and I in him, he will bear much fruit; apart from me you can do nothing.*

What are good works?

GOOD WORKS ARE ALL THINGS DONE IN FAITH.

How did the Pharisee think he could please God? (A. By obeying many man-made rules and regulations) Making and trying to keep man-made rules to please God is worthless and sinful.

Matthew 15:9. *They worship me in vain; their teachings are but rules taught by men.*

What causes us to do God-pleasing works? (A. Our faith, our love for God.)

Where are we told what works please God? (A. In God's Ten Commandments)

John 14:15. *If you love me, you will obey what I command.*

What are good works?

GOOD WORKS ARE ALL THINGS DONE BY CHRISTIANS ACCORDING TO THE TEN COMMANDMENTS.

Summary

The Holy Spirit creates faith in hearts through Baptism and God's Word. The Holy Spirit sanctifies sinners through faith in the Savior. Faith in the Savior makes sinners into loving and obedient children of God. Believers in the Savior express or show their faith by their good works. They want to keep God's commandments.

What are good works in the sight of God?

GOOD WORKS IN THE SIGHT OF GOD ARE ALL THINGS DONE IN FAITH ACCORDING TO THE TEN COMMANDMENTS.

What This Means to Me

I was born in sin. God graciously brought me to faith through Baptism and His Word. He has kept me in the faith. I am now God's child. I am thankful that God through the Holy Spirit brought me to faith and blesses me with forgiveness of sins. Daily I want to show my appreciation to my gracious God by thanking, serving, and obeying Him. I pray that He will give me strength and desire to let my faith shine before people that they may see my works of faith and glorify my Father in heaven. There are many ways I can serve God. For example, I can serve Him by being kind and loving to others, by helping my parents, and by gladly hearing and learning His Word.

For Me to Memorize
Assigned Bible passages

For Me to Do
What work of faith did these people do?
   The widow (Mark 12:41-44)
   Mary and Martha (Luke 10:38-42)

For Me to Prepare for the Next Lesson
Read the Bible story "Jesus' Return for Judgment" (Matthew 25:31-33).
   How will Jesus return on the Last Day?
   Who will be gathered before Him?

Read the Bible story "The Judgment" (Matthew 25:34-46).
   How will Jesus divide all people?
   What will He give to those who believed in Him and served Him?
   What will those receive who did not believe in Him and serve Him?

51. THE RESURRECTION OF THE BODY AND LIFE EVERLASTING

THE THIRD ARTICLE
[I believe that the Holy Ghost] on the Last Day . . . will raise me and all the dead;
And he will give eternal life to me and all believers in Christ.

For Me to Learn
What the Lord will do on the Last Day

For Me to Remember
Who will come in great glory on the Last Day? (A. Christ)
Who will be gathered before Him? (A. All people)

What will Jesus command all the dead to do? What will happen?
John 5:28,29. *Do not be amazed at this, for a time is coming when all who are in their graves will hear his voice and come out.*

Name some people whom Jesus raised from death. (A. Lazarus and the daughter of Jairus)
Who gives us faith to believe in the resurrection of the dead? (A. The Holy Spirit)

What will Christ do on the Last Day?

CHRIST WILL RAISE ALL PEOPLE FROM DEATH.

Who will judge all people on the Last Day?
What will He give to those who believed in Him as their Savior and in faith served Him?
John 3:16. *God so loved the world that he gave his one and only Son, that whoever believes in him shall not perish but have eternal life.*
Only which people will receive the gift of eternal life?
John 3:36. *Whoever believes in the Son has eternal life.*

To whom will God give eternal life?

GOD WILL GIVE ETERNAL LIFE TO ALL BELIEVERS.

Who keeps people in the true faith and gives them eternal life? (A. The Holy Spirit)

Summary
What, then, will the Lord do on the Last Day?

ON THE LAST DAY THE LORD WILL RAISE ALL PEOPLE FROM DEATH AND GIVE ETERNAL LIFE TO THE BELIEVERS.

What This Means to Me

On the Last Day of the world Jesus will come, and I and all people will be gathered before Him. Those who have died He will raise from death. He will send the unbelievers to eternal punishment in hell. Those who believe in Jesus as their Savior will receive eternal life in heaven. There they will live forever with Christ and be free from all sin, pain, sorrow, and death.

Heaven is my eternal home. I look forward to the day when the Holy Spirit will have finished His work of grace and I shall be with Jesus in heaven. There I shall thank and praise my gracious God who brought me to faith and kept me in faith and made me an heir of eternal life in heaven.

For Me to Memorize
Assigned Bible passages
The entire Third Article

For Me to Do
Read Philippians 3:21. What will Christ do with our bodies on the Last Day?
Read Psalm 16:11. What will we experience in heaven?

For Me to Prepare for the Next Lesson
Use the Review and Study Guide (Number 52) to prepare for the next lesson. Write the answers to the questions on a sheet of paper and study them. The review is on lessons 33 - 51.

52. REVIEW AND STUDY GUIDE

(Lessons 33 - 51)

I. *Answer*

Answer these questions.

1. What does God expect us to do with His commandments?
2. What does God threaten to do to those who disobey His commandments?
3. What should we fear?
4. Why does God threaten to punish those who disobey Him?
5. To whom does God show mercy?
6. What does no one deserve from God?
7. Why is God merciful and why does He promise to bless us?

II. *Complete*

Complete these sentences.

1. The second Chief Part of our Catechism is called the ....
2. There are .... articles in the Creed.
3. The true God is one God, but there are .... persons. They are the ...., the ...., the ....

157

4. God made all things with His almighty ....
5. In His goodness God defends us against .... and protects us from ....
6. We can show our appreciation to God for His goodness toward us by .... and .... Him.
7. We can show by our actions that we appreciate God's goodness when we .... and .... Him.
8. Since the fall into sin all people are ....
9. No one can .... himself from eternal death and damnation.
10. God sent His .... to earth to suffer for the .... of all people.
11. Since Jesus is God's Son He is true ....
12. Since Jesus is Mary's Son He is true ....
13. As true God He could keep all of the .... perfectly.
14. As true man Jesus could .... and .... for the sins of all people.
15. Jesus had to be true .... and true .... to be our Savior.

III. Match

Match column A with column B.

A	B
1. Jesus, our High Priest	.... a. made heaven and earth.
2. Jesus, our Prophet	.... b. redeemed us with His blood.
3. Jesus, our King	.... c. kept the Law and suffered and died for us.
4. God, our Creator	.... d. defends and protects us.
5. God, our Provider	.... e. brings us to faith and keeps us in faith.
6. God, our Protector	.... f. preaches the Gospel.
7. Christ, our Redeemer	.... g. gives us what we need.
8. The Holy Spirit	.... h. rules over us with His power and the Gospel.

IV. Underline

Underline the correct answers to these questions.

1. Who is the third Person of the Holy Trinity?
   (Jesus Christ, the Holy Spirit, the Father)
2. What is the work of the Holy Spirit?
   (He protects us from dangers, He suffered for our sins, He brought us to faith and keeps us in faith.)

3. When do people receive the blessings of the Holy Spirit?
   (When they hear God's Word, when they do good works, when they are baptized)
4. Who are members of the holy Christian church?
   (All people who go to church services, all people who listen to God's Word, all people who believe in Jesus as their Savior)
5. For whom did Jesus earn forgiveness of sins?
   (All people, only those who believe in Jesus as their Savior, those who try to lead good lives)
6. Whom does God declare just and forgiven?
   (All people, only those who believe in Jesus as their Savior, those who try to lead good lives)
7. What people can do works that please God?
   (Only those who believe in Christ as their Savior, all those who try to keep the commandments, all those who are members of a visible church)
8. Who will be gathered before Christ on the Last Day?
   (Only the believers, only the people still living on the earth that day, all people who ever lived)
9. To whom will Jesus give eternal life?
   (All those who believed in Jesus as their Savior, all those who tried to lead good lives, all those who went to church)
10. What does the Holy Spirit do so that we can have eternal life in heaven?
    (He protects our bodies from harm, He brings us to faith, He keeps us in faith to the end.)

For Me to Prepare for Lesson 53

Read the Bible story "The Man of Ethiopia" (Acts 8:26-33)
What did the man ask Philip to do as they came near some water?
What did Philip do?

Read the Bible story "Jesus Commands His Disciples" (Matthew 28: 16-20)
Who met with Jesus in Galilee?
How much power has Jesus?
What two things did He command the disciples to do?

THE SACRAMENT OF HOLY BAPTISM

53. THE NATURE OF BAPTISM

FIRST: WHAT IS BAPTISM?

Baptism is not just plain water, but it is water used by God's command and connected with God's Word.

What is the Word of God?

Christ our Lord says in the last chapter of Matthew, "Go and make disciples of all nations, baptizing them in the name of the Father and of the Son and of the Holy Spirit!"

For Me to Learn
What Baptism is

For Me to Remember
What does the word "baptize" mean? (A. To apply water)
With what did Philip baptize the man from Ethiopia? (A. Natural or plain water)
With what did John the Baptist baptize? (A. Plain or natural water)

What is used in Baptism?

SIMPLE WATER IS USED IN BAPTISM.

Who met with Jesus just before He ascended into heaven? (A. His eleven disciples)
What did He command them to do? (A. To teach His Word and to baptize)
Matthew 28:19. *Go and make disciples of all nations, baptizing them in the name of the Father and of the Son and of the Holy Spirit.*
What did Jesus institute by this command? (A. Holy Baptism)
Jesus is true God. He has all power in heaven and on earth.
To whom did God give the command to baptize? (A. All Christians)
Who should be baptized? (A. All people)

Whose command is carried out in Baptism?

GOD'S COMMAND IS CARRIED OUT IN BAPTISM.

In whose name are all people to be baptized?
Matthew 28:19. *Go and make disciples of all nations, baptizing them*

in the name of the Father and of the Son and of the Holy Spirit.
The Word of God must always be used with Baptism.
What does God do when His name or Word is used?
Numbers 6:27. *They will put my name on the Israelites, and I will bless them.*

Whose Word is used in Baptism?

GOD'S WORD IS USED IN BAPTISM.

Summary
Natural or plain water is used in Baptism.
Baptizing does not consist in just applying water.
Baptizing is a holy act commanded by God.
God's Word is used in baptizing.
Read the answers to these questions from your Catechism: "What is baptism?" "Which is that Word of God?"

What, then, is Baptism?

BAPTISM IS WATER USED BY GOD'S COMMAND AND CONNECTED WITH GOD'S WORD.

What This Means to Me
I was baptized when I was very young. I was baptized because God's command to baptize all nations includes little children. I could not be taught God's Word when I was an infant, but I became God's child and received His blessings through holy Baptism. By Baptism the Holy Spirit brought me to faith and I received forgiveness of sins. I thank God that my parents had me baptized so that I became God's child.

For Me to Memorize
Assigned Bible passages
Baptism: What is Baptism? Which is that Word of God?

For Me to Do
Your day of Baptism was an important day in your life.
Ask your parents to show you your baptismal certificate.
Find this information on the certificate:
  Date of your Baptism; place of your Baptism;
  name of the pastor who baptized you; name of your sponsors.

For Me to Prepare for the Next Lesson
Read the Bible story "Pentecost" (Acts 2:1-47).
  What did the disciples do?

What did they tell the people to do?
What were the results of the disciples' preaching?

54. THE BLESSINGS OF BAPTISM

SECOND: WHAT DOES BAPTISM DO FOR US?

Baptism works forgiveness of sin, delivers from death and the devil and gives eternal salvation to all who believe this, as the words and promises of God declare.

What is God's promise?

Christ our Lord says in the last chapter of Mark, "Whoever believes and is baptized will be saved, but whoever does not believe will be condemned."

For Me to Learn
What blessings God gives us in Baptism

For Me to Remember
What did the disciples ask the people to do on Pentecost? (A. To be baptized)
Why should they be baptized?
Acts 2:38. *Repent and be baptized, every one of you, in the name of Jesus Christ so that your sins may be forgiven.*
Who earned forgiveness of sins for *all* people?
Who makes this forgiveness ours in Baptism? (A. The Holy Spirit)

What blessing does God give us in Baptism?

IN BAPTISM GOD GIVES US FORGIVENESS OF SINS.

What is the cause of temporal and eternal death?
Romans 6:23. *The wages of sin is death.*
If we had no sin, we would not have to fear death.
How did Jesus free us from our sins?
Whose righteousness is put on us in Baptism? (A. Christ's righteousness)
Galatians 3:27. *All of you who were baptized into Christ have been clothed with Christ.*

From what death are we delivered or freed? (A. Eternal death)
What death has lost its terrors for us? (A. Temporal death)
To whose kingdom did we belong when we were born? (A. The devil's kingdom)

Whose children did we become in Baptism? (A. God's children)
Whom do we now not have to obey? (A. The devil)

What two additional blessings does God give us in Baptism?

IN BAPTISM GOD DELIVERS US FROM DEATH AND THE DEVIL.

How are all people who believe and are baptized? (A. Saved)
Mark 16:16. *Whoever believes and is baptized will be saved, but whoever does not believe will be condemned.*
What are all baptized believers sure of? (A. Eternal salvation)

What blessings does God give us in Baptism?

IN BAPTISM GOD GIVES US ETERNAL SALVATION.

Summary

Christ earned forgiveness of sins for us and all people.
He overcame the devil and death. Through His work of redemption we have eternal life. All that Christ has earned for us is offered in Baptism. Answer these questions from your catechism: "What does baptism do for us?" "What is God's promise?"

What, then, are the blessings God gives us in Baptism?

IN BAPTISM GOD FORGIVES OUR SINS, DELIVERS US FROM DEATH AND THE DEVIL, AND GIVES US ETERNAL SALVATION.

What This Means to Me

Christ earned forgiveness of sins for me and all people by His holy life and by His suffering and death. Through Baptism this forgiveness becomes mine. Since my sins are forgiven, I am now God's child and no longer under the power of the devil. The devil cannot condemn me because of my sin. I can be sure of eternal life in heaven. I look forward to the day when Jesus will take me to Himself to live with Him forever. I thank God for the blessings I received in my Baptism.

For Me to Memorize

Assigned Bible passages
Baptism Secondly: What does Baptism do for us?
What is God's promise?

For Me to Do
>Read Acts 22:16. What does Baptism do to sin?
>Read 1 Corinthians 6:11. What three words say that our sins are forgiven for Jesus' sake?

For Me to Prepare for the Next Lesson
>Read the Bible story "Naaman Is Healed" (2 Kings 5:1-14).
>>What did Elisha tell Naaman to do?
>>What did Naaman think the water of the Jordan River could not do?
>>Whose word did he trust to heal him?
>>What was the result?

55. THE POWER OF BAPTISM

THIRD: HOW CAN WATER DO SUCH GREAT THINGS?

>It is certainly not the water that does such things, but God's Word which is in and with the water, and faith which trusts this Word used with the water.

>For without God's Word the water is just plain water and not baptism. But with this Word it is baptism. God's Word makes it a washing through which God graciously forgives our sin and grants us rebirth and a new life through the Holy Spirit.

>*Where is this written?*
>St. Paul says in Titus, chapter 3, "God saved us through the washing of rebirth and renewal by the Holy Spirit, whom he poured out on us generously through Jesus Christ our Savior, so that, having been justified by his grace, we might become heirs having the hope of eternal life. This is a trustworthy saying."

For Me to Learn
>How we receive the blessings in Baptism

For Me to Remember
>From what did Jesus save us? (A. From our sins)
>Where is the forgiveness of sins offered that Jesus earned for all people? (A. In Baptism)
>What gives Baptism the power to forgive sins? (A. God's Word)
>Ephesians 5:25,26. *Christ loved the church and gave himself up for her to make her holy, cleansing her by the washing with water through the Word.*

What Word of God is used in Baptism? (A. God's promise and God's command)

What is God's command?

Rx Matthew 28:19. *Go and make disciples of all nations, baptizing them in the name of the Father and of the Son and of the Holy Spirit.*

What is God's promise?

Rx Mark 16:16. *Whoever believes and is baptized will be saved, but whoever does not believe will be condemned.*

How do we receive God's blessings in Baptism?

WE RECEIVE THE BLESSINGS OF BAPTISM FROM THE WORD OF GOD.

Whose word did Naaman believe when he washed himself in the Jordan River? (A. God's Word)
What was the result? (A. He was healed)
Whose Word are we to believe in Baptism? (A. God's Word)
What will God do with those who believe His Word of command and promise?
Mark 16:16. *Whoever believes and is baptized will be saved, but whoever does not believe will be condemned.*
Faith is the "hand" by which we receive the great blessings offered in Baptism.

How do we receive God's blessings in Baptism?

WE RECEIVE THE BLESSINGS OF BAPTISM THROUGH FAITH.

Summary

The Word of God offers great blessings in Baptism. Faith in that Word of God makes those blessings ours.

Read the answer to this question from your Catechism? "How can water do such great things?"

How, then, do we receive God's great blessings in Baptism?

WE RECEIVE THE BLESSINGS OF BAPTISM THROUGH FAITH IN GOD'S WORD.

What This Means to Me

When I was baptized, water was poured or sprinkled on my head as the pastor spoke these words, "I baptize you in the name of the Father and of the Son and of the Holy Spirit." Through Baptism my sins were washed away and I became God's child. It was not the water that made me God's child and gave me all the great blessings of God in Baptism, but it was the Word of God that was connected with the water. God, the Holy Spirit, gave me the faith to believe God's Word, and He will keep me in faith unto everlasting life.

For Me to Memorize
Assigned Bible passages
Baptism "Third"

For Me to Do
Baptism has the power to forgive our sin and to make us members of God's kingdom. Little babies also are sinful and in need of forgiveness. Therefore they are in need of being baptized.
Read Mark 10:13,14. What does Jesus want parents to do with their children? Why?
Read John 3:5,6. Who only can enter the Kingdom of God?

56. THE MEANING OF BAPTISM FOR US

FOURTH: WHAT DOES BAPTIZING WITH WATER MEAN?

It means that our old Adam with his evil deeds and desires should be drowned by daily contrition and repentance, and die, and that day by day a new man should arise, as from the dead, to live in the presence of God in righteousness and purity now and forever.

Where is this written?
St. Paul says in Romans, chapter 6, "We were buried with Christ through baptism into death in order that, just as Christ was raised from the dead through the glory of the Father, we too may live a new life."

For Me to Learn
What baptizing with water means for us

For Me to Remember

How are all people since Adam and Eve sinned? (A. Sinful)
What desire do sinful people have? (A. To do evil)
What does the Bible call that sinful desire? (A. The old self)
What can those people do who believe and are baptized? (A. Overcome the old self)
Colossians 3:9. *You have taken off your old self with its practices.*

With whom are we buried in Baptism? (A. With Christ)
Romans 6:4. *We were . . . buried with him through baptism into death.*
God now looks upon us as though we had died and were buried without sins. Baptism gives us the power to overcome our sinful desires, to drown the Old Adam.
What will we do when we do fall into sin? (A. Repent)

What does baptizing with water mean for us?

BAPTIZING WITH WATER MEANS THAT WE DROWN OUR SINFUL DESIRES BY DAILY REPENTANCE.

What kind of a spiritual man does Baptism create? (A. A new spiritual man)
Ephesians 4:24. *Put on the new self, created to be like God in true righteousness and holiness.*
Whose righteousness is ours when we put on the New Man? (A. Christ's righteousness)
How will the new self want to live? (A. In righteousness and true holiness)

What does baptizing with water mean for us?

BAPTIZING WITH WATER MEANS THAT WE ARE MADE NEW PEOPLE WHO LIVE TO PLEASE GOD.

Summary

Read the questions and answers under "Fourth" in your Catechism.

What, then, does baptizing with water mean to us?

BAPTIZING WITH WATER MEANS THAT WE DROWN OUR SINFUL DESIRES BY DAILY REPENTANCE AND LEAD GOD-PLEASING LIVES.

What This Means to Me

I pray that God will never let me forget the blessings I received at my Baptism and what Baptism should mean to me. In Baptism I became a new person. I received Jesus' righteousness. God no longer sees my sins. But I still have the Old Adam, the desire to do evil things. Only with God's strength can I overcome temptations to sin. My Baptism assures me that God will give me strength to overcome sin and to lead a life pleasing to Him.

For Me to Memorize

Assigned Bible passages
Baptism "Fourth"

For Me to Do

Read 2 Corinthians 5:14,15.
    What should make us want to please God?
    For whom do those in Christ not want to live?
    For whom do those in Christ want to live?

THE MINISTRY OF THE KEYS

57. THE KEYS OF THE KINGDOM OF HEAVEN

For Me to Learn
What the keys of the kingdom of heaven are

For Me to Remember
Who is the head of the kingdom of heaven? (A. Christ)
Matthew 28:18. *All authority in heaven and on earth has been given to me.*
What has Jesus the authority to do with heaven? (A. To lock or unlock heaven to people)
What locks or closes heaven to people? (A. Their sins)
Romans 3:23. *All have sinned and fall short of the glory of God.*

Who has paid the penalty for all sins and earned eternal life for all people?
2 Timothy 1:10. *Our Savior, Christ Jesus, . . . has destroyed death and has brought life and immortality to light through the gospel.*
Who has everlasting life and will enter the kingdom of heaven?
John 3:36. *Whoever believes in the Son has eternal life.*
What is this good news called? (A. The Gospel)

Where is the Gospel found? (A. In the Word of God)

What, then, is the key of the kingdom of heaven?

THE GOSPEL IN THE WORD IS THE KEY OF THE KINGDOM OF HEAVEN.

Whose word is used in the sacrament of Baptism (A. God's Word)
What is God's Word of promise in Baptism?
Mark 16:16. *Whoever believes and is baptized will be saved.*
What is this good news for the sinner called? (A. The Gospel)
What is unlocked or opened to those who believe the Gospel in the sacrament of Baptism? (A. Heaven)

What, then, is the key of the kingdom of heaven?

THE GOSPEL IN THE SACRAMENT OF BAPTISM IS THE KEY OF THE KINGDOM OF HEAVEN.

Who instituted Holy Communion? (A. Jesus)
For whom did Jesus give His body and shed His blood?
Luke 22:19,20. *This is my body given for you. This cup is the new covenant in my blood, which is poured out for you.*
This Word of God is the good news or Gospel that all people hear when they partake of Holy Communion.
What do those have who believe this Word of God? (A. Forgiveness of sins)
What is opened to them? (A. Heaven)

What, then, is the key of the kingdom of heaven?

THE GOSPEL IN THE SACRAMENT OF HOLY COMMUNION IS THE KEY OF THE KINGDOM OF HEAVEN.

Summary

The Gospel is the good news that Jesus saved all people from their sins and that all who believe this Gospel have eternal life. God has given us the Gospel in His Word and in the sacraments of Baptism and Holy Communion. Through them God opens heaven to all believers.

What, then, are the keys of the kingdom of heaven?

THE KEYS OF THE KINGDOM OF HEAVEN ARE THE GOSPEL IN THE WORD AND SACRAMENTS.

What This Means to Me

I am thankful to my gracious God that He has opened heaven for me. Through the Gospel in the sacrament of holy Baptism I became God's child and received forgiveness of sins. Whenever I hear or read the Gospel, my faith is strengthened and I am assured of my forgiveness for Jesus' sake. Later, after confirmation, I will receive those same blessings through the Gospel in the sacrament of Holy Communion.

For Me to Memorize

Assigned Bible passages

For Me to Do

Draw the symbol for the keys of the kingdom of heaven. On top of the drawing print the title THE KEYS OF THE KINGDOM OF HEAVEN. Beneath the drawing print THE GOSPEL IN THE WORD   THE GOSPEL IN THE SACRAMENTS.

58. THE USES OF THE KEYS OF THE KINGDOM OF HEAVEN

I. The Keys

FIRST: WHAT IS THE USE OF THE KEYS?

The use of the keys is that special power and right which Christ gave to his church on earth, to forgive the sins of penitent sinners, but to refuse forgiveness to the impenitent as long as they do not repent.

Where is this written?

The holy Evangelist John writes in Chapter 20, "Jesus breathed on his disciples and said, 'Receive the Holy Spirit. If you forgive anyone his sins, they are forgiven, if you do not forgive them, they are not forgiven.'"

For Me to Learn

How the church is to use the keys of the kingdom of heaven

For Me to Remember

To whom did Jesus give the keys of the kingdom of heaven? (A. To His church on earth)

What are the keys of the kingdom of heaven? (A. The Gospel in the Word and in the sacraments)

When does the church use the keys of the kingdom of heaven? (A. Whenever the Gospel is preached or taught and the sacraments are administered)

Matthew 28:19. *Go and make disciples of all nations, baptizing them in the name of the Father and of the Son and of the Holy Spirit.*

What do the people receive who repent of their sins and believe the Gospel? (A. Forgiveness of sins)

Luke 24:47. *Repentance and forgiveness of sins will be preached in his name to all nations.*

How, then, does the church use the keys of the kingdom of heaven?

THE CHURCH USES THE KEYS OF THE KINGDOM OF HEAVEN TO FORGIVE THE SINS OF PENITENT SINNERS.

Some people do not repent of their sins. They do not believe in Jesus as their Savior.
What does God say of those who despise his Gospel?
Proverbs 13:13. *He who scorns instruction will pay for it.*
What do we call sinners who do not repent of their sins? (A. Impenitent sinners)
What do they not receive from God? (A. Forgiveness)
What is retained? (A. Their sin)
Read the answers to these questions in your Catechism? "What is the use of the keys?" "Where is this written?"

How, then, does the church use the keys of the kingdom of heaven?

THE CHURCH USES THE KEYS OF THE KINGDOM OF HEAVEN TO RETAIN THE SINS OF THE IMPENITENT SINNERS.

Summary

Christ gave the keys of the kingdom of heaven to his church on earth. The church uses the keys of the kingdom of heaven when it preaches and teaches the Gospel and when it administers the sacraments. Those who believe the Gospel and repent of their sins receive forgiveness. Those who do not believe the Gospel and do not repent of their sins do not receive forgiveness.

How, then, does the church use the keys of the kingdom of heaven?

THE CHURCH USES THE KEYS OF THE KINGDOM OF HEAVEN WHEN IT FORGIVES THE SINS OF THE PENITENT SINNERS AND REFUSES FORGIVENESS TO THE IMPENITENT.

What This Means to Me

I know that my sins can separate me from God. Every day I will want to repent of my sins and ask God to forgive me for Jesus' sake. I know that only those have their sins forgiven who are penitent and who believe in Jesus as their Savior. May God give me a penitent and believing heart!

For Me to Memorize

Assigned Bible passages
"What is the use of the keys?" "Where is this written?"

59. THE CALLED MINISTERS OF THE GOSPEL

SECOND: HOW DOES A CHRISTIAN CONGREGATION USE THE KEYS?

A Christian congregation with its called pastor uses the keys in accordance with Christ's command, by forgiving those who repent of their sin and are willing to amend, and by excluding from the congregation those who are plainly impenitent that they may repent. I believe that when it does so this is as valid and certain in heaven also, as if Christ, our dear Lord, dealt with us himself.

Where is this written?

Jesus says in Matthew, chapter 18, "Whatever you bind on earth will be bound in heaven, and whatever you loose on earth will be loosed in heaven."

For Me to Learn

How the Christian congregation uses the keys of the kingdom of heaven

For Me to Remember

What is the duty of everybody in the church of Christ? (A. To proclaim the Gospel and to administer the sacraments)

How is this done by the members of the congregation? (A. They teach the Word of God in their homes and to other individuals; they administer the sacraments in cases of necessity.)

Why do not all Christians do so publicly in the congregation? (A. This would cause disorder and confusion.)

I Corinthians 14:40. *Everything should be done in a fitting and orderly way.*

Whom does God call through congregations to preach, teach, and administer the sacraments?

1 Corinthians 4:1. *Men ought to regard us as servants of Christ and as those entrusted with the secret things of God.*

How does the Christian congregation use the keys of the kingdom of heaven?

THE CHRISTIAN CONGREGATION CALLS MINISTERS TO PREACH THE GOSPEL AND ADMINISTER THE SACRAMENTS.

What authority did Christ give to His church on earth? (A. To forgive sins)
John 20:23. *If you forgive anyone his sins, they are forgiven.*
Who pronounces forgiveness in our church services and to individuals when they come to him? (A. The minister)
He does so in the name of Christ and by the authority of the church that called him.

How, then, does the Christian congregation use the keys of the kingdom of heaven?

THE CHRISTIAN CONGREGATION CALLS MINISTERS TO PRONOUNCE FORGIVENESS TO PENITENT SINNERS.

Not all people in a congregation are penitent sinners. Some may even commit grievous sins, persist in their sins, and deny their faith in the Savior. The members of the congregation together with their minister will admonish them many times.
What will the congregation have to do if they do not repent?
1 Corinthians 5:13. *Expel the wicked man from among you.*
What will the called minister in the name of the congregation have to tell the openly impenitent sinner? (A. That he has no forgiveness and heaven is closed to him until he repents)
John 20:23. *If you forgive anyone his sins, they are forgiven; if you do not forgive them, they are not forgiven.*

How, then, do Christian congregations use the keys?

CHRISTIAN CONGREGATIONS CALL MINISTERS TO DEAL WITH OPENLY IMPENITENT SINNERS.

Summary

Christ has given the power and right of the keys of the kingdom of heaven to His church on earth. Groups of Christians call ministers who carry out the power and right given to the church of Christ.

How, then, is the power and right given by Christ to His church carried out?

> **THE POWER AND RIGHT OF THE CHURCH IS CARRIED OUT BY CALLED MINISTERS.**

What This Means to Me

I daily sin in thought, word, and deed. My unforgiven sins separate me from God. Daily I must repent of my sins and humbly ask God to forgive me for Jesus' sake. I ask God to make me truly penitent and help me to believe in the forgiveness of all my sins for Jesus' sake. May the words of forgiveness spoken by my minister comfort me and assure me of my forgiveness.

For Me to Memorize

Assigned Bible passages
"How does the Christian congregation use the Keys?"
"Where is this written?"

For Me to Do

Read Matthew 18:12-14.
   With what does Jesus compare sinners who are lost because they have not repented of their sins? What does God want that should not happen to them? What are we to do so they will be saved?

For Me to Prepare for the Next Lesson

Read the Bible story "The Prodigal Son" (Luke 15:11-32).
   What did the son do with the money his father gave him?
   What kind of life did the son lead?
   To whom did he return?
   What did he admit?
   What did the father do to show he had forgiven his son?

Read the Bible story "David's Sin and Repentance" (2 Samuel 11,12).
   What grievous sins did David commit?
   Who accused David of his sins?
   What did David say to Nathan?
   Of what did Nathan assure David?

60. CONFESSION

II. Confession

FIRST: WHAT IS CONFESSION?

Confession has two parts. The one is that we confess our sins; the other, that we receive absolution or forgiveness from the pastor as from God himself, not doubting but firmly believing that our sins are thus forgiven before God in heaven.

SECOND: WHAT SINS SHOULD WE CONFESS?

Before God we should plead guilty of all sins, even those we are not aware of, as we do in the Lord's Prayer.

But before the pastor we should confess only those sins which we know and feel in our hearts.

THIRD: HOW CAN WE RECOGNIZE THESE SINS?

Consider your place in life according to the Ten Commandments. Are you a father, mother, son, daughter, employer or employee? Have you been disobedient, unfaithful or lazy? Have you hurt anyone by word or deed? Have you been dishonest, careless, wasteful or done other wrong?

FOURTH: HOW WILL THE PASTOR ASSURE A PENITENT SINNER OF HIS FORGIVENESS?

He will say, "According to the command of our Lord Jesus Christ, I forgive you your sins in the name of the Father and of the Son and of the Holy Spirit. Amen."

For Me to Learn

What confession means

For Me to Remember

How are all people by nature from their birth? (A. Sinful)
Who alone knows all the sins we commit? (God)
Of how many sins will the penitent sinner plead guilty? (A. Of *all* sins)
What will the penitent sinner ask God to do? (A. Forgive him *all* sins)
Psalm 19:12. *Who can discern his errors? Forgive my hidden faults.*

For whose sake will God forgive the sins of the penitent sinner? (A. For Jesus' sake)

What does confession before God mean?

CONFESSION OF SINS BEFORE GOD MEANS TO PLEAD GUILTY OF ALL SINS AND TO RECEIVE FORGIVENESS FROM GOD.

Against whom did the prodigal son sin when he left home and squandered the money his father had given him? (A. His father)
To whom did he confess his sins? (A. His father)
What should we want to do when we wrong someone by what we say or do? (A. Confess our sins to him and ask for forgiveness)
James 5:16. *Confess your sins to each other.*

What does confession before our neighbor mean?

CONFESSION BEFORE OUR NEIGHBOR MEANS TO PLEAD GUILTY OF SINS WE HAVE COMMITTED AGAINST HIM AND TO RECEIVE FORGIVENESS.

To whom did David confess the sins that greatly troubled him? (A. The prophet Nathan)
Of what did Nathan assure him? (A. Of God's forgiveness)
Of what are we certain when the minister pronounces forgiveness to a penitent sinner? (A. That his sins are forgiven by God)
Matthew 18:18. *Whatever you bind on earth will be bound in heaven, and whatever you loose on earth will be loosed in heaven.*

What does confession before the minister mean?

CONFESSION BEFORE THE MINISTER MEANS TO PLEAD GUILTY OF SINS THAT ESPECIALLY TROUBLE US AND TO RECEIVE FORGIVENESS.

Summary

The penitent sinner is troubled by his sins and wants forgiveness. He will plead guilty of all his sins (the known and unknown) before God and ask for forgiveness. He will go to his neighbor whom he has offended and confess his sins and ask for forgiveness. He may confess to his pastor the sins that especially trouble him so that he can be comforted with forgiveness.

What, then, is meant by Confession?

CONFESSION MEANS TO PLEAD GUILTY OF OUR SINS AND TO RECEIVE FORGIVENESS.

What This Means to Me

Read the questions and answers under "Confession" in your Catechism. I daily sin much; only God knows how often. I can't name and number all my sins. I need forgiveness of my many sins. Daily I want to ask God to forgive them *all* for Jesus' sake. In my work and play I sin by offending and hurting my parents, brothers, sisters, friends, and others. As God's child I will want to go to them, confess my sins, and ask for their forgiveness. When I am especially troubled by what I have said or done, I may go to my pastor and in private confess my sins and be assured by him that my sins are forgiven for Jesus' sake.

For Me to Memorize

Assigned Bible passages
"What is confession?"
"What sins should we confess?"

For Me to Do

In the communion service the Christians confess their sins and receive forgiveness spoken by the minister. Read the words of confession and absolution to your class from your hymnal. See page 16.

For Me to Prepare for the Next Lesson

Read the Bible story "The Institution of the Lord's Supper" (Matthew 26:17-28).
- What feast was Jesus celebrating with His disciples?
- What did Jesus give His disciples to eat and to drink?
- What did He say of the bread?
- What did He say of the wine?

THE SACRAMENT OF HOLY COMMUNION AND THE MEANS OF GRACE

61. THE MEANING OF THE SACRAMENT OF HOLY COMMUNION

FIRST: WHAT IS THE SACRAMENT OF HOLY COMMUNION?

It is the true body and blood of our Lord Jesus Christ together with the bread and wine, instituted by Christ for us Christians to eat and to drink.

Where is this written?
The holy Evangelists Matthew, Mark, Luke and the Apostle Paul tell us: The Lord Jesus, on the night he was betrayed, took bread; and when he had given thanks, he broke it, gave it to his disciples and said, "Take and eat. This is my body, which is given for you. Do this in remembrance of me."
In the same way after supper he took the cup, gave thanks, gave it to them and said, "Drink from it, all of you. This cup is the new covenant in my blood, which is poured out for you for the forgiveness of sins. Do this, whenever you drink it, in remembrance of me."

For Me to Learn
   What the sacrament of Holy Communion is

For Me to Remember
   Who instituted the sacrament of Holy Communion? (A. Jesus Christ)
   What did Jesus give His disciples to eat when He instituted Holy Communion? (A. Unleavened bread)
   What did Jesus say as He gave them the bread? (A. "This is my body, which is given for you.")
   What did Jesus give His disciples to drink? (A. Wine)

What did He say as He gave them the wine? (A. "This cup is the new covenant in my blood.")
What do people receive with the bread and wine in Holy Communion?
What visible elements are used in Holy Communion? (A. Bread and wine)
Whose Word is used in Holy Communion? (A. God's Word)

Summary
Holy Communion is a sacrament because it was instituted by Christ who is true God, because visible elements are used, because it is connected with God's Word, and because God offers spiritual benefits through Holy Communion.
In Holy Communion we receive the body and blood of Christ in and with the bread and wine.

What, then, is Holy Communion?

HOLY COMMUNION IS A SACRAMENT IN WHICH WE RECEIVE THE BODY AND BLOOD OF CHRIST WITH THE BREAD AND THE WINE.

What This Means to Me
Jesus Himself tells me that in Holy Communion I will receive His body and blood in and with the bread and wine. My mind cannot understand this, but I believe what Jesus says, because He is true God. I am grateful that the Lord Jesus has given His believers the sacrament of Holy Communion as a means through which they can receive blessings for their souls.

For Me to Memorize
"What is the sacrament of Holy Communion?"
"Where is this written?"

For Me to Do
God inspired four men to describe the institution of Holy Communion. Read these accounts of the institution in your Bibles:
Matthew 26:26-29; Mark 14:22-25; Luke 22:15-20; 1 Corinthians 11:23-26

62. THE BLESSINGS OF HOLY COMMUNION

SECOND: WHAT BLESSING DO WE RECEIVE THROUGH THIS EATING AND DRINKING?

That is shown us by these words, "Given and poured out for you for the forgiveness of sins."

Through these words we receive forgiveness of sins, life and salvation in this sacrament.

For where there is forgiveness of sins, there is also life and salvation.

For Me to Learn
What blessings does God give us in Holy Communion?

For Me to Remember
What does everyone receive with the bread in Holy Communion? (A. Christ's body)
What does everyone receive with the wine in Holy Communion? (A. Christ's blood)
For whom did Christ give His body into death and shed His blood? (A. All people)
Why did Christ shed His blood and die? (A. For the forgiveness of our sins)
What words of Jesus tell us that? (A. "Given and poured out for you for the forgiveness of sins.")
Ephesians 1:7. *In him we have redemption through his blood, the forgiveness of sins.*

What blessing does God give us in Holy Communion?

IN HOLY COMMUNION GOD GIVES US FORGIVENESS OF SINS.

Forgiveness of sins is a great and wonderful blessing of God. Without that blessing we would be eternally lost. How should we feel toward God for His great goodness? (A. Thankful, grateful)
What will we want to do to show our appreciation to God for this undeserved goodness? (A. Please Him)
Psalm 119:32. *I run in the path of your commands, for you have set my heart free.*
What does the forgiveness of sins in Holy Communion give us the desire and strength to do? (A. To lead godly lives)

What blessing does God give us in Holy Communion?

IN HOLY COMMUNION GOD GIVES US THE DESIRE TO LEAD GODLY LIVES AND THE STRENGTH TO RESIST TEMPTATION.

All people who have forgiveness of sins are holy in the sight of God. They rejoice in the salvation that God has provided for them.
Of what does Holy Communion make them sure? (A. Of their eternal salvation)

What blessing does God give us in Holy Communion?

IN HOLY COMMUNION GOD GIVES US ETERNAL SALVATION.

Summary

In Holy Communion God assures each person that his sins are forgiven. Christ's body and blood and Christ's words, "Given and poured out for *you* for the forgiveness of sins," makes each person sure that his sins are forgiven. When a person has forgiveness of sins, he also has a new spiritual life and finally eternal salvation in heaven.

What blessings, then, does God give us in Holy Communion?

IN HOLY COMMUNION GOD GIVES US FORGIVENESS OF SINS, LIFE, AND SALVATION.

What This Means to Me

In Holy Communion Jesus offers forgiveness of sins in a special way. In Holy Communion I will receive Christ's body and blood with the bread and wine, and I am told by Jesus, "This is given and poured out for you for the forgiveness of your sins." These words of my Lord and Savior make me sure that my sins are forgiven.

For Me to Memorize

Assigned Bible passages
"What blessings do we receive through this eating and drinking?"

For Me to Do

Write the name for the sacrament of Holy Communion that you find in each of these Bible passages:
1 Corinthians 11:20   Acts 2:42   1 Corinthians 10:16   1 Corinthians 10:21

For Me to Prepare for the Next Lesson
Read the Bible story "Naaman is Healed" (2 Kings 5:1-14).
What did Elisha tell Naaman to do?
What did Naaman think the water of the Jordan River could not do?
Whose word did he trust to heal him?

63. THE POWER OF HOLY COMMUNION

THIRD: HOW CAN EATING AND DRINKING DO SUCH GREAT THINGS?

It is certainly not the eating and drinking that does such things, but the words, "Given and poured out for you for the forgiveness of sins."

These words are the main thing in this sacrament, along with the eating and drinking.

And whoever believes these words has what they plainly say, the forgiveness of sins.

For Me to Learn
What gives Holy Communion the power to bless us with forgiveness of sins, life, and salvation?

For Me to Remember
What did Jesus give His disciples to eat and to drink? (A. Bread and wine)
What power does that eating and drinking not have? (A. To forgive sins)
What did Jesus say of the bread and wine? (A. This is my body; this is my blood.)
What words of promise did Jesus speak as He gave the disciples the bread to eat and the wine to drink? (A. "Given and poured out for you for the forgiveness of sins.")
What does Jesus offer and promise in Holy Communion? (A. Forgiveness of sins)

What, then, gives Holy Communion the power to bless us?

CHRIST'S WORDS OF PROMISE GIVE HOLY COMMUNION THE POWER TO BLESS US.

What may some people who partake of Holy Communion not believe?
(A. Christ's promise of forgiveness in Holy Communion)
What do they not receive? (Forgiveness of sins)

1 Corinthians 11:27. *Whoever eats the bread or drinks the cup of the Lord in an unworthy manner will be guilty of sinning against the body and blood of the Lord.*

How, then, do we receive the blessings of Holy Communion?

WE RECEIVE THE BLESSINGS OF HOLY COMMUNION THROUGH FAITH IN CHRIST'S WORDS.

Summary
Both the believers and unbelievers who partake of Holy Communion receive the body and blood of Christ with the bread and wine. But the unbelievers do not receive forgiveness of sins. They do not believe the promise of Christ, "Given and poured out for you for the forgiveness of sins." These words of Christ are the chief thing in Holy Communion. Only those who believe Christ's words of promise have forgiveness of sins.

What, then, gives Holy Communion the power to bless the believers with forgiveness of sins, life, and salvation?

CHRIST'S PROMISE OF FORGIVENESS GIVES HOLY COMMUNION THE POWER TO BLESS THE BELIEVERS.

What This Means to Me
When I will partake of Holy Communion, I will receive Christ's body and blood with the bread and wine, but the eating and drinking are not the most important thing in Holy Communion. The words Christ spoke when He instituted Holy Communion are most important. It is most important and necessary that I believe the words of Christ, "Given and poured out for you for the forgiveness of sins." All believers in Jesus' promise of forgiveness receive the blessings of Holy Communion.

For Me to Memorize
Assigned Bible passages
"How can eating and drinking do such great things?"

64. PREPARATION FOR HOLY COMMUNION

FOURTH: WHO THEN IS PROPERLY PREPARED TO RECEIVE THIS SACRAMENT?

Fasting and other outward preparations may serve a good purpose, but he is properly prepared who believes these words, "Given and poured out for you for the forgiveness of sins."

But whoever does not believe these words or doubts them is not prepared, because the words "for you" require nothing but hearts that believe.

For Me to Learn
Who are blessed by partaking of Holy Communion?

For Me to Remember
What do we receive with the bread and wine in Holy Communion? (A. Christ's body and blood)
Can we understand how this is possible?
Why do we believe this to be true? (A. Because Jesus said, "Take and eat. This is my body, which is given for you. Drink from it, all of you. This is my blood poured out for you.")
What are we to believe when we partake of Holy Communion? (A. That we receive the true body and blood in Holy Communion)

Who, then, is blessed by partaking of Holy Communion?

ALL THOSE ARE BLESSED WHO BELIEVE THAT THEY RECEIVE THE BODY AND BLOOD OF CHRIST IN HOLY COMMUNION.

For what purpose did Christ give us the sacrament of Holy Communion? (A. To make us sure of the forgiveness of our sins)
Of what should we then repent? (A. Of our sins)
Not only should we be sorry for our sins, but what should we believe? (A. Jesus' words: "Given and poured out for you for the forgiveness of your sins.")
1 John 1:7. *The blood of Jesus, his Son, purifies us from every sin.*

Who, then, is blessed by partaking of Holy Communion?

ALL THOSE ARE BLESSED WHO REPENT OF THEIR SINS AND BELIEVE THAT THEIR SINS ARE FORGIVEN FOR JESUS' SAKE.

Summary

What will we be doing if we are not properly prepared to participate in Holy Communion? (A. Sinning)
What should we do before we partake of Holy Communion? (A. Examine ourselves)
What are we to believe that God gives us with the bread and wine?
How are we to feel about our sins?
What are we to believe that God has done with our sins?

Who, then, is blessed by partaking of Holy Communion?

ALL THOSE ARE BLESSED WHO REPENT OF THEIR SINS AND BELIEVE THAT THEY RECEIVE THE BODY AND BLOOD OF JESUS FOR THE FORGIVENESS OF THEIR SINS.

What This Means to Me

God has graciously given us the sacrament of Holy Communion through which He blesses us with forgiveness of sins, life, and salvation. After I am confirmed I will want to partake of Holy Communion often so that I may be assured of the forgiveness of my sins. I pray that God will make me worthy and well-prepared to partake of this sacrament. He alone can give me a repentant and believing heart and the desire to lead a life pleasing to Him.

For Me to Memorize

Assigned Bible passages
"Who, then, is properly prepared to receive this sacrament?"

For Me to Do

Only people who agree with us and our church in the doctrines of God's Word may participate with us in Holy Communion. The reason is found in Acts 2:42. Read this Bible passage to your class and discuss it. We cannot participate in Holy Communion with people in churches that do not agree with us in the teachings of God's Word. The reason is found in Romans 16:17. Read that Bible passage to your class and discuss it.

For Me to Prepare for the Next Lesson

Read the Bible story "The Great Banquet" (Luke 14:15-24).
   What did a certain man prepare?
   Whom did he send out to invite the people?
   What did the servant say?
   Why did the servant have to be sent out several times?

65. THE MEANS OF GRACE

For Me to Learn
What God's Means of Grace are

For Me to Remember
What did the apostles preach to the people? (A. God's Word)
Who earned salvation for all people? (A. Jesus Christ)
What is that good news in God's Word called? (A. The Gospel)
Romans 1:16. *I am not ashamed of the gospel, because it is the power of God for the salvation of everyone who believes.*
What does the Holy Spirit create through the Gospel? (A. Faith)
Romans 10:17. *Faith comes from hearing the message, and the message is heard through the Word of Christ.*
All who believe the Gospel are saved by God's grace.

What, then, is the Gospel in the Word?

THE GOSPEL IN THE WORD IS A MEANS OF GOD'S GRACE.

How did Jesus earn salvation for all people? (A. By His holy life and by His suffering and death)
What do all have who believe that Jesus is their Savior? (A. Forgiveness)
Where is this forgiveness offered to all, even to babies? (A. Baptism)
Acts 2:38,39. *Repent and be baptized, every one of you, in the name of Jesus Christ so that your sins may be forgiven. . . . The promise is for you and your children and for all who are far off.*
What is the good news in Baptism called? (A. The Gospel)
All who believe the good news (Gospel) are saved by God's grace.

What, then, is the Gospel in Baptism?

THE GOSPEL IN BAPTISM IS A MEANS OF GOD'S GRACE.

What do we eat and drink in Holy Communion? (A. The body and blood of Christ with the bread and wine)
From what did Christ redeem all people by giving His body and blood? (A. From their sins)
Ephesians 1:7. *In him we have redemption through his blood, the forgiveness of sins.*
What does Jesus say to all who partake of Holy Communion? (A. "Given and poured out for you for the forgiveness of sins.") This is the Gospel.
What do all receive who believe Christ's Word? (A. All who believe these words are saved by God's grace.)

What, then, is the Gospel in Holy Communion?

THE GOSPEL IN HOLY COMMUNION IS A MEANS OF GOD'S GRACE.

Summary

We have learned these Gospel truths:
God in His great love gave His Son Jesus Christ to keep the Law in our place and to suffer and die for our sins.
God has declared us righteous for His Son's sake.
All people who believe the Gospel message are saved by the grace of God.

What means does God use to offer and give us the free gifts of His grace, the forgiveness of sins, life, and salvation? (A. The Gospel in His Word and the Gospel in the sacraments of Baptism and Holy Communion)

What, then, are God's Means of Grace?

THE MEANS OF GRACE ARE THE GOSPEL IN WORD AND SACRAMENTS.

What This Means to Me

Jesus, my Savior, has earned forgiveness of sins, life, and salvation for me. God graciously gave me those gifts of His grace when I was baptized. Again and again God through the Holy Spirit blesses me with those gifts when I hear and read his Gospel. When I am confirmed, I shall have the joy and privilege of receiving those gifts as

I partake of Holy Communion. I pray that throughout my life I will always make the fullest use of God's Means of Grace.

For Me to Memorize
Assigned Bible passages

For Me to Prepare for the Next Lesson
Use the Review and Study Guide (Lesson 66) to prepare for the next lesson. Write the answers on a sheet of paper and study them.

66. REVIEW AND STUDY GUIDE

(Lessons 53 - 65)

I. *Answer*

Answer these questions.

1. Who commanded that all people should be baptized?
2. What visible element is to be used in Baptism?
3. Whose word is used in Baptism?
4. In whose name are people to be baptized?
5. What blessing does Baptism give people?
6. From what does Baptism deliver those who are baptized?
7. What gives Baptism its power?
8. Through what do people receive the blessings of Baptism?
9. What should we drown by daily repentance?
10. What kind of lives should we lead?

II. *Complete*

Complete these sentences.

1. .... is the head of the kingdom of heaven.
2. .... locks heaven to people who do not repent.
3. The good news that Jesus redeemed all people from their sins is called the ....
4. .... is opened to all who are sorry for their sins and believe that Jesus is their Savior.
5. The .... in God's Word is a key to the kingdom of heaven.
6. The .... is used in the sacrament of Baptism.
7. God's Word says, "Whoever .... and is baptized will be saved."
8. The .... is used in the sacraments of Holy Communion.

9. God's Word says, "Given and poured out for you for the .... of sins."
10. The Gospel in the .... and the two .... are the keys of the kingdom of heaven.

III. *Underline*

Underline the correct answers to these questions. (More than one answer may be correct.)

1. By whom was Holy Communion instituted?
   (Moses, the disciples of Jesus, Jesus Christ)
2. What visible elements did Jesus use in Holy Communion?
   (Bread, wine, water, meat)
3. What do people eat and drink when they partake of Holy Communion?
   (Only bread and wine, the body and blood of Christ with the bread and wine)
4. For whom did Jesus give His body into death and pour out His blood?
   (For the believers, for those who are sorry for their sins, for all people)
5. Who receives forgiveness of sins in Holy Communion?
   (All people, all who are sorry for their sins and believe in Jesus as their Savior, all who are sorry for their sins)
6. What gives Holy Communion the power to forgive sins?
   (The promise of Jesus: "Given and poured out for you for the forgiveness of sins," the eating and drinking)
7. What is necessary to receive the blessings of Holy Communion?
   (Fasting, repentance, faith in Jesus' promise of forgiveness)

IV. *Choose*

To which Means of Grace do these Bible passages refer: The Gospel in the Word? The Gospel in Baptism? The Gospel in Holy Communion?

1. Repent and be baptized, every one of you, in the name of Jesus Christ so that your sins may be forgiven (Acts 2:38).
2. Go and make disciples of all nations, baptizing them in the name of the Father and of the Son and of the Holy Spirit (Matthew 28:19).
3. Whoever believes and is baptized will be saved, but whoever does not believe will be condemned (Mark 16:16).
4. This is my blood of the covenant, which is poured out for many for the forgiveness of sins (Matthew 26:28).
5. Take and eat; this is my body (Matthew 26:26).

6. Repentance and forgiveness of sins will be preached in his name to all nations (Luke 24:47).
7. He who scorns instruction will pay for it (Proverbs 13:13).
8. We were . . . buried with him through baptism into death (Romans 6:4).
9. Do this in remembrance of me (Luke 22:19).
10. Blessed . . . are those who hear the word of God and obey it (Luke 11:28).

Catechism Lessons
Course Two

I. THE BIBLE AND THE CATECHISM

For Me to Learn
   How we can learn to know the true God

For Me to Remember
   What do we know from the wonders and beauty of nature? (A. That there is a God)
   What do the wonders of nature tell us about God? (A. That He is wise and powerful)
   Hebrews 3:4. *Every house is built by someone, but God is the builder of everything.*

   What do many people worship who do not know the true God? (A. Idols)
   Whom can people not learn to know from nature? (A. The true God)
   Who moved men to tell us about the true God? (A. The Holy Spirit)
   2 Peter 1:21. *Men spoke from God as they were carried along by the Holy Spirit.*
   Whose word did the holy men write? (A. God's Word)
   What do we call the book that is God's Word? (A. The Bible)

   Whose word, then, is the Bible?

THE BIBLE IS GOD'S WORD.

   What do the writings of people often contain? (A. Mistakes and untruths)
   How is everything that is told us in the Bible? (A. True)
   God is holy. Therefore His Word is also holy and true.
   John 17:17. *Sanctify them by the truth; your word is truth.*

What only does the Bible contain?

THE BIBLE CONTAINS ONLY THE TRUTH.

Summary
How is everything the Bible says about God? (A. True)
How is everything the Bible says about what God has done, still does, and will do? (A. True)

Where, then, can we learn to know the true God?

WE CAN LEARN TO KNOW THE TRUE GOD FROM THE BIBLE.

We cannot study the entire Bible in school.
What booklet did Luther write to help us study the most important teachings of God's Word? (A. The Catechism)
How many chief parts are in the Catechism? (A. Six)

What This Means to Me
The Bible is my most precious book because it is God's Word. In it God tells me about Himself. He tells me what He had done for me, what He is still doing for me, and what He will do for me. I will want to listen very carefully whenever God's Word is read and when it is taught in the religion lessons. God has promised to bless me when I attentively hear and read His Word.
Luke 11:28. *Blessed . . . are those who hear the word of God and obey it.*

For Me to Memorize
Assigned Bible passages

For Me to Do
Practice reading correctly the names of the books of the Bible.

For Me to Prepare for the Next Lesson
Read the Bible story "The Baptism of Jesus" (Matthew 13:13-17).
  Whom did John baptize?
  Who came down in the form of a dove?
  Who spoke from heaven?
  What did He say?

THE APOSTLES' CREED

2. THE ONLY TRUE GOD

For Me to Learn
Who the only true God is

For Me to Remember
What do all people know when they see the wonders of nature? (A. That there is a God)
When they do wrong, they have a guilty feeling.
What does their mind tell them? (A. That they have disobeyed God)
This is called a natural knowledge of God.
Psalm 14:1. *The fool says in his heart, "There is no God."*
What do people not learn from the natural knowledge of God? (A. Who the true God is, what He has done, what He still does, and what He will do for us)
Where only can we learn to know the true God?
2 Timothy 3:16. *All Scripture is God-breathed and is useful for teaching, rebuking, correcting and training in righteousness.*

How many true Gods are there?
1 Corinthians 8:4. *There is no God but one.*

How many true Gods, then, are there?

THERE IS BUT ONE TRUE GOD.

What three persons of the godhead were present at the Baptism of Jesus? (A. The Son, the Holy Spirit, the Father)
What is Jesus since He is God's Son? (A. True God)

Psalm 2:7. *You are my Son; today I have become your Father.*
Whom should we honor as God? (A. Jesus Christ)
John 5:23. *All may honor the Son just as they honor the Father.*
What is the Holy Spirit called in the story of Ananias and Sapphira? (A. God)
In whose name are people to be baptized?
Matthew 28:19. *Go and make disciples of all nations, baptizing them in the name of the Father and of the Son and of the Holy Spirit.*

How does the Bible describe the one true God?

THERE ARE THREE PERSONS IN THE ONE TRUE GOD.

Summary

There is only *one* God, but since there are three persons in the one true God, we say that the true God is a *tri* (three) *une* (in one) God. Who are the three persons in the *one* God?

Who, then, is the only true God?

THE ONLY TRUE GOD IS THE TRIUNE GOD, FATHER, SON, AND HOLY SPIRIT.

What This Means to Me

I cannot understand how it is possible that there is one true God and yet *three* persons in the one true God. A triangle helps illustrate what the Bible tells me. A triangle with equal sides is *one* drawing of *three* lines that are equal to one another. God is *one* being of three persons who are equal one to another. Even though my mind cannot understand that the true God is a three-in-one God, I believe it is true because the Bible teaches it, and the Bible is God's word. God grant that I will always worship the one true God, Father, Son, and Holy Spirit.

For Me to Memorize

Assigned Bible passages

For Me to Prepare for the Next Lesson

Make a simple symbol that illustrates the Triune God.
Continue to learn the correct pronunciation of the books of the Bible.

3. KNOWLEDGE OF GOD

For Me to Learn
What God is like

For Me to Remember
We cannot see God. He is invisible.
John 4:24. *God is spirit.*

How does the Bible describe God?
THE BIBLE SAYS THAT GOD IS SPIRIT.

When did God already exist? (A. Before the Creation)
Psalm 90:2. *Before the mountains were born or you brought forth the earth and the world, from everlasting to everlasting you are God.*
God had no beginning and will have no end.

How does the Bible describe God?
THE BIBLE SAYS THAT GOD IS EVERLASTING.

Why can no one hide from God? (A. God is all over.)
Jeremiah 23:24. *"Can anyone hide in secret places so that I cannot see him?" declares the Lord. "Do not I fill heaven and earth?" declares the Lord.*
God is all over at the same time. He is always present.

How does the Bible describe God?
THE BIBLE SAYS THAT GOD IS EVER-PRESENT.

God showed His great power and might when He made the world.
Is there anything that God cannot do?
Luke 1:37. *Nothing is impossible with God.*
God can do whatever He pleases.

How does the Bible describe God?
THE BIBLE SAYS THAT GOD IS ALMIGHTY.

What does God know? (A. Everything)
Psalm 139:1,2. *O Lord, you have searched me and you know me. You know when I sit and when I rise; you perceive my thoughts from afar.*
Everything is known to God.

How does the Bible describe God?

THE BIBLE SAYS THAT GOD IS ALL-KNOWING.

God is without sin. What word describes Him? (A. The word "holy")
Isaiah 6:3. *Holy, holy, holy is the Lord Almighty.*
Everything God does it right.

How does the Bible describe God?

THE BIBLE SAYS THAT GOD IS HOLY.

How is everything God says? (A. True)
Psalm 33:4. *The word of the Lord is right and true; he is faithful in all he does.*
God faithfully keeps His Word. He does what He promises.

How does the Bible describe God?

THE BIBLE SAYS THAT GOD IS FAITHFUL.

How is God toward all creatures? (A. Good)
Psalm 145:9. *The Lord is good to all; he has compassion on all he has made.*
God has pity on those who need help and shows mercy to them.

How does the Bible describe God?

THE BIBLE SAYS THAT GOD IS MERCIFUL.

Not only is God merciful to us, but He gives good things to us even though we deserve only punishment from Him.
Exodus 34:6. *The Lord [is] the compassionate and gracious God.*

God in His grace gives us spiritual and bodily gifts that we do not deserve.

How does the Bible describe God?

THE BIBLE SAYS THAT GOD IS GRACIOUS.

What This Means to Me

God's Word tells me that the true God is a great and wonderful God. My mind cannot begin to understand the greatness, might, and wisdom of God. Only in heaven will I know Him in the fullness of His glory. May I always believe in Him as the only true God and worship Him as my Lord and Savior.

For Me to Memorize
Assigned Bible passages

For Me to Do
Be prepared to read Psalm 100 to your class.
Practice locating the books of the Old Testament in your Bible.

For Me to Prepare for the Next Lesson
Read the Bible story "The Healing of the Centurion's Servant" (Luke 7:1-10).
About whom had the centurion heard?
What did he ask the elders of the Jews to do?
Why did he not want Jesus to come to his house?
What did he think Jesus would have to do to heal the servant?

4. FAITH IN GOD

For Me to Learn
What it means to have faith in God

For Me to Remember
Whom must we know to have eternal life?
John 17:3. *This is eternal life: that they may know you, the only true God, and Jesus Christ, whom you have sent.*
How can we learn to know the true God? (A. By hearing and reading God's Word)
What does God give us through His Word? (A. Faith)
Romans 10:17. *Faith comes from hearing the message, and the message is heard through the word of Christ.*

What does it mean to have faith in God?

TO HAVE FAITH IN GOD MEANS TO KNOW THE TRUE GOD.

Many people read and study the Bible, but they do not accept as true what God's Word tells them. What do those who have faith in the true God say about God's Word?
John 17:17. *Your word is truth.*

What does it mean to have faith in God?

TO HAVE FAITH IN GOD MEANS TO ACCEPT AS TRUE WHAT THE BIBLE SAYS OF GOD.

In whom do those trust who have faith in the true God?
Psalm 31:14. *I trust in you, O Lord; I say, "You are my God."*

What does it mean to have faith in God?

TO HAVE FAITH IN GOD MEANS TO TRUST IN GOD.

Summary

To have faith in God means to know God from the Bible. It means to believe as true what the Bible says about God. It means to trust in God and His Word.

What, then, does it mean to have faith in God?

FAITH IN GOD MEANS TO KNOW GOD, TO ACCEPT AS TRUE WHAT THE BIBLE SAYS OF GOD, AND TO TRUST IN HIM.

What This Means to Me

The Bible tells me about God. From the Bible I learn to know who the true God is, what He has done, what He still does, and what He will do. I accept as true what the Bible tells me because I believe that the Bible is God's Word. I have complete trust in God and firmly believe everything that He says in His word. May God strengthen my faith as I continue to read and study His holy Word.

For Me to Memorize

Assigned Bible passages

For Me to Do

Hymn 396 (TLH) is a prayer asking God for a strong faith in Him and His promises. Be prepared to read this prayer in the next religion period.

5. GOD THE FATHER ALMIGHTY

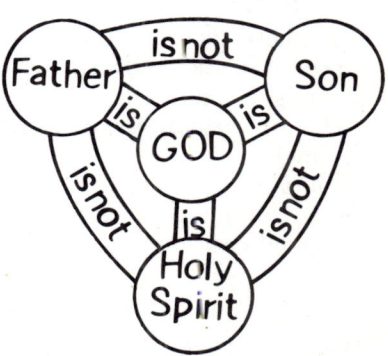

THE FIRST ARTICLE
I believe in God the Father Almighty, Maker of heaven and earth.

For Me to Learn
Why the first person of the Trinity is called Father

For Me to Remember
Who are the three persons in the Holy Trinity? (A. Father, Son, and Holy Spirit)
Matthew 28:19. *Go and make disciples of all nations, baptizing them in the name of the Father and of the Son and of the Holy Spirit.*

In whom do we confess our faith in the First Article of the Apostles' Creed? (A. God the Father)
Whose Father was He from all eternity? (A. Jesus Christ's Father)
What does God the Father call Jesus?
Matthew 3:17. *This is my Son, whom I love; with him I am well pleased.*
What does Jesus call God the Father?
John 20:17. *I am returning to my Father.*

Why is God called Father?
GOD IS THE FATHER OF JESUS CHRIST.

What effect did the sin of Adam and Eve have on all people? (A. It made them all sinful.)
Ephesians 2:3. *We were by nature objects of wrath.*
All people are sinful by nature.

Under whose wrath and condemnation are they? (A. Under God's condemnation)
Sin separated them from their heavenly Father.

What did God do to make it possible to adopt us and all people as His children? (A. He sent His Son to redeem all people.)

Galatians 4:4,5. *When the time had fully come, God sent his Son, born of a woman, born under law, to redeem those under law, that we might receive the full rights of sons.*

Who are the children of God? (A. Those who believe in Jesus as their Savior)

Galatians 3:26. *You are all sons of God through faith in Christ Jesus.* Whose children are all people who believe in Jesus as their Savior? (A. God's children)

Why, then, is God called Father?

GOD THE FATHER IS THE FATHER OF JESUS CHRIST AND OF ALL BELIEVERS IN THE SAVIOR.

Summary

God the Father is the Father of Jesus Christ from eternity. God the Father is the Father of all people who believe in Jesus Christ as their Savior.

Why, then, is the first Person of the Trinity called Father?

GOD THE FATHER IS THE FATHER OF JESUS CHRIST AND OF ALL BELIEVERS IN THE SAVIOR.

What This Means to Me

God is my almighty and loving Father. He made me, protects me, and provides for me. He showed His great love for me when He sent His own dear Son to earth to redeem me from sin, death, and the devil. He gave me faith to believe that Jesus is my Savior. Now I am God's child and He is my Father. I pray that God will always be my loving Father and I His dear child.

For Me to Memorize

Assigned Bible passages

For Me to Do

Find the Bible passages in today's lesson in your Bible.

For Me to Prepare for the Next Lesson
Read the Bible story "The Creation" (Genesis 1:1-27)
When did God create heaven and earth?
What did God create on each of the six days? List them on a sheet of paper.

6. THE CREATION

THE FIRST ARTICLE
I believe in God the Father Almighty, Maker of heaven and earth.

What does this mean?
I believe that God has made me and every creature.

For Me to Learn
How all things were created

For Me to Remember
Where does God tell us how all things were created? (A. In Genesis chapter one)
By whom were all things created? When did God create all things?
Genesis 1:1. *In the beginning God created the heavens and the earth.*
What two kinds of things did God create? (A. Visible and invisible)
Colossians 1:16. *By him all things were created: things in heaven and on earth, visible and invisible.*
The visible creation consists of things we can see, such as man, plants, animals. The invisible creation consists of things that we cannot see, such as angels, gravity.

In how many days did God create all things?
Genesis 1:31. *God saw all that he had made, and it was very good. And there was evening, and there was morning — the sixth day.*

GOD CREATED ALL THINGS IN SIX DAYS.

Who alone existed before the Creation? (A. God) God had nothing and needed nothing to create all things. What did God say when He created light? When He created the firmament?
What did God use to create all things? (A. His Word)
Psalm 33:9. *He spoke, and it came to be.*

We cannot understand how God could create all things by simply saying, "Let there be."

Why do we believe that God created the world and all things by His almighty Word? (A. Because His holy Word tells us that He did) Hebrews 11:3. *By faith we understand that the universe was formed at God's command.*

How were all things created?

GOD CREATED ALL THINGS THROUGH HIS ALMIGHTY WORD.

Summary

The almighty God created heaven and earth and all things in six days. He used the power of His almighty Word to create all things.

How were all things created?

GOD CREATED ALL THINGS IN SIX DAYS THROUGH HIS ALMIGHTY WORD.

What This Means to Me

The creation of heaven and earth and all creatures is a miracle of God. All around me and wherever I travel I see what God has done with the power of His Word. The sky with its sun, moon, and stars are His creation. The plains, mountains, rivers, and oceans came into being by His Word. The millions of creatures great and small were formed by Him out of nothing. All creation is a gift of a loving God. May I always appreciate His gifts and use them to His glory and for my good and for the good of other people.

For Me to Memorize

Assigned Bible passages

For Me to Do

Read Psalm 33:1-9. Which three verses tell about God's creation? Read them to your class.

For Me to Prepare for the Next Lesson

Read Genesis 2:7. What did God do when He created man?
Read Genesis 1:26,27. In whose image did God make man?

7. THE CREATION OF MAN

THE FIRST ARTICLE

I believe in God the Father Almighty, Maker of heaven and earth.

What does this mean?

I believe that God made me and every creature and that he gave me my body and soul, eyes, ears and all my members, my mind and all my abilities.

For Me to Learn

Why man is the most important creature

For Me to Remember

When did God create the first man? (A. On the sixth day of creation)
How did God create the body of man?
Genesis 2:7. *The Lord God formed man from the dust of the ground and breathed into his nostrils the breath of life, and man became a living being.*
When God made all the other creatures, He simply spoke or commanded and they were there, but God gave more attention to the creation of man. He formed his body.

Why, then, is man the most important creature?

GOD FORMED THE BODY OF MAN.

What did God do after He had formed the body of man?
Genesis 2:7. [*He*] *breathed into his nostrils . . . and man became a living being.*
Only what creature has a soul? (A. Man)
What can the soul do? (A. Understand, reason, learn about God)
The soul is living. It will never die. It is immortal.

Why is man the most important creature?

GOD GAVE MAN A SOUL.

What did God say when He was going to create man?
Genesis 1:26. *Let us make man in our image, in our likeness.*
Whom did man know well since he had the image of God? (A. He knew God.)

Colossians 3:10. *Put on the new self, which is being renewed in knowledge in the image of its Creator.*
How was man since he had the image of God? (A. He was holy.)
Ephesians 4:24. *Put on the new self, created to be like God in true righteousness and holiness.*

Why is man the most important creature?

MAN WAS CREATED IN THE IMAGE OF GOD.

Summary
God created man in a special way by forming his body from the ground. Then He gave man a soul that can reason, think, and learn to know God. Man was made in the image of the Triune God. Man was holy and had a perfect knowledge of God. (The image of God was lost when Adam and Eve disobeyed God.)

Why, then, is man the most important creature?

> **GOD FORMED MAN.**
> **GOD GAVE MAN A SOUL.**
> **MAN WAS MADE IN GOD'S IMAGE.**

What This Means to Me
In the First Article I confess, "I believe that God made me and every creature and that he gave me my body and soul, eyes, ears and all my members, my mind and all my abilities." Abilities refers to such things as seeing, hearing, speaking.

God has given me a wonderful body. He has given me eyes to see the wonders and beauties of His creation. I can see my parents, friends, and relatives; I can hear and understand what they say. With my mouth I can speak and sing. With my feet I can walk and run. With my hands I can work and play. I can reason, learn, and understand. For all this I praise my Creator.

Psalm 139:14. *I praise you because I am fearfully and wonderfully made.*

For Me to Memorize
The First Article and the first paragraph of the explanation
Assigned Bible passages

For Me to Do
Read Genesis 2:21,22. How did God create the first woman?

For Me to Prepare for the Next Lesson
   Read the Bible story "Joseph Provides for His Family" (Genesis 45: 1-13).
      Who came to Egypt to buy grain?
      Who had gathered grain during the good years?
      What was Joseph able to do for his family?

   Read the Bible story "The Rescue of Moses" (Exodus 2:1-10).
      How did the mother protect Moses?
      How did Pharaoh's daughter keep danger away from Moses?

8. GOD, THE PRESERVER

THE FIRST ARTICLE

I believe that God still preserves me by richly and daily providing clothing and shoes, food and drink, house and home, wife and children, land, cattle and all I own, and all that I need to keep my body and life, and by defending me against all danger and guarding and protecting me from all evil.

For Me to Learn
   How God preserves me

For Me to Remember
   In what country did God cause crops to grow that fed the people during a famine? (A. Egypt)
   Through whom did God provide food for Jacob's family? (A. Joseph)
   Genesis 45:5. *It was to save lives that God sent me ahead of you.*

   What does God cause to grow to feed people and animals?
   Psalm 104:14. *He makes grass grow for the cattle, and plants for man to cultivate — bringing forth food from the earth.*
   Growing things give work to many people who turn these into food, clothing, homes, and many useful things. God gives work to people, but only when does their work benefit them? (A. When God blesses them)
   Psalm 127:1. *Unless the Lord builds the house, its builders labor in vain.*

How does God preserve us?

GOD PROVIDES FOR OUR BODILY NEEDS.

Through whom did God protect Moses? (A. Through Pharaoh's daughter)
Whom does God send to keep His children from harm?
Psalm 91:11. *He will command his angels concerning you to guard you in all your ways.*
Psalm 91:10. *No harm will befall you, no disaster will come near your tent.*

How does God preserve us?

GOD DEFENDS US AGAINST DANGER AND GUARDS AND PROTECTS US FROM EVIL.

Summary
God has given us body and life. Our bodies need food, clothing, and shelter. God provides for those bodily needs. Our bodies need protection. God defends us, guards and protects us.
What words of the First Article tell us how God preserves us?

How, then, does God preserve us?

GOD PROVIDES FOR OUR BODILY NEEDS AND DEFENDS, GUARDS, AND PROTECTS US.

What This Means to Me
God preserves me by giving me all I need for my body and life. God does not preserve me in the way He did the Children of Israel in the wilderness when He protected them with a pillar of fire and a cloud and let bread and meat come down from heaven to feed them. God gives sunshine and rain for crops to grow. These crops must be planted and harvested. God gives people health and skills to turn crops and vegetation into things I need for my body and life. God guards and protects me through my parents, through policemen, through teachers, and through my government. Without God's blessing nothing would grow and nothing would be provided and I would have no protection. I must rely altogether on God to preserve me.

For Me to Memorize
First Article and first two paragraphs of the explanation
Assigned Bible passages

For Me to Do
   Be prepared to read those verses of Psalm 104 which tell us that God preserves us.

For Me to Prepare for the Next Lesson
   Read the Bible story "The Youth of Nain" (Luke 7:11-15).
      How did Jesus feel when He saw the sorrowing mother?
      How did He show His goodness to her?

   Read the Bible story "The Centurion of Capernaum" (Luke 7:1-10).
      Why did the centurion himself not go to Jesus and ask for His help?
      Why did the centurion not want Jesus to come to his home?

9. GOD'S GOODNESS AND MERCY

THE FIRST ARTICLE

All this God does only because he is my good and merciful Father in heaven, and not because I have earned or deserved it.

For Me to Learn
   Why God preserves us

For Me to Remember
   How did Jesus feel toward the widow who had lost her son? (A. He had compassion on her.) He pitied her. How did He show His goodness toward her? (A. He brought her son back to life.)

   How does the Lord feel toward those who fear Him?
   Psalm 103:13. *As a father has compassion on his children, so the Lord has compassion on those who fear him.*
   What does God do in His divine goodness? (A. He helps us and preserves us.)

   Why does God preserve us?

GOD PRESERVES US OUT OF FATHERLY, DIVINE GOODNESS.

What did God in His mercy not do to Adam and Eve after they had sinned? (A. Kill or destroy them)
What did He promise to do in His mercy? (A. To send His Son to save them)

Where can we see evidences of God's mercy? (A. In all He does)
Psalm 145:9. *The Lord is good to all; he has compassion on all he has made.*
What does God do for us? (A. He preserves us.)

Why does God preserve us?

GOD PRESERVES US OUT OF DIVINE MERCY.

What do we not deserve from God? (A. His goodness and mercy)
Why do we not deserve God's goodness and mercy? (A. We are disobedient to Him; we sin daily.)
Of what are we unworthy?
Genesis 32:10. *I am unworthy of all the kindness and faithfulness you have shown your servant.*
There is nothing that we have done or can do that should cause God to be good and merciful to us.

What is not the reason for God preserving us?

GOD PRESERVES US WITHOUT ANY MERIT OR WORTHINESS IN US.

Summary

Our heavenly Father provides for our bodily needs; He protects us from evil, and He defends us against dangers. He does that all out of His fatherly, divine goodness, and mercy. There is nothing we do that makes us worthy of God's goodness toward us.
What words of the First Article tell us why God preserves us?

Why, then, does God preserve us?

GOD PRESERVES US OUT OF FATHERLY, DIVINE GOODNESS, AND MERCY.

What This Means to Me

I believe that my heavenly Father made me and that He will preserve me by giving me what I need every day. I know that I do not deserve the least of the many things that God gives me. I am a sinner and am unworthy of God's goodness, but God has pity on me, and in His mercy He preserves me from day to day. I praise and thank Him for the undeserved blessings He gives me.

For Me to Memorize

First Article and the entire explanation except the last paragraph
Assigned Bible passages

For Me to Do
  Read Mark 6:30-44. How did Jesus show His goodness to the people?

For Me to Prepare for the Next Lesson
  Read the Bible story "The Healing of the Lame Man" (Acts 3:1-9).
  Why was the man helpless?
  How did Peter help him?
  What did the man do after he was healed?

10. OUR APPRECIATION FOR GOD'S GOODNESS AND MERCY

THE FIRST ARTICLE
For all this I ought to thank and praise, to serve and obey him. This is most certainly true.

For Me to Learn
  How we show that we appreciate God's goodness and mercy

For Me to Remember
  What did God do for the lame man? (A. He healed him.)
  How did the man show his appreciation for what God had done? (A. He thanked and praised God.)
  How do we show our appreciation to God for His goodness?
  Psalm 118:1. *Give thanks to the Lord, for he is good; his love endures forever.*
  For what do we praise God? (A. For His blessings or benefits)
  Psalm 103:2. *Praise the Lord, O my soul, and forget not all his benefits.*

How, then, do we show that we appreciate God's goodness and mercy?

WE THANK AND PRAISE GOD FOR HIS GOODNESS AND MERCY.

We not only show our appreciation to God by thanking and praising

213

Him with words, but there are other ways in which we can do this.
Psalm 116:12. *How can I repay the Lord for all his goodness to me?*
What do we do when we willingly obey God's commandments? (A. We honor or glorify God.)
1 Corinthians 6:20. *You were bought at a price. Therefore honor God with your body.*
For whose benefits should we use the gifts God gives us? (A. Our own and our neighbor's benefits)
Galatians 6:10. *As we have opportunity, let us do good to all people.*

How, then, do we show that we appreciate God's goodness and mercy?

WE SERVE AND OBEY GOD FOR HIS GOODNESS AND MERCY.

Summary

We show that we truly appreciate God's goodness and mercy by thanking and praising Him and by obeying Him. We also show our appreciation to God by using the blessings He has given us to help and serve our neighbor.

What words of the First Article tell us how we show our appreciation for God's goodness?

How, then, do we show that we appreciate God's goodness and mercy?

WE THANK, PRAISE, SERVE, AND OBEY GOD FOR HIS GOODNESS AND MERCY.

What This Means to Me

I believe that my body and soul and all that I have and ever will have are gifts from God. I do not deserve any of them. God gives them to me out of His goodness and mercy. Every day I want to thank and praise Him for the many undeserved blessings He gives me. I also want to show my appreciation to Him by willingly obeying His commandments and by helping and serving my neighbor. May God help me to show that I sincerely appreciate His goodness.

For Me to Memorize

First Article with explanation
Assigned Bible passages

For Me to Do

Read Hymn 570 (TLH). On a sheet of paper write the blessings mentioned in this hymn for which we praise God.

For Me to Prepare for the Next Lesson
Use the Review and Study Guide (Number 11) to prepare for the next lesson. Write the answers on a sheet of paper and study them.

II. REVIEW AND STUDY GUIDE

(Lessons 1 - 10)

I. *Answer*

Answer these questions.

1. What do all people know from nature?
2. Whom can people not learn to know from nature?
3. From what book can we learn to know the true God?
4. Whose Word is the Bible?
5. How many true gods are there?
6. How many persons are in the true God?
7. What are the names of the persons in the true God?
8. What is the true God called since there are three persons in one God?

II. *Match*

Match column A with column B

A	B
...........1. almighty	a. He is without sin.
...........2. is spirit	b. He is always with us.
...........3. holy	c. He has all power.
...........4. ever-present	d. He knows everything.
...........5. everlasting	e. He forgives our sins.
...........6. all-knowing	f. He has no body.
...........7. gracious	g. He has no beginning and no end.
...........8. faithful	h. He keeps His word.

III. *Complete*

Complete these sentences.

1. To have faith in God means to accept as .... what the Bible says of God.
2. To have faith in God means to put our .... in the true God.
3. The .... is the first Person of the Holy Trinity.
4. .... is the Father of Jesus Christ.

5. God is the Father of all who .... in Jesus Christ as their Savior.
6. The .... tells us how all things were created.
7. God created all things in .... days.
8. God used His .... Word to create the world.
9. Only .... existed before the Creation.

IV. *Choose*

Choose the correct answer to each question.

1. How did God make the body of man?
   (God spoke and man was there. God formed him from ground.)
2. In what way were Adam and Eve like God?
   (They were holy. They looked like God.)
3. Who is the most important of God's creations?
   (Angels, man)
4. Why does God preserve and protect us?
   (Because He is good and merciful, because we try to keep His commandments)
5. What do we deserve from God?
   (Kindness and mercy, punishment)
6. Why do we thank and praise God?
   (Because God commands us to do so, because we appreciate God's goodness and mercy)
7. Why do we serve and obey God?
   (Because we want to receive more gifts from Him, because we appreciate His goodness toward us)

12. JESUS CHRIST, TRUE GOD

THE SECOND ARTICLE
I believe in Jesus Christ, his only Son, our Lord; who was conceived by the Holy Ghost; born of the Virgin Mary.

What does this mean?
I believe that Jesus Christ, true God, begotten of the Father from eternity, and also true man, born of the Virgin Mary, is my Lord.

For Me to Learn
How we know that Jesus Christ is true God

For Me to Remember
What are some names that the Bible gives to Jesus Christ that only God can have? (A. Son of God, true God, Christ the Lord, Savior, Lord)
We call them divine names.
Jeremiah 23:6. *This is the name by which he will be called: The Lord Our Righteousness.*
Luke 2:11. *Today in the town of David a Savior has been born to you; he is Christ the Lord.*

What kind of names does God's Word give to Jesus Christ?

GOD'S WORD GIVES DIVINE NAMES TO JESUS CHRIST.

What must Jesus Christ be since God's Word gives Him divine names? (A. True God)
What does Jesus Christ know?
John 21:17. *Lord, you know all things.*
What must Jesus be since He is all-knowing? (A. True God)
How is Jesus since He never changes? (A. Unchangeable and eternal)
Hebrews 13:8. *Jesus Christ is the same yesterday and today and forever.*
How much power does Jesus have?
Matthew 28:18. *All authority in heaven and on earth has been given to me.*

Who is Jesus since He is all-knowing, unchangeable, eternal, and almighty? (A. True God)

How does God's Word describe Jesus?

GOD'S WORD DESCRIBES JESUS AS GOD.

What must Jesus Christ be since the Bible describes Him as God? (A. True God)
Name some miracles that Jesus did. (A. He stilled the storm, healed ten lepers, raised Jairus' daughter from the dead.)
Who only can do such miracles? (A. God)
What great power does Jesus have?
Matthew 9:6. *The Son of Man has authority on earth to forgive sins.*
Who only can forgive sin? (A. God)

What does God's Word tell us about the work of Jesus?

GOD'S WORD TELLS US THAT JESUS CAN DO DIVINE WORKS.

What must Jesus Christ be since He can do divine works? (A. True God)
To whom should the same honor be given as to the Father?
John 5:23. *All may honor the Son just as they honor the Father.*
To honor Jesus as the Father in heaven is honored means to give Jesus divine honor.

How does God's Word tell us to honor Jesus Christ?

GOD'S WORD TELLS US TO GIVE JESUS CHRIST DIVINE HONOR.

What must Jesus Christ be since we are to give Him divine honor? (A. True God)

Summary

The Word of God contains many evidences that Jesus Christ is true God. We believe that God's Word is true. We believe everything that God's Word tells us; therefore, we believe everything it tells us about Jesus Christ.

How, then, do we know that Jesus Christ is true God?

GOD'S WORD TELLS US THAT JESUS CHRIST IS TRUE GOD.

What This Means to Me
From God's Word I know that Jesus Christ is true God. He is equal to God the Father. In the Second Article I confess: "I believe that Jesus Christ, true God, begotten of the Father from eternity . . . is my Lord." This is most certainly true.

For Me to Memorize
Assigned Bible passages

For Me to Do
Read Luke 22:69,70. What question did the Jews ask Jesus? What did He answer them?
Read John 10:30. What did Jesus say of the Father and Himself?

For Me to Prepare for the Next Lesson
Read Luke 1:26-35.
  Whom did Mary conceive in her womb?
  By whose power did she conceive Jesus?

Read Luke 2:1-7.
  Who went to Bethlehem?
  Who is the mother of Jesus?

13. JESUS CHRIST, TRUE MAN

THE SECOND ARTICLE

I believe in Jesus Christ, his only Son, our Lord; who was conceived by the Holy Ghost; *born of the Virgin Mary.*

What does this mean?
I believe that Jesus Christ, true God, begotten of the Father from eternity, and also *true man, born of the Virgin Mary, is my Lord.*

For Me to Learn
How we know that Jesus Christ is true man

For Me to Remember
Who was the mother of Jesus Christ?

219

What is Jesus since He was born of a woman? (A. True man) This is told us in the Bible: "She [Mary] gave birth to her firstborn, a son [Jesus]" (Luke 2:7).

How, then, do we know that Jesus Christ is true man?

GOD'S WORD TELLS US THAT JESUS CHRIST WAS BORN OF A WOMAN.

To whom did Jesus say that He had flesh and bones? (A. The disciples) Jesus had a body like all people. Just before Jesus was to suffer and die He said, "My soul is overwhelmed with sorrow."
What does Jesus have that all people have? (A. A soul) The Bible tells us that Jesus has the natural parts of man, namely body and soul.

How, then, do we know that Jesus Christ is true man?

GOD'S WORD TELLS US THAT JESUS CHRIST HAS A BODY AND A SOUL.

How was young Jesus like other children? (A. He learned more and more every day. He grew taller and stronger.)
Luke 2:52. *Jesus grew in wisdom and stature, and in favor with God and men.*
How did Jesus become when He went without food for several days? He needed food just as we do. What did Jesus need after being awake for some time? (A. Rest) Jesus was in need of sleep just as we are in need of sleep. What did Jesus feel when He was crowned with thorns and crucified? (A. Pain) Jesus felt pain just as all people feel pain. What did Jesus finally do on the cross? (A. He died.) The Bible tells us that Jesus was man in these and other ways.

How, then, do we know that Jesus Christ is true man?

GOD'S WORD TELLS US THAT JESUS CHRIST WAS MAN IN WHAT HE FELT AND DID.

What does the Bible call Jesus besides calling Him God? (A. Man)
1 Timothy 2:5. *There is one God and one mediator between God and men, the man Christ Jesus.*

How, then, do we know that Jesus Christ is true man?

GOD'S WORD GIVES JESUS CHRIST THE NAME "MAN."

Summary

God's Word contains many evidences that Jesus Christ is true man. We accept these evidences as true because the Word of God is true. We can believe everything God's Word tells us; therefore, we believe everything God's Word tells us about Jesus Christ.

How, then, do we know that Jesus Christ is true man?

GOD'S WORD TELLS US THAT JESUS CHRIST IS TRUE MAN.

What This Means to Me

From God's Word I know that Jesus Christ is true man. But there is one great difference between Jesus Christ and all other people. Jesus Christ is holy, without sin.

The Bible contains many evidences that make me sure that Jesus is true man. I can believe these because God's Word is true. It is reliable. I cannot understand how it is possible that Jesus is both true God and true man, but I believe that it is most certainly true.

For Me to Memorize

Assigned Bible passages

14. THE TWO NATURES OF CHRIST

THE SECOND ARTICLE

I believe in Jesus Christ, his only Son, our Lord; who was conceived by the Holy Ghost; born of the Virgin Mary.

What does this mean?

I believe that Jesus Christ, true God, begotten of the Father from eternity, and also true man, born of the Virgin Mary, is my Lord.

For Me to Learn

Why Jesus Christ had to be true God and true man

For Me to Remember

What does God demand of all people? (A. That they be holy, that they be without sin and obey His commandments perfectly)
Leviticus 19:2. *Be holy because I, the Lord your God, am holy.*
But what have all people done? (A. Sinned)
Whom have they not satisfied? (A. God)
Romans 3:23. *All have sinned and fall short of the glory of God.*

No person can obey the Law of God. Yet God demands that every person obey the Law perfectly.

What did God do for us? (A. He had His Son become a man and obey the Law which we cannot obey.)

Galatians 4:4,5. *When the time had fully come, God sent his Son, born of a woman, born under law, to redeem those under law.*

What did Jesus do for us as true God and true man?

JESUS OBEYED THE LAW IN OUR PLACE.

What is the punishment for sin? (A. Eternal death in hell)
Ezekiel 18:20. *The soul who sins is the one who will die.*
Who suffered and died for our sin?
John 1:29. *Look, the Lamb of God, who takes away the sin of the World!*
What did Jesus give as a ransom to pay for the punishment of our sins? (A. His life)
Mark 10:45. *The Son of Man did not come to be served, but to serve, and to give his life as a ransom for many.*

What did Jesus do for us as true man and true God?

JESUS SUFFERED AND DIED FOR OUR SINS AS OUR SUBSTITUTE.

Summary

What did Jesus obey perfectly while He was a man on earth? (A. The Law, the Ten Commandments) Why could He obey the Law perfectly? (A. He was true God) What did Jesus suffer as a man while He was on earth? (A. Great pain and death on the cross) In whose stead did He suffer and die? From what did Jesus free all people with His suffering and death? What did Jesus have to be to suffer and die? (A. True man) What did Jesus have to be to suffer and die for our sins? (A. True God)

Why, then, did Jesus Christ have to be true God and true man?

JESUS CHRIST HAD TO BE TRUE GOD AND TRUE MAN IN ORDER TO REDEEM US.

What This Means to Me

As true man Jesus Christ obeyed the Law in my place. He could obey the Law perfectly for me because He is true God.

As true man Jesus Christ suffered the pain and death that I should suffer as a sinner.

Jesus could suffer and die in my place as my substitute and pay for my sins because He is true God. Now I am a redeemed child of God. This is most certainly true!

For Me to Memorize
  Assigned Bible passages

For Me to Do
  What is Jesus called in these Bible passages?
  Matthew 16:16;   John 20:28;   Luke 2:7;   Matthew 2:13.

15. JESUS CHRIST, OUR HIGH PRIEST

THE SECOND ARTICLE
I believe in Jesus Christ, his only Son, our Lord.

What does this mean?
I believe that Jesus Christ, true God, begotten of the Father from eternity, and also true man, born of the Virgin Mary, is my Lord. He *has redeemed me.*

For Me to Learn
  How Christ is our High Priest

For Me to Remember
  What had destroyed the perfect relation between God and the people? (A. Sin)
  What were the Old Testament priests to do with their prayers and sacrifices? (A. To restore peace and good will between God and the people)
  Of whom were the sacrifices symbols or shadows? (A. Of Christ who was to come)
  Who is our holy High Priest? (A. Jesus Christ)
  Hebrews 7:26,27. *Such a high priest meets our need — one who is holy, blameless, pure, set apart from sinners, exalted above the heavens. Unlike the other high priests, he does not need to offer sacrifices day after day, first for his own sins, and then for the sins of the people. He sacrificed for their sins once for all when he offered himself.*
  What did Christ obey perfectly in our stead? (A. The Law of God)

How, then, is Christ our High Priest?

CHRIST OBEYED THE LAW OF GOD FOR US.

What do all people deserve because they have transgressed God's Law? (A. Eternal death in hell)
Ezekiel 18:20. *The soul who sins is the one who will die.*
The sinners must be punished for disobeying God, for not keeping God's commandments.
Who took our place and suffered our punishment?
Ephesians 5:2. *Christ loved us and gave himself up for us as a fragrant offering and sacrifice to God.*
Christ Jesus was God's sacrifice for our sins.

How, then, is Christ our High Priest?

CHRIST SACRIFICED HIMSELF FOR US.

What does Jesus Christ still do for us? (A. He prays for us.)
1 John 2:1. *If anybody does sin, we have one who speaks to the Father in our defense — Jesus Christ, the Righteous One.*
Christ is our lawyer. He pleads our case before God and asks Him to be patient with us and to forgive us for the sake of His suffering and death.

How, then, is Christ our High Priest?

CHRIST PLEADS FOR US BEFORE OUR HEAVENLY FATHER.

Summary

As our High Priest Christ redeemed us by fulfilling the Law of God in our place.
As our High Priest Christ redeemed us by sacrificing Himself for us.
As our High Priest Christ pleads for us.

How, then, is Christ our High Priest?

CHRIST IS OUR HIGH PRIEST BECAUSE HE REDEEMED US AND NOW PLEADS FOR US BEFORE OUR HEAVENLY FATHER.

What This Means to Me

God demands that I must lead a holy life by obeying all of His commandments. But I am sinful and daily disobey God. As my High Priest Jesus obeyed the Law for me. I deserve to be punished by

God with eternal death because I am a sinner. As my High Priest Jesus suffered and died in my place. My High Priest has redeemed me and made peace between God and me. For all of this I want to thank, praise, and serve Jesus, my High Priest. I know that even now He prays the heavenly Father to be good to me and to forgive my sins for the sake of His suffering and death. I pray that I will always believe that the blood of Jesus Christ, my Savior and High Priest, cleanses me of all my sins.

For Me to Memorize
Assigned Bible passages

For Me to Do
Read 1 Timothy 2:5,6. Who is the mediator (go-between) between God and man?
How did He free us from sin and the punishment we deserved?

For Me to Prepare for the Next Lesson
Read Luke 4:16-22.
  What did Jesus do in the synagogue?
  What had the Spirit of the Lord anointed Him to do?

Read Matthew 28:16-20.
  What command did Jesus give His disciples?
  What did He promise them?

16. JESUS CHRIST, OUR PROPHET

THE SECOND ARTICLE
I believe in Jesus Christ, his only Son, our Lord.

What does this mean?
I believe that Jesus Christ, true God, begotten of the Father from eternity, and also true man, born of the Virgin Mary, is my Lord.
He has redeemed me.

For Me to Learn
How Jesus Christ is our Prophet

For Me to Remember
Whom did God send to be our Prophet? (A. Jesus Christ)

Deuteronomy 18:15. *The Lord your God will raise up for you a prophet like me from among your own brothers. You must listen to him.*

What did Jesus do as Prophet while He was on earth? (A. He preached to the people.)

What did He preach? (A. The Gospel of salvation)

What does the Gospel tell us and all people?

John 3:16. *God so loved the world that he gave his one and only Son, that whoever believes in him shall not perish but have eternal life.*

This is the Gospel of salvation which Jesus preached.

How, then, is Jesus Christ our Prophet?

JESUS CHRIST PREACHED THE GOSPEL OF SALVATION.

What command did Jesus give His disciples before He left this earth? Matthew 28:19. *Go and make disciples of all nations.*

Who speaks to us when we hear our parents, pastors, and teachers tell us the good news of our salvation? (A. Jesus)

Luke 10:16. *He who listens to you listens to me; he who rejects you rejects me.*

Through whom does Jesus Christ, our Prophet, speak to us today? (A. Through his believers)

How, then, is Jesus Christ our Prophet?

JESUS CHRIST HAS THE GOSPEL OF SALVATION PREACHED THROUGH HIS BELIEVERS.

Summary

As our Prophet Jesus Christ preached and taught the Gospel of salvation while He was on earth. As our Prophet Jesus Christ has the Gospel of salvation preached and taught through His believers.

How, then, is Jesus Christ our Prophet?

JESUS CHRIST PREACHED THE GOSPEL OF SALVATION AND HAS THE GOSPEL PREACHED THROUGH HIS BELIEVERS.

What This Means to Me

Jesus Christ is my Prophet. God sent Him to earth and said, "Listen to Him!" Although I cannot hear Jesus' voice as did Mary and Martha, He still speaks to me. He speaks to me whenever I listen to my parents, pastors, teachers, and others preach or teach the Gospel of salvation. What Jesus has to say to me is most important. Therefore I will want to listen to Him as often as I can, and I will want to listen very carefully as He talks to me through the people He has chosen to speak His word. I will also want to invite and urge others to hear the Gospel of salvation.

For Me to Memorize
Assigned Bible passages

For Me to Do
Read Ephesians 4:11. Whom has Christ chosen to preach and teach the Gospel of Salvation?

For Me to Prepare for the Next Lesson
Read the Bible story "Jesus Stills the Storm" (Matthew 8:23-27).
What did the disciples say to Jesus?
How did Jesus stop the storm?
What had to obey Jesus?

17. JESUS CHRIST, OUR KING

THE SECOND ARTICLE
I believe in Jesus Christ, his only Son, *our Lord.*

What does this mean?
I believe that Jesus Christ, true God, begotten of the Father from eternity, and also true man, born of the Virgin Mary, *is my Lord.* He has redeemed me.

For Me to Learn
How Jesus Christ is our King

For Me to Remember
How great is the power of Jesus Christ? (A. He is almighty.)
Over what does He rule with His almighty power?
Matthew 28:18. *All authority in heaven and on earth has been given to me.*
What does "heaven and earth" include? (A. All creatures in heaven and on earth and all other created things.)

How, then, is Jesus Christ our King?

JESUS CHRIST RULES EVERYTHING WITH HIS ALMIGHTY POWER.

What did Jesus make known while He was on earth? (A. The way to eternal salvation)
What is the good news about eternal salvation through Jesus called? (A. The Gospel)
What are those people called who believe the Gospel? (A. The church or believers)
Acts 20:28. *Be shepherds of the church of God, which he bought with his own blood.*
With what, then, does Jesus Christ rule His church? (A. The Gospel)

How, then, is Christ our King?

JESUS CHRIST RULES THE CHURCH WITH THE GOSPEL OF SALVATION.

Where will Jesus take all people who believed in Him as their Savior? (A. To heaven)
2 Timothy 4:18. *The Lord will rescue me from every evil attack and will bring me safely to his heavenly kingdom.*
Where will Jesus receive all who believe in Him? (A. Into glory)
Psalm 73:24. *You guide me with your counsel, and afterward you will take me into glory.*
In heaven Jesus rules in His glory.

How, then, is Jesus Christ our King?

JESUS CHRIST WILL RULE OVER US IN HIS GLORY IN HEAVEN.

Summary

Jesus Christ has a three-fold kingdom.
He rules over the believers with His Gospel of salvation, which is the Means of Grace. This is His Kingdom of Grace.
He rules over the world with His almighty power. This is His Kingdom of Power.
He rules the believers in heaven where they will be with Him in all His glory. This is His Kingdom of Glory.

How, then, is Jesus Christ our King?

JESUS CHRIST RULES OVER HIS KINGDOM OF POWER, OVER HIS KINGDOM OF GRACE AND OVER HIS KINGDOM OF GLORY.

What This Means to Me
It gives me great comfort to know that the almighty Jesus Christ rules everything. He is all-wise and just. Everything that happens in the world and in my life is for my good, because in His grace, Jesus controls everything. God has made me a member of His church on earth. I believe and trust the Gospel of salvation through which Jesus rules all His believers. When I die in faith, Jesus will take me to heaven to live with Him forever in His Kingdom of Glory.

For Me to Memorize
Assigned Bible passages

For Me to Do
Read Philippians 2:9-11. What will all people have to confess on the Last Day?
Read Colossians 1:12-14. To whose kingdom do all those belong who have redemption by the blood of Christ?

For Me to Prepare for the Next Lesson
Read the Bible story "The Fall into Sin" (Genesis 3:1-7).
  In whose image did God make Adam and Eve?
  How did they sin?

Read the Bible story "The Parable of the Lost Sheep" (Luke 15:4-7).
  Where was the sheep lost?
  Why did the man leave the 99 sheep?

18. LOST AND CONDEMNED SINNERS

THE SECOND ARTICLE
I believe that Jesus Christ, true God, begotten of the Father from eternity, and also true man, born of the Virgin Mary is my Lord.
He has redeemed me, a lost and condemned creature.

For Me to Learn
Why Christ had to redeem all people

For Me to Remember

In whose image did God make Adam and Eve? (A. In His own image)
How were they therefore? (A. Holy)
Who tempted Eve to sin? (A. The devil)
What did Adam and Eve lose because they sinned? (A. God's image)
How are all people since the Fall into sin? (A. Sinful)
Psalm 51:5. *Surely I have been a sinner from birth.*
What does this sinful nature cause people to do? (A. Sin)
Matthew 15:19. *Out of the heart come evil thoughts, murder, adultery, sexual immorality, theft, false testimony, slander.*

Why can no one obey the Law of God?
Ecclesiastes 7:20. *There is not a righteous man on earth who does what is right and never sins.*

Why did Christ have to redeem all people?

NO ONE CAN OBEY THE LAW OF GOD PERFECTLY.

From whom has sin separated all people? (A. From God)

What are they not able to do? (A. To save themselves)
They are lost and helpless to save themselves.

Why did Christ have to redeem all people?

ALL PEOPLE ARE LOST SINNERS.

What is God's punishment for sinners? (A. Temporal and eternal death)
Romans 6:23. *The wages of sin is death.*
Who has condemned all people? (A. God has condemned all people because they are sinful.)

Why did Christ have to redeem all people?

ALL PEOPLE ARE CONDEMNED SINNERS.

Summary

Since the Fall into sin all people are sinful and commit sins. Sin has separated them from God. They are in the power of Satan. They are lost and cannot save themselves. They cannot keep God's Law. Instead of keeping the Law, they daily disobey God's Law. Unless they rely on God to save them, they will suffer the dreadful torments of hell prepared for the devil and his angels.

Why, then, did Christ have to redeem all people?

ALL PEOPLE ARE LOST AND CONDEMNED SINNERS.

What This Means to Me

I was born with a sinful nature. This sinful nature causes me to sin and makes it impossible for me to keep the commandments of God perfectly. But God demands that I must be holy and keep His Law perfectly or I will be lost eternally. I know that I cannot keep God's Law and that I cannot do anything that will cause God to take away my sins. I need a savior to redeem me.

Galatians 3:13. *Christ redeemed us from the curse of the law by becoming a curse for us.*

God, in His goodness, sent His only Son, Jesus Christ, to keep the Law for me and to pay for my sin and guilt.

For Me to Memorize

Assigned Bible passages

For Me to Do

Read Romans 3:23. How many people have sinned?
Read Psalm 49:7. What can no person do?

For Me to Prepare for the Next Lesson

Read the Bible story "The Resurrection of Jesus" (Matthew 28:1-6). What did the angel tell the woman who had come to the grave of Jesus?

Read the Bible story "The Temptation of Jesus" (Matthew 4:1-11). How did the devil tempt Jesus?
What was the devil not able to do?
What did the devil have to do when Jesus said to him, "Worship the Lord your God, and serve him only"?

19. CHRIST, OUR REDEEMER

THE SECOND ARTICLE

I believe that Jesus Christ, true God, begotten of the Father from eternity, and also true man, born of the Virgin Mary, is my Lord.
He has redeemed me, a lost and condemned creature, *purchased and won me from all sins, from death and from the power of the devil.*

For Me to Learn
From what Christ has redeemed all people

For Me to Remember
Whom did God send to earth to redeem all people?
Galatians 4:4,5. *When the time had fully come, God sent his Son, born of a woman, born under law, to redeem those under law, that we might receive the full rights of sons.*

What does God demand of all people? (A. That they should be holy and obey all His commandments perfectly)
Matthew 5:48. *Be perfect . . . as your heavenly Father is perfect.*
Why can no person keep God's commandments? (A. Because all people are sinful)
Who obeyed the commandments for all people?
Whose righteousness becomes our righteousness?
Romans 5:19. *Through the obedience of the one man the many will be made righteous.*
On whom did God place the sins of all people?
Isaiah 53:6. *The Lord has laid on him the iniquity of us all.*
What did Jesus have to do in our place?

From what did Christ redeem all people?

CHRIST REDEEMED ALL PEOPLE FROM THE GUILT AND PUNISHMENT OF SIN.

What should all people suffer because they are sinful? (A. Death)
Romans 5:12. *Death came to all men, because all sinned.*
Death on earth is the result of sin.
Eternal death in hell is the final punishment for sin.

What did Jesus remove by His suffering, death, and resurrection? (A. Eternal death in hell)
2 Timothy 1:10. *Our Savior, Christ Jesus, . . . has destroyed death and has brought life and immortality to light through the gospel.*
Of what can we be sure? (A. That we shall rise from death and live forever in heaven with Jesus)
John 14:19. *Because I live, you also will live.*

From what has Christ redeemed all people?

CHRIST HAS REDEEMED ALL PEOPLE FROM DEATH.

What does the devil try to make all people do? (A. Commit sin)
What did Jesus do to the devil when He suffered and died for the sins of all people? (A. He took away the devil's power.)
1 John 3:8. *The reason the Son of God appeared was to destroy the devil's work.*

From what has Christ redeemed all people?

CHRIST HAS REDEEMED ALL PEOPLE FROM THE POWER OF THE DEVIL.

Summary

All people were lost and condemned sinners. No one could save himself from sin, death, and the power of the devil. Jesus came to earth and redeemed all people from the guilt and punishment of sin, from eternal death, and from the power of the devil.

From what has Christ redeemed all people?

CHRIST REDEEMED ALL PEOPLE FROM SIN, DEATH, AND THE POWER OF THE DEVIL.

What This Means to Me

I believe that Jesus Christ redeemed me by keeping all the commandments of God which I cannot keep. He redeemed me by suffering and dying in my place to pay for the punishment of my sins. He redeemed me from the power of the devil who wants to make me sin and who accuses me of sin. Since Christ has redeemed me, I need not fear death on earth because I know that death on earth leads to eternal life in heaven.

For Me to Memorize
   Assigned Bible passages

For Me to Do
   Be prepared to read Isaiah 53:4-6 to your class. In these passages Isaiah foretells how the Savior would redeem all people.

20. THE COST OF OUR REDEMPTION

THE SECOND ARTICLE

I believe that Jesus Christ, true God, begotten of the Father from eternity, and also true man, born of the Virgin Mary, is my Lord.

He has redeemed me, a lost and condemned creature, purchased and won me from all sins, from death and from the power of the devil, *not with gold or silver, but with his holy, precious blood and with his innocent suffering and death.*

All this he did that I should be his own, and live under him in his kingdom, and serve him in everlasting righteousness, innocence and blessedness, just as he has risen from death and lives and rules eternally.
This is most certainly true.

For Me to Learn
   How Jesus redeemed all people

For Me to Remember
   What did Jesus suffer while He was on earth? (A. He was hated, despised, and rejected by many people. He experienced grief, sorrow, and pain.)
   Isaiah 53:3. *He was despised and rejected by men, a man of sorrows, and familiar with suffering.*
   Who ordered that Jesus should be scourged, crowned with thorns, and crucified? (A. Pontius Pilate)
   In whose place was Jesus bruised and wounded?
   Isaiah 53:5. *He was pierced for our transgressions, he was crushed for our iniquities.*

What did Jesus shed to pay for the sins of all people? (A. His precious blood)
1 John 1:7. *The blood of Jesus, his Son, purifies us from every sin.*

How did Jesus redeem all people?

JESUS SUFFERED AND SHED HIS BLOOD TO REDEEM ALL PEOPLE.

How did Jesus die? (A. By crucifixion)
Why should Jesus not have been condemned to be crucified? (A. He was innocent; He is the holy Son of God.)
Jesus willingly let Himself be crucified, and He died willingly.
1 Corinthians 15:3. *Christ died for our sins according to the Scriptures.*

How did Jesus redeem all people?

JESUS DIED FOR ALL PEOPLE.

Summary

Jesus has redeemed all people from sin, from death, and from the power of the devil. He did this not with gold and silver but with His holy precious blood and with His innocent suffering and death.

How, then, did Jesus redeem all people?

JESUS SUFFERED, SHED HIS BLOOD, AND DIED TO REDEEM ALL PEOPLE.

What This Means to Me

Jesus has bought or redeemed me with His holy, precious blood and with His innocent suffering and death.
1 Corinthians 6:19,20. *You are not your own; you were bought at a price.*
I now belong to Jesus. He is my Savior and my Lord. He paid for the guilt of my sins. I do not have to fear death because Jesus has earned eternal life for me in heaven. The devil cannot claim me as his own, because Jesus has freed me from the devil's power. My heart is filled with thanksgiving to my dear Savior. All my life I will want to live in joyful obedience to Him and in heaven serve Him in everlasting righteousness and holiness.

For Me to Memorize

Second Article and first two paragraphs of the explanation
Assigned Bible passages

For Me to Do
Be prepared to read stanzas 1-3 of Hymn 181 (TLH) to your class.

21. THE RESURRECTION OF JESUS

THE SECOND ARTICLE

I believe in Jesus Christ, his only Son, our Lord; who was conceived by the Holy Ghost; born of the Virgin Mary; suffered under Pontius Pilate; was crucified, dead and buried; he descended into hell; *the third day he rose again from the dead.*

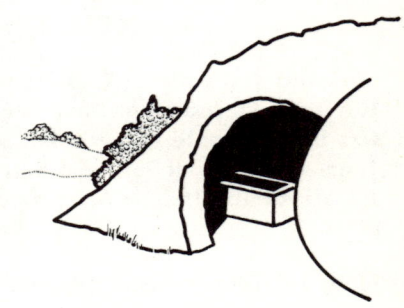

For Me to Learn
What the resurrection of Jesus means to us

For Me to Remember
What did Jesus say He would do on the third day after His death?
John 2:19. *Destroy this temple [Jesus' body], and I will raise it again in three days.*
Who only can make a dead body live again? (A. God)

What did Jesus prove by raising His body from death? (A. That He is the Son of God)
Romans 1:4. *[Jesus] was declared with power to be the Son of God by his resurrection from the dead.*

What does the resurrection of Jesus mean to us?

THE RESURRECTION OF JESUS MEANS THAT HE IS THE SON OF GOD.

What did God the Father place on Jesus? (A. Our sins or offenses)
Romans 4:25. *He [Jesus our Lord] was delivered over to death for our sins and was raised to life for our justification.*
Jesus endured the punishment for the sins of all people. How do we know that God the Father was satisfied with Jesus' work of redemption? (A. Jesus was raised from the dead.)
1 Corinthians 15:17. *If Christ has not been raised, your faith is futile; you are still in your sins.*

Whose work of redemption did God accept? (A. Jesus' work of redemption)
By raising Jesus from death God declared that all people are righteous for Jesus' sake.

What does the resurrection of Jesus mean to us?

THE RESURRECTION OF JESUS MEANS THAT GOD ACCEPTED JESUS' WORK OF REDEMPTION.

What does Jesus promise to do with all people who die? (A. To make them alive on the Last Day)
Why do we know that He is able to keep that promise? (A. Because He was able to raise Himself from death)
John 14:19. *Because I live, you also will live.*
What does Jesus promise to all those who believe in Him as the Savior? (A. They will continue to live with Him forever.)
John 11:25,26. *I am the resurrection and the life. He who believes in me will live, even though he dies, and whoever lives and believes in me will never die.*
The believers in the Savior will be raised from death and live with Him forever.

What does the resurrection of Jesus mean to us?

THE RESURRECTION OF JESUS MEANS THAT JESUS WILL RAISE US TO ETERNAL LIFE.

Summary
The resurrection of Jesus means
that Jesus is the Son of God,
that God accepted Jesus' work of redemption,
that Jesus will raise us to eternal life.

What This Means to Me
1 Corinthians 15:17. *If Christ has not been raised, your faith is futile; you are still in your sins.*
In the Bible I can find evidence that Jesus rose from the dead. He showed Himself alive more than ten times. This is a great comfort to me. I know that He is the Son of God and the promised Savior from sin. Jesus came to earth to suffer and die for my sins and the sins of all people. God the Father was satisfied with Jesus' great sacrifice. By raising His Son from the dead, God said that I and all people are forgiven. Jesus showed by His resurrection that He has power over death. On the Last Day He will raise me and all

people from death and give to me and all believers in Him eternal life in heaven.

For Me to Memorize
Assigned Bible passages
Second Article with explanation

For Me to Do
Read Luke 24:36-45. What did Jesus do to prove to the disciples that He was the living Jesus?

For Me to Prepare for the Next Lesson
Read the Bible story "The Ascension of Jesus" (Luke 24:50,51 and Acts 1:9-11).
What did Jesus do as He blessed His disciples?
What did the two angels say that Jesus would do?

22. CHRIST'S ASCENSION AND RULE

THE SECOND ARTICLE

I believe in Jesus Christ, his only Son, our Lord; who was conceived by the Holy Ghost; born of the Virgin Mary; suffered under Pontius Pilate; was crucified, dead and buried; he descended into hell; the third day he rose again from the dead; *he ascended into heaven, and is sitting at the right hand of God the Father Almighty*; from thence he shall come to judge the living and the dead.

For Me to Learn
Why Jesus' ascension and rule give us great comfort

For Me to Remember
Why did the disciples know that Jesus ascended? (A. He told them that He would ascend, and they saw Him go to heaven.)
With whom does Jesus want to share the glories of heaven? (A. With His believers)
John 17:24. *Father, I want those you have given me to be with me where I am, and to see my glory.*

Why could Jesus return in triumph to heaven? (A. His work of redemption was completed.)
What had He prepared for all people? (A. Heaven)
What will He do on the Last Day? (A. Take those who believe in Him to heaven)
John 14:2,3. *In my Father's house are many rooms; if it were not so, I would have told you. I am going there to prepare a place for you. And if I go and prepare a place for you, I will come back and take you to be with me that you also may be where I am.*

Of what does Jesus' ascension make us sure?

JESUS' ASCENSION MAKES US SURE THAT HE HAS PREPARED A PLACE FOR US IN HEAVEN.

How much power does Jesus have?
Matthew 28:18. *All authority in heaven and on earth has been given to me.*
Jesus rules all creatures and things in heaven and on earth with His almighty power.
With what does He rule His believers? (A. With His Gospel)
Through the Gospel He keeps us in the true faith until we reach the heaven He has prepared for us.
Jesus ascended to heaven with a human body. He is no longer with us as a visible man. But what do we know? (A. That He is present everywhere)
Matthew 28:20. *Surely I will be with you always, to the very end of the age.*

Of what does Jesus' ascension make us sure?

JESUS' ASCENSION MAKES US SURE THAT HE IS WITH US AND KEEPS US SAFE UNTO EVERLASTING LIFE IN HEAVEN.

Summary
Jesus' ascension makes us sure that He has prepared a place for us in heaven.
Jesus' ascension makes us sure that He is with us and keeps us safe unto eternal life.

Why, then, does Jesus' ascension give us great comfort?

WE KNOW THAT JESUS EARNED HEAVEN FOR US AND THAT HE KEEPS US SAFE UNTO EVERLASTING LIFE.

What This Means to Me
>I believe that Jesus earned forgiveness for all my sins and has prepared a place for me in heaven. Now He rules with His almighty power. He is my Lord and Savior. He guards and protects me and keeps me in the true faith. On the last day of the world He will return and take me and all believers to heaven to live with Him in His glory.

For Me to Memorize
>Assigned Bible passages
>Second Article with explanation

For Me to Do
>Read Ephesians 4:10-12. Whom does the ascended Jesus choose to preach and teach His Gospel?

For Me to Prepare for the Next Lesson
>Read the Bible story "The Day of Judgment" (Matthew 25:31-46).
>>Who will come with Christ on Judgment Day?
>>Who will be gathered before Christ's throne of glory?
>>Into how many classes will Jesus divide all people?
>>Where will Jesus take those on His right hand?
>>Where will He send those on His left hand?

23. THE SECOND COMING OF CHRIST

THE SECOND ARTICLE

>I believe in Jesus Christ, his only Son, our Lord; who was conceived by the Holy Ghost; born of the Virgin Mary; suffered under Pontius Pilate; was crucified, dead and buried; he descended into hell; the third day he rose again from the dead; he ascended into heaven, and is sitting at the right hand of God the Father Almighty; *from thence he shall come to judge the living and the dead.*

For Me to Learn
>How Christ will reveal Himself on Judgment Day

For Me to Remember
>What are some of the signs that tell us that Judgment Day is coming? (A. Wars, false prophets, great wickedness, signs in the heavenly bodies, earthquakes, the Gospel preached over all the world)

Who will come with Christ on Judgment Day? (A. His holy angels) Who will announce Jesus' coming? (A. An archangel) Where will Jesus sit? (A. On His throne of glory) What will Jesus do to all the people who have died? (A. Raise them to life)
Where will all people be gathered? (A. Before Christ's throne of glory)

How will Christ reveal Himself on Judgment Day?

CHRIST WILL REVEAL HIMSELF IN ALL HIS GLORY.

As what did God appoint Jesus? (A. As Judge of the living and the dead)
Acts 10:42. *He is the one whom God appointed as judge of the living and the dead.*
Into what two groups or classes will Jesus divide all people on Judgment Day? (A. Believers and unbelievers) What will show that they were believers or unbelievers? (A. Their works) Whose Word will Christ use to judge all people? (A. His own Word)
John 12:48. *That very word which I spoke will condemn him at the last day.*
What is that Word?
Mark 16:16. *Whoever believes and is baptized will be saved, but whoever does not believe will be condemned.*
Where will Christ, the Judge, take all believers? (A. To heaven)
Where will Christ, the Judge, send all unbelievers? (A. To hell)

How will Christ reveal Himself on Judgment Day?

CHRIST WILL REVEAL HIMSELF AS THE JUST JUDGE.

Summary

On Judgment Day Christ will come in all His glory. All His holy angels and all the people who ever lived on earth will be gathered around Christ's throne of glory. There He will judge them justly by His Word.

How, then, will Christ reveal Himself on Judgment Day?

CHRIST WILL REVEAL HIMSELF IN ALL HIS GLORY AS THE JUST JUDGE.

What This Means to Me

Jesus is my Savior. He has redeemed me with His blood. Therefore I don't have to fear death or Judgment Day. I know and believe that when I die Jesus will take my soul to heaven. On Judgment Day He will unite my soul and body and take me and all believers to live with Him in everlasting righteousness, innocence, and blessedness. I pray God to keep me faithful to my wonderful Savior.

For Me to Memorize
Assigned Bible passages
Entire Second Article

For Me to Do
Name some signs of the coming Judgment Day that you have heard or read about.

For Me to Prepare for the Next Lesson
Use the Review and Study Guide (Number 24) to prepare for the next lesson. Write the answers on a sheet of paper and study them.

24. REVIEW AND STUDY GUIDE

(Lessons 12 - 23)

I. *Answer*
Answer these questions.

1. What divine name does the Bible give to Jesus Christ?
2. What must Jesus Christ be since the Bible gives Him divine names?
3. What did Jesus do on earth to prove that He is true God?
4. How does God's Word tell us to honor Jesus?
5. What did Jesus, God's Son, become when He was born?
6. What two natural parts of man does Jesus have?
7. Name some things that Jesus felt and did to prove that He is true man.
8. What did Jesus keep and fulfill for us?
9. What did Jesus have to be to suffer and die?
10. What did Jesus have to be in order to redeem us?

II. *Match*
Write *Priest, Prophet* or *King* behind each of these statements.

1. Jesus rules everything with His almighty power. ....
2. Jesus fulfilled the Law for us. ....
3. Jesus sacrificed Himself for us. ....
4. Jesus will rule over the believers in heaven. ....
5. Jesus preached the Gospel of salvation. ....

6. Jesus rules the believers with the Gospel. ....
7. Jesus has the Gospel preached by His believers. ....
8. Jesus pleads for us before the heavenly Father. ....

III. *Complete*

Complete these sentences.

1. Since .... and .... sinned all people are sinful.
2. It is impossible for people to keep the .... of God.
3. All people are .... and .... sinners.
4. Jesus Christ came to .... all people.
5. Christ redeemed all people from the .... and .... of sin.
6. Christ redeemed all people from eternal ....
7. Christ redeemed all people from the power of the ....
8. Christ redeemed all people by .... great pain.
9. Christ redeemed all people by .... His blood.
10. Christ redeemed all people by .... on the cross.

IV. *Choose*

Complete these sentences by choosing the correct word on the right side of the sheet.

1. The resurrection of Jesus means that God has .... Jesus' work of redemption.
2. Jesus' resurrection .... that He is God's Son.
3. The resurrection of Jesus means that He will .... us to eternal life.
4. The ascension of Jesus makes us sure that Jesus has .... a place for us in heaven.
5. The ascension of Jesus makes us sure that Jesus will .... us safe to eternal life in heaven.
6. Jesus will .... on Judgment Day.
7. On Judgment Day we shall see Jesus in all His ....
8. On Judgment Day Jesus will .... all people.

proves
prepared
accepted
glory
keep
return
judge
raise

25. THE PERSON OF THE HOLY SPIRIT

THE THIRD ARTICLE
(Of Sanctification)

I believe in the Holy Ghost; the holy Christian church, the communion of saints; the forgiveness of sins; the resurrection of the body; and the life everlasting. Amen.

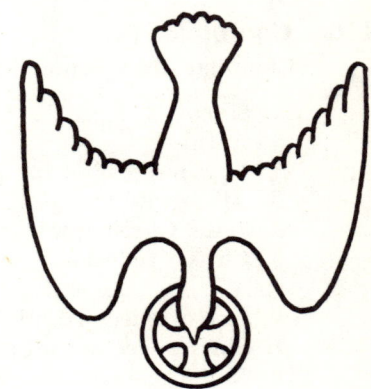

For Me to Learn
  Who the Holy Spirit is

For Me to Remember
  To whom did Ananias lie? (A. To the Holy Spirit) What did Peter tell Ananias? (A. That he lied to God when he lied to the Holy Spirit) God is a divine name.
  The Holy Spirit is divine. He is holy.

What kind of name does the Holy Spirit have?

THE HOLY SPIRIT HAS A DIVINE NAME.

  The Holy Spirit has the power to be everywhere. (See Psalm 139:7-10)
  Who only has that power? (A. God)
  This is a divine power.
  What does the Holy Spirit know? (A. Everything)
  1 Corinthians 2:10. *The Spirit searches all things, even the deep things of God.*
  Who only is all-knowing? (A. God)
  This is a divine power.

What kind of power does the Holy Spirit have?

THE HOLY SPIRIT HAS DIVINE POWER.

  In what great work did the Holy Spirit take part? (A. The creation of the world)
  Psalm 33:6. *By the word of the Lord were the heavens made, their starry host by the breath of his mouth.*

Who only can create? (A. God)
This is a divine work.

What kind of works can the Holy Spirit do?
THE HOLY SPIRIT CAN DO DIVINE WORKS.

What three words in the following Bible passage give glory to the Father, the Son, and the Holy Spirit? (A. Holy, holy, holy)
Isaiah 6:3. *Holy, holy, holy is the Lord Almighty; the whole earth is full of his glory.*
Who only should receive divine honor and glory?

What kind of honor should the Holy Spirit receive?
THE HOLY SPIRIT SHOULD RECEIVE DIVINE HONOR.

Summary
    The Holy Spirit has a divine name.
    The Holy Spirit has divine power.
    The Holy Spirit does divine works.
    The Holy Spirit should receive divine honor.

Who, then, is the Holy Spirit?
THE HOLY SPIRIT IS TRUE GOD.

What This Means to Me
    Matthew 28:19. *Go and make disciples of all nations, baptizing them in the name of the Father and of the Son and of the Holy Spirit.*
    In the Third Article I confess, "I believe in the Holy Ghost." I believe that the Holy Spirit is true God with the Father and the Son, Jesus Christ. Therefore I want to give Him divine honor and glory.

For Me to Memorize
    Assigned Bible passages

For Me to Do
    Read these Bible passages: John 14:26; I Corinthians 6:11; Galatians 4:6.
    What name is used for the Holy Spirit in each passage?

For Me to Prepare for the Next Lesson
    Read the Bible story "The Great Supper" (Luke 14:16-24)

What did the man do after the supper was prepared?
What did many who were invited not do?
Who was able to enjoy the supper?

26. THE CALL BY THE HOLY SPIRIT

THE THIRD ARTICLE

I believe that I cannot by my own thinking or choosing believe in Jesus Christ, my Lord, or come to him. But *the Holy Ghost has called me by the gospel.*

For Me to Learn
How the Holy Spirit brings us to faith

For Me to Remember
Whom did God the Father give to save all people? (A. His Son)
What is this good news called? (A. The Gospel)
Who will have everlasting life? (A. All who believe that Jesus is their Savior)
John 3:16. *God so loved the world that he gave his one and only Son, that whoever believes in him shall not perish but have eternal life.*
Why can people not believe this good news by their own power? (A. They are dead in sin.)
Ephesians 2:1. *You were dead in your transgressions and sins.*
What means does the Holy Spirit use to bring us to Christ? (A. The Gospel)
Matthew 11:28. *Come to me, all you who are weary and burdened, and I will give you rest.*
In the Gospel we receive rest for our souls through the forgiveness of sins.

How does the Holy Spirit bring us to faith?

THE HOLY SPIRIT BRINGS US TO FAITH BY THE GOSPEL.

Who only can move people to believe the Gospel? (A. The Holy Spirit)
1 Corinthians 12:3. *No one can say, "Jesus is Lord," except by the Holy Spirit.*
What does the Holy Spirit work in the hearts of people through the Gospel?
Ephesians 2:8. *By grace you have been saved, through faith — and this not from yourselves, it is the gift of God.*
Faith in Jesus is a gift of the Holy Spirit.

What does the Holy Spirit do for us?

THE HOLY SPIRIT BRINGS US TO FAITH IN JESUS.

Summary

God has prepared eternal salvation for everyone. He offers this salvation in the Gospel. The Holy Spirit calls us through the Gospel. The Holy Spirit gives us faith to believe the Gospel. He gives us faith to believe in Jesus as our Savior.

How, then, does the Holy Spirit call or bring us to faith?

THE HOLY SPIRIT CALLS US TO FAITH IN JESUS THROUGH THE GOSPEL.

What This Means to Me

I could never believe the good news that Jesus saved me if the Holy Spirit had not called me to believe. Through the Gospel He moved me to accept Jesus as my only Savior. Through the Gospel He keeps me in the true faith. The Gospel is the most important message I will ever hear. Therefore, I will want to hear, read, and learn God's Word diligently all my life. May God grant me the will and strength to do so!

For Me to Memorize

Assigned Bible passages

For Me to Do

Read Romans 1:16. What power does the Gospel have?
Read Philippians 2:13. Who gives us the will to believe?

For Me to Prepare for the Next Lesson

Read the Bible story "The Emmaus Disciples" (Luke 24:13-35).
  Why were the disciples sad?
  What did Jesus tell them?
  Why were they happy when they returned to Jerusalem?

27. THE ENLIGHTENMENT BY THE HOLY SPIRIT

THE THIRD ARTICLE
But the Holy Ghost has called me by the gospel, *enlightened me with his gifts.*

For Me to Learn
What the Holy Spirit does when He enlightens us with His gifts

For Me to Remember
Who cannot understand and believe what God says in His Word? (A. Natural man)
What are the truths of God to natural man? (A. Foolishness)
1 Corinthians 2:14. *The man without the Spirit does not accept the things that come from the Spirit of God, for they are foolishness to him.* Natural man cannot see and understand what God has done for him and still wants to do for him. He is in spiritual darkness. Who removes his spiritual darkness? (A. God, the Holy Spirit)
1 Peter 2:9. *God . . . called you out of darkness into his wonderful light.* The Holy Spirit enlightens us with His gifts. Whom does the Holy Spirit make known to us?
2 Corinthians 4:6. *[God] made his light shine in our hearts to give us the light of the knowledge of the glory of God in the face of Christ.*

What does the Holy Spirit do when He enlightens us with His gifts?

THE HOLY SPIRIT MAKES GOD KNOWN TO US AS OUR LOVING FATHER IN HEAVEN.

What did Jesus use to enlighten the Emmaus disciples? (A. His Word)
What did they then believe? (A. That Jesus their Savior had risen from the dead)
Who enlightens us to believe that we are justified by faith in Jesus Christ?
1 Corinthians 6:11. *You were sanctified, you were justified in the name of the Lord Jesus Christ and by the Spirit of our God.*

What does the Holy Spirit do when He enlightens us?

THE HOLY SPIRIT MOVES US TO BELIEVE THAT WE ARE JUSTIFIED BY FAITH IN JESUS CHRIST.

What condemns natural man? (A. His unbelief) Natural man has no hope of everlasting life in heaven. Why are the people who are enlightened by the Holy Spirit not condemned by God? (A. By God's grace they believe that they are justified through Jesus Christ.)
Romans 8:1. *There is ... no condemnation for those who are in Christ Jesus.*
Of what are enlightened people sure? (A. Of everlasting life)

What does the Holy Spirit do when He enlightens us with His gifts?

THE HOLY SPIRIT GIVES US THE HOPE OF ETERNAL LIFE IN HEAVEN.

Summary
Through the Gospel the Holy Spirit enlightens us with many gifts. Some gifts are:
to know and believe that God is our loving Father,
to know and believe that we are justified by faith in Christ Jesus,
to know and believe that God will not condemn us because of our sins but give us eternal life.

What, then, does the Holy Spirit do when He enlightens us?

THE HOLY SPIRIT GIVES US MANY SPIRITUAL GIFTS WHEN HE ENLIGHTENS US.

What This Means to Me
Whenever I hear or read the Gospel, the Holy Spirit enlightens me with His gifts. He makes my faith grow stronger by assuring me again and again that Jesus is my Savior and that God has declared me free from all of my sins. He also makes me sure that I will live forever with Jesus in the glories of heaven.

For Me to Memorize
Assigned Bible passages

For Me to Prepare for the Next Lesson
Read the Bible story "The Pharisee and the Tax Collector" (Luke 18:9-14)
About what did the Pharisee boast?

How did the tax collector show that he depended on God to save him?

Read the Bible story "The Paralytic Man" (Matthew 9:1-7)
Why was the man brought to Jesus?
What did Jesus do for the man?

28. THE GIFT OF FORGIVENESS

THE THIRD ARTICLE

I believe in the Holy Ghost; the holy Christian church, the communion of saints; *the forgiveness of sins.*

For Me to Learn
How we receive the gift of forgiveness of sins

For Me to Remember
How are all people from their very beginning? (A. Sinful)
Psalm 51:5. *Surely I have been a sinner from birth.*
What do we commit every day? (A. Sins)
Romans 3:23. *All have sinned and fall short of the glory of God.*
From whom do sins separate people? (A. From God)
Isaiah 59:2. *Your iniquities have separated you from your God.*
With what must our just God punish sins? (A. Eternal death)
Ezekiel 18:20. *The soul who sins is the one who will die.*
Who suffered and died for the sins of all people? (A. Jesus)
John 1:29. *Look, the Lamb of God, who takes away the sin of the world!*

What did Jesus earn for all people?

JESUS EARNED FORGIVENESS FOR ALL PEOPLE.

On whom did God lay the sins of the whole world? (A. On His holy Son Jesus) Our sins were transferred to Jesus who has no sin. What did God transfer to us? (A. Jesus' righteousness)
2 Corinthians 5:21. *God made him who had no sin to be sin for us, so that in him we might become the righteousness of God.*

How does God declare all people for Jesus' sake?

GOD DECLARES ALL PEOPLE RIGHTEOUS FOR JESUS' SAKE.

What good news did Jesus tell the paralytic man? (A. That his sins were forgiven)

What word do we use for the good news of forgiveness of sins? (A. Gospel)

What gift does God offer through the Gospel?

GOD OFFERS THE GIFT OF FORGIVENESS THROUGH THE GOSPEL.

Not all people accept or believe this offer of free forgiveness. Why did the Pharisee not ask for mercy and forgiveness? (A. He believed he was just and needed no forgiveness.) Why did the tax collector pray for mercy and forgiveness? (A. He knew he was a sinner and believed that God could and would forgive his sins.)
Who gives us faith to believe in the forgiveness of sins?
Ephesians 2:8. *By grace you have been saved, through faith — and this not from yourselves, it is the gift of God.*
The good news of forgiveness is found in the Gospel of Jesus Christ.

Who gives us faith to believe the Gospel?

THE HOLY SPIRIT GIVES US FAITH TO BELIEVE THE GOSPEL.

Summary
All people are born in sin and sin daily.
Sin separates people from God.
All people need forgiveness of sins to be saved.
Jesus earned forgiveness of sins for all people.
God declared all people righteous for Jesus' sake.
This is the good news or Gospel.
The Holy Spirit gives us faith to believe the Gospel.

How, then, do we receive forgiveness of sins?

THE HOLY SPIRIT GIVES US FORGIVENESS OF SINS THROUGH FAITH IN THE GOSPEL.

What This Means to Me
I was born in sin, and I daily sin in thought, word, and deed. I cannot save myself. God's Son suffered and died to save me. God put all my sins on Jesus and declared me righteous in His sight. The Gospel tells me this good news, and the Holy Spirit gives me faith to believe that all my sins are forgiven. Forgiveness of sins is the greatest gift of God. I pray that the Holy Spirit will move many people to accept this wonderful gift.

For Me to Memorize
Assigned Bible passages

For Me to Do
Read Titus 2:14. What will we who have received the gift of forgiveness be eager to do?

For Me to Prepare for the Next Lesson
Read the Bible story "The Thief on the Cross" (Luke 23:39-41).
What did the first thief scornfully say to Jesus?
What did the other thief say that showed he believed Jesus was innocent?
What did he ask Jesus to do for him?

Read the Bible story "The Pharisee and the Tax Collector" (Luke 18:9-14).
About what did the Pharisee boast?
What did Jesus say about the two men?

Read the Bible story "Zacchaeus" (Luke 19:1-10)
Whom did Zacchaeus receive with joy?
What did he say he would do with his riches?

29. SANCTIFICATION BY THE HOLY SPIRIT

THE THIRD ARTICLE

But *the Holy Ghost has* called me by the gospel, enlightened me with his gifts, *sanctified* and kept *me* in the true faith.

For Me to Learn
What it means to be sanctified by the Holy Spirit

For Me to Remember
What did Peter tell the people to do when he preached to them on Pentecost Day? (A. To repent and be baptized) What gift does the Holy Spirit give to those who are baptized in the name of Jesus Christ? (A. Forgiveness of sins)
Acts 2:38. *Repent and be baptized, every one of you, in the name of Jesus Christ so that your sins may be forgiven.*

How are people who have faith in Jesus as their Savior? (A. They are sanctified or justified.) That means that they are holy in the sight of God. Who sanctifies them? (A. The Holy Spirit)
1 Corinthians 6:11. *You were sanctified, you were justified in the name of the Lord Jesus Christ and by the Spirit of our God.*

What, then, does it mean to be sanctified by the Holy Spirit?

THE HOLY SPIRIT MAKES US HOLY THROUGH FAITH IN JESUS CHRIST.

Who dwells or lives in the hearts of all believers? (A. The Holy Spirit)
With what does He fill their hearts? (A. Love toward God)
What does the Holy Spirit give the believers the strength to do? (A. To overcome the temptation to sin) This work of the Holy Spirit is called sanctification.
1 Corinthians 3:16. *Don't you know that you yourselves are God's temple and that God's Spirit lives in you?*

What, then, does it mean to be sanctified by the Holy Spirit?

WE ARE SANCTIFIED WHEN THE HOLY SPIRIT GIVES US STRENGTH TO OVERCOME SIN.

What kind of life did Zacchaeus lead before he became a believer in the Savior? (A. A sinful life)
How did he show that he had changed after he came to faith in Jesus? (A. He no longer wanted to cheat people. He wanted to help them.)
What happens to people who become believers in Jesus Christ? (A. They become new creatures.)
Whom do they want to obey and serve? (A. God)
The Holy Spirit, who lives in their hearts, gives them the power to lead holy lives.
This work of the Holy Spirit is called sanctification.

What, then, does it mean to be sanctified by the Holy Spirit?

WE ARE SANCTIFIED WHEN THE HOLY SPIRIT GIVES US POWER TO LEAD A HOLY LIFE.

Summary
To sanctify means to make holy.
Only faith in Jesus as our Savior can sanctify us.
The Holy Spirit sanctifies us when He gives us faith to believe in Jesus Christ.
The Holy Spirit gives us power to overcome sin.
The Holy Spirit gives us strength to lead holy lives.

What, then, does it mean to be sanctified by the Holy Spirit?

WE ARE SANCTIFIED WHEN THE HOLY SPIRIT MAKES US HOLY THROUGH FAITH IN CHRIST AND GIVES US THE STRENGTH TO OVERCOME SIN TO LEAD A HOLY LIFE.

What This Means to Me

The Holy Spirit brought me to faith in Jesus my Savior. God now sees me as His holy or sanctified child. The Holy Spirit lives in my heart and fills it with love for God. He gives me the power to hate sin and to overcome the temptations of my enemies, the devil, the wicked world, and my sinful desires. He also gives me strength to think, say, and do those things that please God. I know that my good works are not perfect and that I sin much. Therefore, I daily ask God to forgive my sins for Jesus' sake and to strengthen my faith through the gift of the Holy Spirit.

For Me to Memorize
Assigned Bible passages

For Me to Do
Read Psalm 1 to your class. How are the believers different from the unbelievers?

For Me to Prepare for the Next Lesson
Read Matthew 26:31-35 and 69-75.
In whom did Peter trust to remain faithful to Jesus?
What did Peter do when he was accused of being a disciple of Jesus?

30. PRESERVATION IN THE FAITH

THE THIRD ARTICLE

But *the Holy Ghost has* called me by the gospel, enlightened me with his gifts, sanctified and *kept me in the true faith.*

For Me to Learn
How our faith is preserved

For Me to Remember
What can we not do by our own will and strength? (A. Remain in the true faith)
By whose power are we preserved in the faith?
1 Peter 1:5. *Through faith [you] are shielded by God's power until the coming of the salvation.*
What does the Holy Spirit do for us? (A. He keeps us in the true faith unto salvation.)
How long will the Holy Spirit preserve us in the true faith? (A. Until we die and until Judgment Day)
Philippians 1:6. *Being confident of this, that he who began a good work in you will carry it on to completion until the day of Christ Jesus.*

Who preserves our faith?

THE HOLY SPIRIT PRESERVES OUR FAITH.

What does the Holy Spirit use to preserve our faith? (A. The Gospel)
Romans 1:16. *I am not ashamed of the gospel, because it is the power of God for the salvation of everyone who believes.*
Only through the Gospel does the Holy Spirit preserve us in the true faith. There is no other way.

How, then, is our faith preserved?

OUR FAITH IS PRESERVED THROUGH THE GOSPEL.

Summary
We cannot preserve our faith by our own will or strength.
The Holy Spirit has the power to preserve our faith.
The Holy Spirit preserves our faith through the Gospel.

How, then, is our faith preserved?

THE HOLY SPIRIT PRESERVES OUR FAITH THROUGH THE GOSPEL.

What This Means to Me
It is only because of God's grace and mercy that I believe in Jesus Christ as my Savior. Through the Gospel in Baptism and through the Gospel in His Word the Holy Spirit brought me to faith and keeps me in the true faith. When I will partake of the sacrament of the Lord's Supper, the Holy Spirit will strengthen my faith through the Gospel in the Lord's Supper. When I refuse to hear the Gospel, the Holy

Spirit will not work faith in my heart. I thank God for the gift of faith which the Holy Spirit gives me through the Gospel.

For Me to Memorize
Assigned Bible passages
Third Article including the first two paragraphs of the explanation

For Me to Do
Read 1 Timothy 2:4. How many people does God want saved? What does God want all people to know?

For Me to Prepare for the Next Lesson
Read the Bible story "Pentecost" (Acts 2:37-41).
What did the people ask Peter after they heard his sermon?
What did Peter tell them they would receive in Baptism?
How many people did the Holy Spirit add to the church on Pentecost?

31. THE COMMUNION OF SAINTS

(The Invisible Church)
THE THIRD ARTICLE

I believe in the Holy Ghost; *the holy Christian church, the communion of saints*; the forgiveness of sins; the resurrection of the body; and the life everlasting. Amen.

What does this mean?
I believe that I cannot by my own thinking or choosing believe in Jesus Christ, my Lord, or come to him.
But *the Holy Ghost has called me by the gospel, enlightened me with his gifts, sanctified and kept me in the true faith. In the same way he calls, gathers, enlightens and sanctifies the whole Christian church on earth, and keeps it with Jesus Christ in the one true faith.*
In this Christian church he daily and fully forgives all sins to me and all believers.
On the Last Day he will raise me and all the dead;

And he will give eternal life to me and all believers in Christ. This is most certainly true.

For Me to Learn
Who belongs to the communion of saints?

For Me to Remember
Through what does the Holy Spirit call people to believe? (A. The Gospel)
What does the Holy Spirit work in their hearts? (A. Faith in the Savior)
How does God look upon all believers? (A. As saints)
What unites or gathers together all believers in the Savior? (A. Faith)

Who belongs to the communion of saints?

ALL PEOPLE WHO ARE CALLED TO FAITH BY THE HOLY SPIRIT BELONG TO THE COMMUNION OF SAINTS.

What do people not understand before they are called to faith? (A. God's Word)
In whom do they not trust and believe? (A. In God)
They are in the dark about the way to eternal salvation.
What does the Holy Spirit do through the Gospel? (A. He enlightens them.)
Ephesians 5:8. *You were once darkness, but now you are light in the Lord.*

Who belongs to the communion of saints?

ALL PEOPLE WHO ARE ENLIGHTENED BY THE HOLY SPIRIT BELONG TO THE COMMUNION OF SAINTS.

What kind of works can people not do with their own will or strength? (A. God-pleasing works)
Who gives Christians the will and power to do God-pleasing works? (A. The Holy Spirit)
Through what does the Holy Spirit sanctify people so they do good works? (A. The Gospel)
Galatians 5:22,23. *The fruit of the Spirit is love, joy, peace, patience, kindness, goodness, faithfulness, gentleness and self-control.*

Who belongs to the communion of saints?

ALL PEOPLE WHO ARE SANCTIFIED BY THE HOLY SPIRIT BELONG TO THE COMMUNION OF SAINTS.

The Holy Spirit brings people to faith in the Savior. To inherit everlasting life they must keep that faith until they die.
What can people not do with their own will or strength? (A. Remain in the faith)
Through whose power are people kept in the faith?
1 Peter 1:5. *Through faith [you] are shielded by God's power until the coming of the salvation.*

Who belongs to the communion of saints?

ALL PEOPLE WHO ARE KEPT IN THE TRUE FAITH BY THE HOLY SPIRIT BELONG TO THE COMMUNION OF SAINTS.

Summary

All people whom the Holy Spirit "calls, gathers, enlightens and sanctifies, . . . and keeps . . . in the one true faith" belong to the communion of saints or the holy Christian church.
John 8:31. *To the Jews who had believed him, Jesus said, "If you hold to my teaching, you are really my disciples."*
Faith in Jesus as the Savior is necessary to belong to the communion of saints. All those who believe in the Savior have been called, gathered, enlightened, sanctified, and kept in the one true faith by the Holy Spirit.

Who, then, belongs to the communion of saints?

ALL PEOPLE WHO BELIEVE IN JESUS CHRIST AS THEIR SAVIOR BELONG TO THE COMMUNION OF SAINTS.

What This Means to Me

I thank God that I am a member of God's holy family, the communion of saints or the holy Christian church. All who believe in Jesus as their Savior are members of this holy group of believers. Daily God richly forgives our sins, and on the Last Day He will give me and all believers in Christ eternal life. This is most certainly true.

For Me to Memorize

Assigned Bible passages
Third Article with explanation

For Me to Do
The Bible gives other names to the communion of saints. What name is given to the communion of saints in each of these Bible passages? 1 Peter 2:9,10; 1 Corinthians 3:16,17; Revelation 21:2; Ephesians 1:22,23.

32. THE TRUE VISIBLE CHURCH

For Me to Learn
Which is the true visible church?

For Me to Remember
Who are Christ's disciples? (A. Those who believe in Him as the Savior)
Whose Word do the disciples of Christ believe and teach? (A. God's Word)
John 8:31. *To the Jews who had believed him, Jesus said, "If you hold to my teaching, you are really my disciples."*
An assembly or group of people that worship together is called a visible church. Why is it called a visible church? (A. We know or can see who belongs to that church.) Not all visible churches teach God's Word purely or correctly. What are such churches called? (A. False churches)

Which is the true visible church?

THE TRUE VISIBLE CHURCH IS A CHURCH THAT TEACHES GOD'S WORD IN ITS TRUTH AND PURITY.

What does Christ command His believers to teach? (A. What God says in his Word)
Matthew 28:19,20. *Go and make disciples of all nations, baptizing them in the name of the Father and of the Son and of the Holy Spirit, and teaching them to obey everything I have commanded you.*
God's Word is a Means of Grace. Through that Word we receive forgiveness of sins. What other Means of Grace did Christ give His believers? (A. The sacraments of Holy Baptism and Lord's Supper or Holy Communion)
How must the church observe these sacraments? (A. As Christ commanded)

Not all visible churches observe the sacraments as Christ instituted them. What are such churches called? (A. False churches)

Which is the true visible church?

THE TRUE VISIBLE CHURCH IS A CHURCH THAT OBSERVES THE SACRAMENTS AS CHRIST INSTITUTED THEM.

Summary

The visible churches consist of people who worship together. There are many different visible churches. They differ from one another in what they teach and believe. A church is a *true* visible church when its doctrines agree with God's Word. All its doctrines are taught in truth and purity.

Which, then, is the true visible church?

THE TRUE VISIBLE CHURCH IS THAT CHURCH WHICH TEACHES THE DOCTRINES OF THE BIBLE IN TRUTH AND PURITY.

What This Means to Me

1 John 4:1. *Do not believe every spirit, but test the spirits to see whether they are from God, because many false prophets have gone out into the world.*

It is important that I study and examine the teachings of the church in which I worship because many churches do not teach God's Word in all its truth and purity. It would be sinful for me to become a member of a church which permits teachings and practices that do not agree with God's Word.

I am thankful that I have the opportunity to study the doctrines of the true Word of God in our catechism course. As we study the teachings of our church we turn to God's Word to show that they are true and correct. May God keep me faithful to His Word all my life and may my church always be a true visible church.

For Me to Memorize

Assigned Bible passages

For Me to Do

Ask your teacher or pastor to give you the following information:
    the number of people who belong to our church,
    the number of confirmed people (communicants) in our church,

the name of our church body,
the number of churches in our church body.

For Me to Prepare for the Next Lesson
Use the Review and Study Guide (Number 33) to prepare for the next lesson. Write the answers on a sheet of paper and study them.

33. REVIEW AND STUDY GUIDE

(Lessons 25 - 32)

I. *Complete*

Complete these sentences.

1. The Holy Spirit is true God because the Bible gives Him .... names.
2. The Holy Spirit is true God because He has divine ....
3. The Holy Spirit is true God because He can do divine ....
4. Since the Holy Spirit is true God, He should receive divine ....
5. The good news that Jesus suffered and died to save us is called the ....
6. All who .... that Jesus is their Savior from sin have everlasting life.
7. Sinful man cannot believe the Gospel by his own ....
8. The .... brings people to faith.
9. The Holy Spirit .... people by the Gospel.
10. The Holy Spirit gives people faith to .... the Gospel.

II. *Answer*

Answer these questions.

1. Who cannot understand and believe what God tells us in His Word?
2. Who moves man to understand and believe God's Word?
3. Whom does the Holy Spirit make known to us through God's Word?
4. What does the Holy Spirit move us to believe?
5. What hope does the Holy Spirit give us?
6. Through what does the Holy Spirit enlighten us with His gifts?
7. For how many people did Jesus earn forgiveness of sins?

8. How did God declare all people because Jesus paid for their sin and guilt?
9. Through what means does God offer forgiveness of sins?
10. Who gives us faith to accept the forgiveness offered by God?

III. *Choose*

Choose the correct answers from the list of answers at the right.

1. In whom must we have faith to do good works?
2. Who gives us faith and power to do good works?
3. Who cannot do God-pleasing works?
4. What is the work of the Holy Spirit called that gives us power to do good works?
5. Who only can do works that please God?
6. What must we have to do good works?
7. Where does God tell us which works please Him and which do not?
8. Through what does the Holy Spirit keep us in the faith?

the Holy Spirit

faith in Christ

the Gospel

sanctification

Jesus Christ

the Ten Commandments

unbelievers

believers

IV. *Choose*

Each of the following sentences describes either the invisible church (the communion of saints) or the visible church. Number your paper 1 - 5 and write either *Visible Church* or *Invisible Church* after each numeral.

1. All people throughout the world who are called by the Holy Spirit to believe the Gospel.
2. All people who belong to a congregation.
3. All people who go to church services.
4. All people who are kept in the faith by the Holy Spirit.
5. All people who believe that Jesus Christ is their Savior.

For Me to Prepare for the Lesson 34.

Read the Bible story "The Giving of the Law" in the Bible history book. Your teacher will help you locate the story.

34. LAW AND GOSPEL

For Me to Learn
What the Law and the Gospel teach us

For Me to Remember
How does God want all people to be?
Leviticus 19:2. *Be holy because I, the Lord your God, am holy.*
How were Adam and Eve after God had created them? (A. Holy)
They knew God, and they knew what was right and wrong.
Where had God written the law, so that they knew God's will? (A. In their hearts)
What made the law unclear in the hearts of all people? (A. Sin)
Where did God give the Law the second time? (A. On Mt. Sinai)
What does God tell us to do in His Law?
Matthew 22:37,39. *Love the Lord your God with all your heart and with all your soul and with all your mind. Love your neighbor as yourself.*
In the Ten Commandments God tells what we should do to show our love for Him and for our neighbor.
What does God tell us not to do in His Law?
1 John 3:4. *Everyone who sins breaks the law; in fact, sin is lawlessness.*
In the Ten Commandments God also tells us what we should not do to show our love for Him and for our neighbor.

What, then, does the Law teach us?

THE LAW TEACHES US WHAT WE SHOULD AND SHOULD NOT DO.

God demands that every commandment must be obeyed perfectly to be safe from eternal punishment.
What can sinful man not do? (A. Keep God's commandments)
What did God do in His great love?
John 3:16. *God so loved the world that he gave his one and only Son, that whoever believes in him shall not perish but have eternal life.*

What did Jesus do to redeem us from the curse of the Law? (A. He obeyed the Law in our place, and He suffered and died for our sins.)
What does God in His grace give us for Jesus' sake? (A. He gives us eternal salvation.)
John 1:17. *The law was given through Moses; grace and truth came through Jesus Christ.*
This is God's good news or the Gospel.

What, then, does the Gospel teach us?

THE GOSPEL TEACHES US WHAT GOD HAS DONE FOR OUR SALVATION.

What This Means to Me

The Law of God, the Ten Commandments, tells me that God demands that I love Him with my whole being and that I love all people as I love myself. I know I have not done that; I know I have not kept the commandments. Therefore I am a guilty sinner and deserve to be rejected by God and to be punished eternally. But in His great love God had pity on me and all people. He sent His own Son to be my substitute. He kept the commandments that I could not keep and He suffered the punishment that I should suffer for the many sins I commit. I shall want to thank, praise, serve, and obey my Lord and Savior all my life for His undeserved goodness toward me and all people.

For Me to Memorize

Assigned Bible passages

For Me to Do

Which one of these Bible passages is Law? Which one of these passages is Gospel?   Galatians 3:13   Deuteronomy 27:26

For Me to Prepare for the Next Lesson

Read the Bible story "The Three Men in the Fiery Furnace" (Daniel 3). Read the story in your Bible history book.
What law did the king make?

What was to be done with those who disobeyed?
What did the three Jewish men refuse to do?
In whom did they trust?
How did God save them?

35. THE LORD YOUR GOD

THE FIRST COMMANDMENT
You shall have no other gods.

What does it mean?
We should fear, love and trust in God above all things.

For Me to Learn
   What God forbids and commands in the First Commandment

For Me to Remember
   Where has God told us what He wants us to do and not to do? (A. In the Ten Commandments)
   What sin did the people commit who worshiped the gold statue? (A. Idolatry)
   What does God forbid? (A. He forbids us to worship and to trust in idols.)
   Isaiah 42:8. *I am the Lord; that is my name! I will not give my glory to another or my praise to idols.*
   An idol is anything or anyone that we fear (greatly respect), love, or trust more than God.

   What does God forbid in the First Commandment?

GOD FORBIDS US TO FEAR, LOVE, AND TRUST ANYONE OR ANYTHING MORE THAN HIM.

   What did the three Jews refuse to worship? (A. The golden statue)
   What did they not fear, love, and trust? (A. The statue)
   Whom did they fear, love, and trust? (A. The true God)
   Whom alone does God command us to worship and serve?
   Matthew 4:10. *Worship the Lord your God, and serve him only.*

We worship God when we fear, love, and trust in Him above all things.

What does God command in the First Commandment?

GOD COMMANDS US TO FEAR, LOVE, AND TRUST IN HIM ABOVE ALL THINGS.

What This Means to Me
The Triune God, Father, Son, and Holy Spirit, is the true God. He created and redeemed me. I want to thank, praise, serve, and obey Him for His goodness toward me. I know that I do not always fear, love, and trust in Him above all things. I ask God to forgive my sins for Jesus' sake and to give me strength and willingness to fear, love, and trust Him more than anyone or anything else.

For Me to Memorize
First Commandment
Assigned Bible passages

For Me to Do
List some ways in which people often show that they fear, love, or trust things of this world more than they do God.

For Me to Prepare for the Next Lesson
Read the Bible story "Peter's Denial" (Matthew 26:69-74)
    Of what was Peter accused?
    What did he deny?
    What did he do to convince the accusers that he was telling the truth?

Read the Bible story "The Ten Lepers" (Luke 17:11-19).
    On whom did the lepers call for help?
    What did Jesus do?
    What did only one leper do?

Read the Bible story "The Ark of the Covenant Is Taken" (1 Samuel 4:1-11).
    Who defeated the Israelites?
    What did the elders think would save Israel?
    What did they have some men bring to the battlefield?
    What did the Philistines do?

36. THE NAME OF YOUR GOD

THE SECOND COMMANDMENT
You shall not misuse the name of the Lord your God.

What does this mean?
We should fear and love God that we do not use his name to curse, swear, lie or deceive, or use it superstitiously, but call upon God's name in every trouble, pray, praise and give thanks.

For Me to Learn
What God forbids and commands in the Second Commandment

For Me to Remember
God has given Himself many names. What are some names by which God has made Himself known to us? (A. Creator, Savior, Son of God, Jesus Christ, Holy Spirit.)
God made His name known to us to save us and bless us. God does not want His name misused.

How did Peter misuse God's name? (A. He cursed and swore by God's name that he was telling the truth.)
How is God's name used in vain?
James 3:10. *Out of the same mouth come praise and cursing. My brothers, this should not be.*

Israel put its trust in the Ark. This was a false or superstitious belief. The Children of Israel misused God's name by trusting in the Ark to save them.
Exodus 20:7. *The Lord will not hold anyone guiltless who misuses his name.*

How do false ministers lie and deceive by God's name? (A. They preach their own ideas as if they were the truths of God's Word.)
They sin by using God's name in vain.
Matthew 15:9. *They worship me in vain; their teachings are but rules taught by men.*

What does God forbid in the Second Commandment?

GOD FORBIDS US TO MISUSE HIS NAME.

How did the ten lepers use God's name? (A. To pray to Jesus)
How did the one leper use God's name? (A. To thank Jesus)

What does God ask us to do in time of need?
Psalm 50:15. *Call upon me in the day of trouble; I will deliver you, and you will honor me.*

What does God want us to do for all His goodness?
Psalm 118:1. *Give thanks to the Lord, for he is good; his love endures forever.*

What does God command us to do in the Second Commandment?

> **GOD COMMANDS US TO USE HIS NAME IN WAYS THAT PLEASE HIM.**

What This Means to Me

God's name is holy. I must never use any name that refers to God in a sinful way. I pray God to guard my tongue, so that I never curse or swear falsely. I also pray God to make me eager to use His name often to thank and praise Him. May God grant that my thoughts do not wander as I pray or hear God's Word, for then I would also be using God's name in vain. I pray God to forgive my sins against this and all commandments for Jesus' sake.

For Me to Memorize

The Second Commandment
Assigned Bible passages

For Me to Do

Name some ways in which people do and do not show respect for God's name, God's Word, and things related to God and His Word in homes, schools, and churches.

For Me to Prepare for the Next Lesson

Read the Bible story "The Great Supper" (Luke 14:16-24).
    What did a good man prepare?
    What did the servant say to many people?
    What did they refuse to do?
    Who later accepted the invitation?

Read the Bible story "Mary and Martha" (Luke 10:38-42).
    To whom did Mary listen?
    What did Martha want her to do?
    Who made the better choice?

37. THE SABBATH OF YOUR GOD

THE THIRD COMMANDMENT
Remember the Sabbath day by keeping it holy.

What does this mean?

We should fear and love God that we do not despise preaching and his Word, but regard it as holy, and gladly hear and learn it.

For Me to Learn
What God forbids and commands in the Third Commandment

For Me to Remember
What did the Sabbath mean to the Old Testament believers? (A. Rest for their bodies and their souls)
On what day of the week was their Sabbath? (A. Saturday)
What does God no longer demand? (A. That we worship Him on *certain* days.)
But God *does* want us to find rest for our souls in His Word.
Whom do people despise when they refuse or neglect to hear God's Word? (A. Christ)
Luke 10:16. *He who listens to you listens to me; he who rejects you rejects me; but he who rejects me rejects him who sent me.*

What does God forbid in the Third Commandment?

GOD FORBIDS US TO DESPISE HIS WORD.

What was Mary glad to hear and learn? (A. God's Word)
How did she regard God's Word? (A. Sacred or holy)
How did the early Christians not regard God's Word? (A. As man's word)
1 Thessalonians 2:13. *When you received the word of God, which you heard from us, you accepted it not as the word of men, but as it actually is, the word of God.*

What does God command in the Third Commandment?

GOD COMMANDS US TO REGARD HIS WORD AS HOLY.

What This Means to Me
There are many things for me to hear, read, and learn, but only God's

Word is holy or sacred. I may not neglect to hear, read, and learn God's Word. If I do, I am despising God's Word. I am sinning against the Third Commandment. God has given me many opportunities to hear, read, and learn His sacred Word. I am thankful to God that He has given me a Christian home, school, and church where I can hear and learn His Word. I know that I have not always gladly heard and learned God's Word. At times I have not been attentive when God's Word was read or preached. I pray God to forgive my sins and to help me, so that I do not despise preaching and His Word.

For Me to Memorize
The Third Commandment
Assigned Bible passages

For Me to Do
Do you have family devotions in your home? If not, talk with your parents about having Bible reading and family devotions. Ask your teacher to suggest books that you can use in your devotions at home.

Write a prayer that you can pray silently before the church service begins. In your prayer ask God to help you to be attentive and to bless His Word that you are about to hear.

For Me to Prepare for the Next Lesson
Read the Bible story "Absalom's Rebellion" (2 Samuel 14:25 - 19:39) in your Bible history book.
- What did Absalom want to become in Israel?
- What did he do to turn the people against David?
- What did he make many people do?
- What finally happened to Absalom?

Read the Bible story "Jacob in Egypt" (Genesis 45:16 - 50:26) in your Bible history book.
- Whom did Joseph invite to come to Egypt?
- How did Joseph welcome his father?
- To whom did he introduce his father?

38. THE REPRESENTATIVES OF YOUR GOD

THE FOURTH
COMMANDMENT

Honor your father and mother, that it may go well with you, and that you may enjoy long life on the earth.

What does this mean?

We should fear and love God that we do not dishonor or anger our parents and others in authority, but honor, serve and obey them, and give them love and respect.

For Me to Learn

What God forbids and commands in the Fourth Commandment

For Me to Remember

What do we call all people whom God has placed over us? (A. God's representatives)

Who is God's representative in the home? In the school? In the church? In the state?

Whose place do they take on earth? (A. They take God's place.)

How did Absalom sin? (A. He despised his father and rebelled against him.)

What does God forbid? (A. God forbids us to despise and disobey our parents.)

Proverbs 30:17. *The eye that mocks a father, that scorns obedience to a mother, will be pecked out by the ravens of the valley, will be eaten by the vultures.*

This passage speaks about father and mother, but it means all of God's representatives.

What does God forbid in the Fourth Commandment?

GOD FORBIDS US TO DESPISE AND DISOBEY HIS REPRESENTATIVES.

How did Joseph honor his father? (A. He went out to meet him. He

introduced him to Pharaoh. He took care of him in his old age.)
What does God command us to do? (A. To honor our parents)
Ephesians 6:2,3. *Honor your father and mother — which is the first commandment with a promise — that it may go well with you and that you may enjoy long life on the earth.*
How will we show that we honor and love our parents? (A. We will obey them.)
What does God command us to do? (A. To obey our parents)
Ephesians 6:1. *Children, obey your parents in the Lord, for this is right.*
When God in these Bible passages speaks about father and mother, He means all His representatives.

What does God command us to do in the Fourth Commandment?

GOD COMMANDS US TO HONOR AND OBEY HIS REPRESENTATIVES.

What This Means to Me

God has placed representatives over me for my good. My parents provide me with a home, with food and clothing, and with guidance in the way that I should go. They are my dearest and best friends. God's representatives in the school, church, and state are over me to instruct me, protect me, and guide me. It is a great sin to dishonor and anger my parents, pastor, teachers, and other people who are over me. My love for God and for my neighbor should make me want to honor, serve, and obey all people whom God has placed over me for my good. I pray God to increase my love and respect for my parents and all of my superiors, so that I may always be an obedient child of God.

For Me to Memorize

The Fourth Commandment
Assigned Bible passages

For Me to Do

Read Romans 13:1. "Submit" means to obey. Whom should all people obey?
"Authorities" refers to all governments. Who establishes all governments?

For Me to Prepare for the Next Lesson

Read the Bible story "Cain and Abel" (Genesis 4:1-12).
   How did Cain feel toward Abel?
   What did he do in his anger?

Read the Bible story "The Good Samaritan" (Luke 10:30-37).
What did thieves do to the man on the road to Jericho?
Who did not help him?
How did the Samaritan help him?

39. THE KINDNESS YOUR GOD DEMANDS

THE FIFTH COMMANDMENT
You shall not murder.

What does this mean?
We should fear and love God that we do not hurt or harm our neighbor in his body, but help and be a friend to him in every bodily need.

For Me to Learn
What God forbids and commands in the Fifth Commandment

For Me to Remember
Who made all people? Who only has the right to bring the life of people to an end? (A. God)
Psalm 31:15. *My times are in your hands.*

What is hatred in the sight of God?
1 John 3:15. *Anyone who hates his brother is a murderer.*
How did Cain sin? (A. He hated Abel and murdered him.)
How did the thieves sin who stopped the man on the way to Jericho? (A. They hurt and wounded him.)

What does God forbid in the Fifth Commandment?

GOD FORBIDS US TO HURT OR HARM OUR NEIGHBOR.

What This Means to Me
In this commandment God forbids me to do anything to anyone that may hurt him or put him in danger of getting hurt or harmed. Even anger or hatred in my heart are sins against my neighbor. When someone wrongs me, it is sinful for me to try and get revenge or to "get even" with him. God commands me to love everyone and show my love by helping them and being good friends with them. There are many ways I can help my parents, brothers and sisters, school

mates, and others. I can help the many needy people in the world by praying for them and giving money with which food and clothing can be purchased for them.

I confess that I have sinned many times against the Fifth Commandment. I pray God to forgive me for the sake of Jesus, who never sinned against God or His neighbor.

For Me to Remember

How did the good Samaritan help the wounded man? What should we do for people even when they are our enemies?

Romans 12:20. *If your enemy is hungry, feed him; if he is thirsty, give him something to drink.*

God has blessed all of us in many ways. Name some things God has given us. But with what is God pleased? (A. When I share my blessings with others, especially the needy) That is being a friend to our neighbor.

Hebrews 13:16. *Do not forget to do good and to share with others, for with such sacrifices God is pleased.*

What does God command us to do?

GOD COMMANDS US TO HELP AND BE A FRIEND TO OUR NEIGHBOR.

What This Means to Me

There are many ways in which I can help others and be a friend to them at home, in school, and in my neighborhood. Everybody is my neighbor, but I want to help and be a friend especially to people who are in need of friendship and help. They are the poor, sick, and lonely. I do not help them in order to be praised and rewarded, but I want to help them to show my appreciation for the many blessings God has given me. I want to show my love for God and for my neighbor.

For Me to Memorize

The Fifth Commandment
Assigned Bible passages

For Me to Do

Read Genesis 9:6. This Bible passage speaks about the government. What right has the government?

God has given all of us many opportunities to help people, whether they are young or old.

Name some opportunities you have to help your neighbor.

For Me to Prepare for the Next Lesson
Read the Bible story "Joseph's Purity" (Genesis 39:4-13).
What did the master's wife ask Joseph to do?
What did he say that shows he did not want to sin against God?

40. THE PURITY YOUR GOD DEMANDS

THE SIXTH COMMANDMENT
You shall not commit adultery.

What does this mean?
We should fear and love God that we lead a pure and decent life in words and actions, and that husband and wife love and honor each other.

For Me to Learn
What God forbids and commands in the Sixth Commandment

For Me to Remember
What sinful thought did Potiphar's wife have when she saw Joseph? (A. She wanted him to be like a husband to her.)
What did she commit in her heart? (A. Adultery)
What kind of talk and words does God forbid? (A. Unwholesome or unclean)
Ephesians 4:29. *Do not let any unwholesome talk come out of your mouths.*
What sin do we commit when we use unclean, dirty talk? (A. Adultery)
Potiphar's wife wanted to live with another man as she lived with her husband.
What does God forbid? (A. God forbids breaking up marriages by unfaithfulness on the part of husbands or wives and by a sinful divorce.)
Matthew 19:6. *What God has joined together, let man not separate.*
What things are often done in secret? (A. Shameful things)
Ephesians 5:12. *It is shameful even to mention what the disobedient do in secret.*
What sins do wives and husbands commit who are unfaithful to each other? (A. Adultery)
What sin do those commit who do shameful things with their bodies? (A. Adultery)

What does God forbid in the Sixth Commandment?

GOD FORBIDS US TO COMMIT ADULTERY IN THOUGHT, WORD, OR ACT.

For Me to Remember

How does God want our hearts to be?
Matthew 5:8. *Blessed are the pure in heart.*
Who can give us a pure heart?
Psalm 51:10. *Create in me a pure heart, O God, and renew a steadfast spirit within me.*

What does God want us to do so that we are not tempted to sin?
(A. Avoid people, places, and things that could make us sin.)
2 Timothy 2:22. *Flee the evil desires of youth.*
What should we do every day to protect us from sin?
Matthew 26:41. *Watch and pray so that you will not fall into temptation.*

What does God command in the Sixth Commandment?

GOD COMMANDS US TO LEAD A PURE AND DECENT LIFE.

What This Means to Me

God wants me to have a pure heart. If my heart is pure, my thoughts and talk will be clean and I will do what is decent and God-pleasing. I know that the devil and wicked people will tempt me to commit sins of adultery by putting unclean thoughts into my mind and by causing me to say and do things that are shameful. I need strength from God to resist and overcome such temptations. Therefore I will read and hear God's Word and pray God to give me power to fight against sinful thoughts, words, and acts and the will and power to lead a pure and decent life.

For Me to Memorize

The Sixth Commandment
Assigned Bible passages

For Me to Do

Many TV programs and movies portray sins against this commandment and even make them appear humorous. The devil uses them to put unclean thoughts into our minds. God's children will not watch such programs and movies. This explains why your parents do not permit you to view certain programs.

For Me to Prepare for the Next Lesson
Read the Bible story "The Separation of Abraham and Lot" (Genesis 13:5-11).
Why was it necessary for Abraham and Lot to separate?
What did Abraham tell Lot he could do?

41. THE GIFTS OF YOUR GOD

THE SEVENTH COMMANDMENT
You shall not steal.

What does this mean?
We should fear and love God that we do not take our neighbor's money or property or get it by dishonest dealing, but help him to improve and protect his property and business.

For Me to Learn
What God forbids and commands in the Seventh Commandment

For Me to Remember
How did the thieves on the road to Jericho sin? (A. They robbed a man of his possessions.)
What does God forbid us to do?
How should we gain our possessions?
Ephesians 4:28. *He who has been stealing must steal no longer, but must work, doing something useful with his own hands.*

How do some dishonest people gain possession of other people's money and goods? (A. They do not return borrowed things; they cheat; they overcharge.)
Psalm 37:21. *The wicked borrow and do not repay.*
Getting people's possessions by cheating them is stealing.

What does God forbid in the Seventh Commandment?

GOD FORBIDS US TO STEAL OUR NEIGHBOR'S POSSESSIONS.

What This Means to Me
God has given every man, woman, and child certain possessions. These possessions are theirs until they sell or trade them willingly. I have no right to take anything from them by trickery or force. I sin whenever I get anything, even small items like a pencil, dishonestly from

someone. Even thinking about stealing something is a sin. My love for God and my neighbor should make me want to help my neighbor, so that he does not lose what he owns.

For Me to Remember
What did Lot need for his cattle? (A. Grass and water)
How did Abraham help Lot improve his property? (A. He let Lot choose the best area for his cattle.)
What should make us want to think of ways in which to help our neighbor? (A. Our love for God and our neighbor)
1 Corinthians 13:4,5. *Love . . . is not self-seeking.*
Christians will want to be unselfish and help their neighbor whenever they can.
What does God command us to do when we hear about our neighbor's needs? (A. Give or loan him money, help him with his work, give him advice)
Matthew 5:42. *Give to the one who asks you, and do not turn away from the one who wants to borrow from you.*

What does God command in the Seventh Commandment?

GOD COMMANDS US TO HELP OUR NEIGHBOR IMPROVE HIS POSSESSIONS.

What This Means to Me
I know that I have not always been unselfish. I pray that God will graciously forgive my sins for Jesus' sake. Out of love for God and my neighbor I will want to help improve what God has given to others, and to help them in their need. I pray God to show me ways in which I can help my parents, teachers, classmates, and others, and to make me eager to help all people, especially the poor and needy.

For Me to Memorize
The Seventh Commandment
Assigned Bible passages

For Me to Do
Read Matthew 15:19. Where does the sin of stealing begin?

For Me to Prepare for the Next Lesson
Read the Bible story "Jonathan Defends David" (1 Samuel 19:1-5).
  What did Jonathan offer to do?
  Who thought evil of David?
  What did he want to do with David?
  What did Jonathan say to Saul to defend David?

42. THE TRUTH OF YOUR GOD

THE EIGHTH COMMANDMENT

You shall not give false testimony against your neighbor.

What does this mean?

We should fear and love God that we do not tell lies about our neighbor, betray him or give him a bad name, but defend him, speak well of him and take his words and actions in the kindest possible way.

For Me to Learn

What God forbids and commands in the Eighth Commandment

For Me to Remember

About whom did Potiphar's wife tell a lie? (A. Joseph)
How did this harm Joseph? (A. He lost his good reputation; he lost his good position; he was put into prison.)
What kind of talk does God forbid? (A. Untrue or false talk)
Proverbs 19:5. *A false witness will not go unpunished, and he who pours out lies will not go free.*
Who is a "false witness?" (A. A person who tells an untruth or a lie)

What does God forbid us to say about others? (A. Evil things)
James 4:11. *Do not slander one another.*
How did Absalom hurt his father's good name? (A. He slandered him and hurt his good name and reputation)

How did Judas sin? (A. He betrayed Jesus to the enemies.)

What does God forbid us to do in the Eighth Commandment?

GOD FORBIDS US TO LIE ABOUT OUR NEIGHBOR, BETRAY HIM, OR GIVE HIM A BAD NAME.

What did Jonathan do when King Saul spoke evil of David and wanted him killed? (A. He defended David and spoke well of him.)
What does God want us to do when we hear someone speak evil of others? (A. Defend them and speak well of them)
Proverbs 31:8. *Speak up for those who cannot speak for themselves, for the rights of all who are destitute.*
We should believe and explain in the best and kindest possible way what people say and do.

What does God command in the Eighth Commandment?

GOD COMMANDS US TO DEFEND OUR NEIGHBOR, SPEAK WELL OF HIM, AND TAKE HIS WORDS AND ACTIONS IN THE BEST WAY.

What This Means to Me

I love God, who forgives my sins for Jesus' sake. I can show my love for God by the love I show for my parents, brothers and sisters, schoolmates, teacher, and all people with whom I associate. I will not want to hurt them by speaking evil about them, telling lies about them, or spreading stories about them that make people think evil of them. When I hear evil talk and lying, I will want to defend the person who is being hurt and speak good things about him. I know that the devil tries to make me hurt others by saying harmful things about them and that he makes it hard for me to speak good about people when others say bad things about them. I pray God to give me strength to keep the Eighth Commandment. When I sin, I pray Him to forgive my sins for Jesus' sake who never spoke evil of anyone.

For Me to Memorize

The Eighth Commandment
Assigned Bible passages

For Me to Do

Be prepared to read James 3:7-10 to your class. Your teacher and classmates will discuss this Bible reading in the next religion period.

For Me to Prepare for the Next Lesson

Read the Bible story "Naboth's Vineyard" (1 Kings 21:1-16).
  What did Ahab want very much?
  Why did Naboth not want to give up his possession?
  How did Jezebel scheme to get the property?

Read the Bible story "Abraham Rescues Lot" (Genesis 14:1,2,12,14,16).
  How did Lot lose his possessions?
  What did Abraham do to help Lot regain his possessions?

43. THE HOLY HEART YOUR GOD DEMANDS

THE NINTH COMMANDMENT
You shall not covet your neighbor's house.

What does this mean?
We should fear and love God that we do not scheme to get our neighbor's inheritance or house or obtain it by false claims, but do all we can to help him keep it.

THE TENTH COMMANDMENT
You shall not covet your neighbor's wife or his workers or his animals or anything that belongs to your neighbor.

What does this mean?
We should fear and love God that we do not force or entice away from our neighbor his wife, workers or animals, but urge them to stay and do their duty.

For Me to Learn
What God forbids and commands in the Ninth and Tenth Commandments

For Me to Remember
How are the hearts of all people by nature? (A. Sinful)
What comes out of our sinful hearts? (A. Sinful thoughts, words, and acts)
Matthew 15:19. *Out of the heart come evil thoughts, murder, adultery, sexual immorality, theft, false testimony, slander.*

What is coveting? (A. The sinful desire to have our neighbor's possessions)
What did Ahab covet? Ahab was not happy and satisfied until he got possession of Naboth's property.
How does God not want us to be? (A. Greedy, dissatisfied with what He has given us)
Isaiah 5:8. *Woe to you who add house to house and join field to field till no space is left.*

What does God forbid in the Ninth and Tenth Commandments?

GOD FORBIDS US TO HAVE SINFUL DESIRES FOR OUR NEIGHBOR'S POSSESSIONS.

For Me to Remember

What did Abraham risk to help Lot regain his possessions? (A. His life and his own possessions)

What will we do if we love our neighbor? (A. Help him keep his possessions)

Philippians 2:4. *Each of you should look not only to your own interests, but also to the interests of others.*

What are some of our neighbor's possessions? (A. His inheritance, house, wife, workers, animals)

What does God command in the Ninth and Tenth Commandments?

GOD COMMANDS US TO HAVE HOLY DESIRES SO THAT WE HELP OUR NEIGHBOR KEEP HIS POSSESSIONS.

What This Means to Me

Galations 5:13. *Serve one another in love.*

Love is the opposite of hatred and envy. If I love God and my neighbor as God demands, I will not envy others. I will not be jealous because someone has things that I do not have. I will be satisfied with what God has given me. It is not wrong for me to wish for things I need, but it is sinful for me to have such a strong desire for things, so that I am unhappy and dissatisfied until I somehow possess those things. That is coveting. If I love my neighbor as God demands, I will be happy that God blessed him with the possessions he has, and I will do all I can to help him keep them.

I pray God to take all sinful thoughts and desires out of my heart and to fill it with love for Him and my neighbor.

For Me to Memorize

The Ninth and Tenth Commandments
Assigned Bible passages

For Me to Do

Read James 1:14,15. To what may sinful desires lead?
Read Psalm 51:10. What do we ask God to give us?

For Me to Prepare for the Next Lesson

Read the Bible story "The Flood" (Genesis 6:1-13).
  How were the people on earth?
  What did God threaten to do?
  How did God punish them?

Read the Bible story "Jacob's Return" (Genesis 32:1-10).
How had God blessed Jacob?
How did Jacob show that he believed that it was because of God's mercy that he was blessed?

44. THE ZEAL OF YOUR GOD

THE CONCLUSION

What does God say about all these commandments?
He says, "I, the Lord your God, am a jealous God punishing the children for the sin of the fathers to the third and fourth generation of those who hate me, but showing love to thousands who love me and keep my commandments."

What does this mean?
God threatens to punish all who transgress these commandments. Therefore we should fear his anger and not disobey what he commands. But he promises grace and every blessing to all who keep these commandments. Therefore we should love and trust in him, and gladly obey what he commands.

For Me to Learn

What God threatens and promises in The Conclusion of His commandments

For Me to Remember

What does God insist that we do with His commandments? (A. Keep or obey them perfectly)
How does God become when we transgress His commandments? (A. Angry with us)
What did God threaten to do before the Flood? (A. To destroy all living things)
How did God punish the wicked people because they would not believe His threats and repent of their sins?
What does God threaten to do to all those who do not keep His commandments? (A. To punish them)
Deuteronomy 27:26. *Cursed is the man who does not uphold the words of this law by carrying them out.*
With what will God punish anyone who does not heed His threats and does not repent of his sins? (A. With eternal death in hell)
Romans 6:23. *The wages of sin is death.*

What does God threaten to do to those who transgress His commandments?

> **GOD THREATENS TO PUNISH THOSE WHO TRANSGRESS HIS COMMANDMENTS.**

For Me to Remember

How did Jacob sin against his father? (A. He deceived him.)
Whom did Jacob learn to trust while he was away from home? (A. God)
How did God show mercy to Jacob? (A. He blessed him, so that he became a very rich man.)
What does God promise those who fear, love, and trust Him and keep His commandments?
Psalm 112:1. *Blessed is the man who fears the Lord, who finds great delight in his commands.*
What does God promise to show to those people who fear and love Him?
Luke 1:50. *His mercy extends to those who fear him, from generation to generation.*

What does God promise those who keep His commandments?

> **GOD PROMISES TO SHOW MERCY TO THOSE WHO OBEY HIS COMMANDMENTS.**

What This Means to Me

God has the right to give me His commandments and to expect that I obey every one of them. He has the right to become angry with me when I transgress any one of His commandments, and He has the right to punish me. My sinful heart often tries to make me sin. Then I should remember God's threat to punish anyone who transgresses His commandments. I pray God to give me the will and strength to obey His commandments.

When I remember that Jesus died to save me from my sins and that God in His mercy has forgiven my sins for Jesus' sake, I will want to obey His commandments. God's goodness and mercy should lead me to repentance when I transgress His commandments. I pray that the mercy and love of God will always make me eager to please Him by obeying His commandments.

For Me to Memorize

The Conclusion of the Commandments
Assigned Bible passages

For Me to Prepare for the Next Lesson
Use the Review and Study Guide (Number 45) to prepare for the next lesson. Write the answers on a sheet of paper and study them.

45. REVIEW AND STUDY GUIDE

(Lessons 34 - 44)

I. *Answer*

Answer these questions.

1. What do we call the truths we learn from the Bible?
2. Which are the two great doctrines in the Bible?
3. Where did God put His law first so that people would know what is right and what is wrong?
4. Where did God give the Law the second time?
5. What is another name for the Law of God?
6. What does the Law teach us?
7. What does the Gospel teach us?
8. With what words does Luther's explanation to each of the commandments begin?
9. What does it mean to fear God?
10. How much should we fear and love God?

II. *Complete*

Complete these sentences.

1. The first three commandments tell us about our duty to ....
2. The last seven commandments tell us about our duty to our ....
3. In the First Commandment God commands us to ...., ... and .... Him more than anything or anyone.
4. Some names by which God has made Himself known to us are ...., ..., ...
5. God's name should not be used to .... or ...., nor should we .... or .... by His name.
6. People .... God's Word when they refuse to read, hear, or learn it.
7. God forbids us to .... and .... His representatives.
8. In the Fifth Commandment God forbids us to .... or .... our neighbor.

9. Sins of adultery are committed with shameful and filthy ...., ..., ...
10. In the Seventh Commandment God protects the .... He has given us and our neighbor.
11. In the Seventh Commandment God forbids us to .... our neighbor's property.
12. In the Eighth Commandment God forbids us to say .... or .... things about our neighbor.
13. Our hearts are .... by nature.
14. In the Ninth and Tenth Commandments God forbids us to have sinful .... for our neighbor's possessions.
15. God threatens to .... all who transgress His commandments.

III. *Choose*

Which commandment

1. commands us to respect and obey God's representatives?
2. commands us to have clean thoughts and to live decent lives?
3. commands us to respect God more than anyone else?
4. commands us to pray in God's name?
5. commands us to hear and learn God's Word gladly?
6. commands us to be a friend to others and to help them in their bodily needs?
7. commands us to speak well of others?
8. commands us to help our neighbor improve what he owns?
9. commands us to help others keep what God has given them?
10. commands us to fear, love, and trust God more than anyone or anything?

IV. *Answer*

Answer these questions.

1. What does God threaten to do to all who do not keep His commandments?
2. Why do we all deserve God's punishment?
3. Who obeyed the commandments in our place?
4. What does God promise those who repent of their sins and trust in Jesus as their Savior?
5. What will we want to do to show our love for our merciful God?

46. MEANING OF PRAYER

For Me to Learn
What prayer is

For Me to Remember
What did God intend to do to the wicked city of Sodom?
What did Abraham do to save the city? (A. He prayed to God.)
In his prayer Abraham talked to God.
What did the woman of Canaan do when her daughter became very sick? (A. She prayed to Jesus to heal her.) She fell down and worshiped Jesus as she prayed.
What do we do when we pray to God from our hearts? (A. Worship Him)
Psalm 95:6. *Come, let us bow down in worship. Let us kneel before the Lord our Maker.*

What is prayer?

PRAYER IS AN ACT OF WORSHIP IN WHICH WE SPEAK TO GOD.

What did Abraham ask God to do? What did the woman of Canaan ask Jesus to do?
We call their prayers for help "petitions." They petitioned (asked) God to help them.
Abraham and the woman of Canaan worshiped God with their petitions.

What, then, is prayer?

PRAYER IS AN ACT OF WORSHIP IN WHICH WE PETITION GOD.

What did the angels do when Jesus was born?
Whom did they worship?
Their song of praise was a prayer to God.

What, then is prayer?

PRAYER IS AN ACT OF WORSHIP IN WHICH WE PRAISE GOD.

What did one leper do after he was healed by Jesus?
Whom did he worship with his words of thanks?
How do we worship God? (A. By thanking God)
Psalm 106:1. *Give thanks to the Lord, for he is good; his love endures forever.*

What, then, is prayer?

PRAYER IS AN ACT OF WORSHIP IN WHICH WE THANK GOD.

Summary
In what three ways can we worship God with our prayers?
  We can worship God with our prayers of petition.
  We can worship God with our prayers of praise.
  We can worship God with our prayers of thanks.

What, then, is prayer?

PRAYER IS AN ACT OF WORSHIP IN WHICH WE PETITION, PRAISE, OR THANK GOD.

What This Means to Me
I am God's child. I will want to speak to God often by praying to Him. He is almighty and can and wants to help me in my needs and troubles. He is my Creator, Preserver, and Savior whom I will want to praise. All I have comes from Him. I will want to thank Him every day for His goodness. I pray God to strengthen my faith so that I will want to worship Him with my petitions, praises, and thanks.

For Me to Memorize
Assigned Bible passages
The first part of Luther's Morning Prayer up to "For into. . . ."

For Me to Do
Write a short prayer of petition, praise, or thanks.

For Me to Prepare for the Next Lesson
Read the Bible story "The Prayer of the Tax Collector" (Luke 18: 9-14).
>What did the tax collector ask of God?
>How did God answer his prayer?

47. REASON FOR PRAYING

For Me to Learn
Why we pray to God

For Me to Remember
What does God command us to do in the Second Commandment? (A. To call upon Him)
What does it mean to call upon God? (A. To pray to Him)
When should we pray to God?
Psalm 50:15. *Call upon me in the day of trouble.*
We need to pray because we have troubles of the body and troubles of the soul.
For whom does God also want us to pray?
James 5:16. *Pray for each other.*

Why, then, do we pray to God?

GOD HAS COMMANDED US TO PRAY IN ALL NEEDS.

For what did the tax collector pray? (A. For mercy or forgiveness)
How did God answer his prayer? (A. God forgave him his sins.)
What does God promise to do when we pray to Him? (A. God promises to hear our prayers and to help us.)
Psalm 50:15. *Call upon me in the day of trouble; I will deliver you, and you will honor me.*
God promises to help us in a way and at the time that is best for us.

Why then, do we pray to God?

GOD PROMISES TO HEAR OUR PRAYER.

Summary
We pray to God because He commands us to pray to Him for all needs of the body and the soul.
We pray to God because He promises to hear all our prayers.

Why, then, do we pray to God?

GOD COMMANDS US TO PRAY TO HIM AND PROMISES TO HEAR OUR PRAYERS.

What This Means to Me

Matthew 7:7. *Ask and it will be given to you; seek and you will find; knock and the door will be opened to you.*

My loving God is eager to help me. Therefore He urges me to pray to Him for all my needs and tells me never to give up praying. He is pleased when I talk to Him about the things that trouble my body and my soul. He is also pleased when I thank Him for His goodness and help. I can be sure that God will hear my prayers and help me. I can trust His promise to listen to my prayers and give me what is best for me.

For Me to Memorize

Assigned Bible passages
Luther's Morning Prayer

For Me to Do

In which one of the following Bible passages does God promise to hear our prayers? In which passage does He command us to pray?
1 Thessalonians 5:17   John 16:23

48. PLACE AND TIME FOR PRAYER

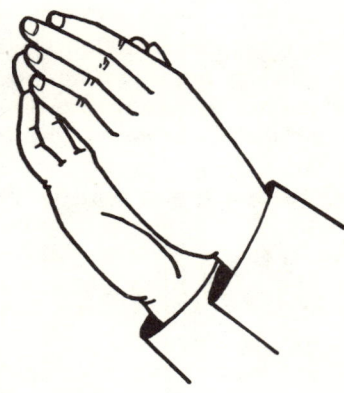

For Me to Learn

When and where God wants us to pray

For Me to Remember
Where did Daniel pray to God? (A. In his home)
Where were the disciples when they prayed, "Lord, save us! We're going to drown!"? (A. On the sea)
Where was the tax collector when he prayed for God's mercy? (A. In the Temple)
Where does God want us to pray to Him?
1 Timothy 2:8. *I want men everywhere to lift up holy hands in prayer.*

GOD WANTS US TO PRAY EVERYWHERE.

When did Daniel and the disciples pray? (A. When they were in danger or trouble)
When did the tax collector pray? (A. When his sins troubled him)
When does God want us to pray to Him?
Psalm 50:15. *Call upon me in the day of trouble.*
A child of God will not pray only in times of trouble. He will make it his habit to pray regularly at certain times of the day.
He will regularly thank God for His goodness and mercy.
He will join his fellow Christians in prayers.
1 Thessalonians 5:17. *Pray continually.*

When does God want us to pray?

GOD WANTS US TO PRAY AT ANY TIME.

Summary
Where and when does God want us to pray?

GOD WANTS US TO PRAY EVERYWHERE AND AT ANY TIME.

What This Means to Me
God is my heavenly Father. I can pray to Him at any time and anywhere. He will hear me because He is everywhere. I can pray to Him at home, on the way to and from school, when riding in a car or bus, on the playground, everywhere. Whenever I am afraid or have troubles, I can pray to God. I will also want to pray regularly mornings, evenings, and at mealtimes. It is a joy for me to join my classmates and teacher in prayer at school and my parents at home. I look forward to praying with other Christians in our church services. I pray God to strengthen my faith, so that I will be diligent in praying to Him.

For Me to Memorize
Assigned Bible passages
Luther's Evening Prayer

For Me to Do
Read Hymn 457 (TLH). List some of the troubles mentioned in the hymn that we can take to the Lord in prayer.

THE LORD'S PRAYER

49. GOD-PLEASING PRAYER

THE ADDRESS
Our Father who art in heaven.

What does this mean?
With these words God tenderly invites us to believe that he is our true Father and that we are his true children, so that we may pray to him as boldly and confidently as dear children ask their dear father.

For Me to Learn
How we should pray to God

For Me to Remember
How do we address or call upon God in the Lord's Prayer? (A. Our Father who art in heaven)
What had separated us from God? (A. Our sins)
Who made peace between us and God? (A. Jesus Christ)
How did Jesus make peace between us and God? (A. He redeemed us from all sins.)
God has adopted us as His children for Jesus' sake.
What can we therefore call God?
1 John 3:1. *How great is the love the Father has lavished on us, that we should be called children of God!*
Who only is truly a child of God and can call God his Father? (A. Only he who has faith in Jesus Christ)
Galatians 3:26. *You are all sons of God through faith in Christ Jesus.*

How, then, should we pray?

WE SHOULD PRAY TO GOD AS OUR FATHER THROUGH JESUS CHRIST.

Why is God able to hear our prayers and to help us? (A. He is always with us, and He is almighty.)
What is God willing to do? (A. To help us)
Matthew 7:11. *If you, then, though you are evil, know how to give good gifts to your children, how much more will your Father in heaven give good gifts to those who ask him!*

Since Jesus has made peace between us and God, we need not be afraid to come to God with our prayers. God also wants to help us, and we know He can help us.

How can we come to God with our prayers? (A. Boldly and confidently believe that God will and can help us)

Hebrews 4:16. *Let us then approach the throne of grace with confidence, so that we may receive mercy and find grace to help us in our time of need.*

How, then, should we pray to God?

WE SHOULD PRAY TO GOD BOLDLY AND CONFIDENTLY.

Summary

Jesus has redeemed us from our sins. We are at peace with God. God has adopted us as His children.

He is our Father for Jesus' sake. We need not fear to come to Him. He is almighty and willing to help us.

How, then, should we pray to God?

WE SHOULD PRAY BOLDLY AND CONFIDENTLY AS CHILDREN OF GOD.

What This Means to Me

In the Lord's Prayer Jesus teaches me that I should pray only to the true God. In this prayer God is called "Our Father who art in heaven." It is through Jesus that God is my Father, and that I am His child. God has other names, but the name "Father" tells me that He loves me dearly as a dear father loves his children. The name "Father" tells me that I need never be afraid to pray to God. I know He will hear all my prayers for Jesus' sake and answers them.

For Me to Memorize

The Address and explanation of the Lord's Prayer
Assigned Bible passages

For Me to Do

Write a short prayer in which you ask God to forgive your sins and to strengthen your faith. Close your prayers with these words: Hear my prayer for Jesus' sake. Amen.

50. THE NAME OF GOD

THE FIRST PETITION
Hallowed be Thy name.

For Me to Learn
What is meant with God's name?

For Me to Remember
Where does God reveal His names to us? (A. In the Bible)
What are some names that God has given to Himself?
Matthew 28:19. *Go and make disciples of all nations, baptizing them in the name of the Father and of the Son and of the Holy Spirit.*
What are some other names by which God has made Himself known to us? (A. Creator, Jesus, Lord)
What name has God given Himself in the Lord's Prayer? (A. Father in heaven or Heavenly Father)

What, then, is meant with God's name?

GOD'S NAME MEANS ALL NAMES THAT STAND FOR GOD.

Ecclesiastes 12:1. *Remember your Creator in the days of your youth.*
Why does the name Creator correctly describe God? (A. Because God created heaven and earth)
Psalm 103:13. *As a father has compassion on his children, so the Lord has compassion on those who fear him.*
Why does the name Lord correctly describe God? (A. Because God is Lord who rules over heaven and earth)
Matthew 1:21. *She will give birth to a son, and you are to give him the name Jesus, because he will save his people from their sins.*
Why does the name Jesus correctly describe Him? (A. Because Jesus means Savior; He saved all people from their sins.)

How are the names of God different from the names of people? (A. The names which God has tell us what He is like and what He has done and still does.)
What are some of the great things God has done? (A. Created the world, made Abraham's descendants into a great nation, saved Israel from the Egyptians, made the Children of Israel into a great nation, sent Jesus to earth to save all people from their sin.)
What great things is God still doing today? (A. Creating new people,

protecting and preserving people, ruling the world, sending sunshine and rain, forgiving sins for Jesus' sake.)
Where does God still tell us what He has done and what He still does? (A. In the Bible)
What should all people do who know what God has done and still does? (A. Honor and praise His name)
Malachi 1:11. *My name will be great among the nations, from the rising to the setting of the sun.*

What, then, is meant with God's name?

GOD'S NAME MEANS EVERYTHING THAT GOD TELLS US ABOUT HIMSELF.

Summary
God's name means all names He has given Himself.
God's name means everything He tells us about Himself.

What, then, is meant with God's name?

GOD'S NAME MEANS ALL NAMES THAT STAND FOR GOD AND EVERYTHING GOD TELLS US ABOUT HIMSELF.

What This Means to Me
God has many names. The Bible tells me His names, but the Bible tells me more. It tells me what God is like and what He has done and what He still does. When I think of God's name and when I read or hear about the great things God has done, I want to honor and praise His holy name.

For Me to Memorize
Assigned Bible passages

51. THE FIRST PETITION

Hallowed be thy name.

What does this mean?
God's name is cerainly holy by itself, but we pray in this petition that we too may keep it holy.

How is God's name kept holy?
God's name is kept holy when his Word is taught in its truth and purity, and we as children of God lead holy lives according to it. Help us to do this, dear Father in heaven!

But whoever teaches and lives contrary to God's Word dishonors God's name among us. Keep us from doing this, dear Father in heaven!

For Me to Learn
What we ask of God in the First Petition

For Me to Remember
God's name and Word are holy.
In the First Petition we ask God to give us strength to hallow His name. We ask God to give us strength to show that we regard God's name as holy by what we say and do.
When is God's name hallowed in what we say or teach? (A. When we speak or teach God's Word faithfully)
Jeremiah 23:28. *Let the one who has my word speak it faithfully.*
God's Word is used faithfully when it is spoken, taught, and preached in its truth and purity.
What are we doing when we speak God's Word in its truth and purity? (A. We are hallowing God's name)
What do people do when they do not teach and preach God's Word truthfully? (A. They disrepect God's Word. They dishonor the name of God.)

What do we ask of God when we pray, "Hallowed be thy name"?

WE ASK GOD TO GRANT THAT WE TEACH HIS WORD TRUTHFULLY.

When do we also show that we hallow God's name? (A. When we do good works according to God's Word)
Matthew 5:16. *Let your light shine before men, that they may see your good deeds and praise your Father in heaven.*
The faith God has given us shows itself in our good works.
People who do not live according to God's Word disgrace God's Word. They dishonor God's name by ungodly living.

What do we ask of God when we pray, "Hallowed be thy name"?

WE ASK GOD TO GRANT US STRENGTH TO LEAD A GODLY LIFE.

Summary
God wants His name to be hallowed or made holy by us.
God's name is hallowed when we speak and teach His Word truthfully.

God's name is hallowed when we lead a godly life according to God's Word.

Only God can make is possible for us to hallow His name.

What do we ask of God when we pray, "Hallowed be thy name"?

WE ASK GOD TO GRANT THAT WE TEACH HIS WORD TRUTHFULLY AND THAT WE LEAD A GODLY LIFE ACCORDING TO IT.

What This Means to Me

When I pray, "Hallowed be thy name," I am asking God to grant that I always speak His Word in all its truth and purity just as He has given it to us in the Bible. When I pray this petition, I am also asking God to grant that all I say and do will be God-pleasing and according to His Word.

For Me to Memorize

The First Petition
Assigned Bible passages

For Me to Do

Mark is ready to leave for a week's vacation at a summer camp. Before he leaves home he prays, "Our Father who art in heaven, hallowed be thy name." He is thinking especially of his week at the camp in his prayer. What is he asking of God in that short prayer?

Karen is a teacher of a Sunday school class. Before she begins teaching her children, she prays, "Our Father who art in heaven, hallowed be thy name." She is thinking especially of the Word of God she is about to teach as she prays that prayer. What is she asking of God in her prayer?

52. THE KINGDOM OF GOD

THE SECOND PETITION
Thy kingdom come.

For Me to Learn

What is meant with the kingdom of God?

For Me to Remember

From what did Jesus redeem us with His suffering and death? (A. From all iniquity or sin)

Whose people did Christ want us to become through His work of redemption? (A. God's people)
In whose kingdom does He want us to live? (A. God's kingdom)
Titus 2:13,14. *Jesus Christ . . . gave himself for us to redeem us from all wickedness and to purify for himself a people that are his very own, eager to do what is good.*

Where are we told what Christ has done for us? (A. In the Gospel)
How do we become members of the kingdom of God? (A. By believing the Gospel)
Mark 1:15. *The kingdom of God is near. Repent and believe the good news!*
What does God in His grace do for those who believe the Gospel of salvation? (A. Forgives their sins) Thereby they become members of God's kingdom.

What is meant with the kingdom of God?

WITH THE KINGDOM OF GOD IS MEANT GOD'S RULE OVER ALL BELIEVERS ON EARTH.

Where will Jesus take all believers on the last day of the world? (A. To heaven)
Over whom will Jesus rule in heaven? (A. Over His saints)
Matthew 25:34. *The King will say to those on his right, "Come, you who are blessed by my Father, take your inheritance, the kingdom prepared for you since the creation of the world."*

What is meant with the kingdom of God?

WITH THE KINGDOM OF GOD IS MEANT GOD'S RULE OVER HIS SAINTS IN HEAVEN.

Summary
Christ established His kingdom by suffering and dying.
He redeemed us to make us His own and to make us members of God's kingdom. On earth God rules in our hearts with His Word. In heaven God will rule over us and all saints.

What, then, is meant with God's kingdom?

WITH GOD'S KINGDOM WE MEAN GOD'S RULE OVER THE BELIEVERS ON EARTH AND IN HEAVEN.

What This Means to Me
Jesus Christ suffered and died to redeem me and make me His own.

The Holy Spirit gives me faith to believe the Gospel of salvation. God in His grace forgives me my sins and thus makes me a member of His Kingdom of Grace. The Holy Spirit keeps me in faith through the Gospel. On the Last Day Jesus will take me and all believers to heaven.

For Me to Memorize
Assigned Bible passages

53. THE SECOND PETITION

Thy kingdom come.

What does this mean?
God's kingdom certainly comes by itself even without our prayer, but we pray in this petition that it may come to us and to many others.

How does God's kingdom come?
God's kingdom comes when our heavenly Father gives his Holy Spirit, so that by his grace we believe his holy Word and lead a godly life now on earth and forever in heaven.

For Me to Learn
What do we ask of God when we pray, "Thy kingdom come"?

For Me to Remember
Who belongs to the Kingdom of Grace? (A. All believers in the Savior)
What can we not do with our own will or strength? (A. Believe God's Word and become members of the Kingdom of Grace)
Who gives us faith to believe?
1 Corinthians 12:3. *No one can say, "Jesus is Lord," except by the Holy Spirit.*
The Kingdom of Grace comes to those whom the Holy Spirit brings to faith in the Savior.
Who are members of the Kingdom of Glory? (A. All people who die believing in the Savior)
What can we not do with our own will or strength? (A. Remain faithful to our Savior)

Who alone can keep us faithful to the end?
2 Timothy 4:18. *The Lord will rescue me from every evil attack and will bring me safely to his heavenly kingdom.*
The Kingdom of Glory comes to those whom the Holy Spirit keeps in faith to the end.

What do we ask of God when we pray, "Thy kingdom come"?

WE ASK GOD TO GIVE US THE HOLY SPIRIT SO THAT WE BELIEVE HIS WORD TO THE END OF OUR LIVES.

How do believers show their faith? (A. By leading a godly life)
Colossians 2:6. *As you received Christ Jesus as Lord, continue to live in him.*
What can we not do with our own will and strength? (A. Good works that please God)
Who only can give us the will and strength to live godly lives? (A. The Holy Spirit)
What do we call the good works that please God? (A. Fruits of the Spirit)
Name some good works.
Galatians 5:22,23. *The fruit of the Spirit is love, joy, peace, patience, kindness, goodness, faithfulness, gentleness and self-control.*
God's kingdom comes to us when the Holy Spirit causes us to live God-pleasing lives.

What do we ask of God when we pray, "Thy kingdom come"?

WE ASK GOD TO GIVE US HIS HOLY SPIRIT, SO THAT WE LEAD GODLY LIVES.

Summary

God's kingdom comes to us when God gives us His Holy Spirit, so that we believe His holy Word and lead a godly life according to it, and finally when He takes us to heaven.

What, then, do we ask of God when we pray, "Thy kingdom come"?

WE ASK GOD TO GIVE US HIS HOLY SPIRIT SO THAT WE BELIEVE HIS WORD TO THE END AND LEAD GODLY LIVES

What This Means to Me

I am a member of God's Kingdom of Grace because the Holy Spirit brought me to faith in Jesus, my Savior. Whenever I pray, "Thy kingdom come," I ask God to keep me in the faith and finally to take me to heaven. I also pray that many people throughout the world become and remain members of the kingdom of God. This is the prayer Jesus has asked all believers to pray.

Matthew 9:38. *Ask the Lord of the harvest . . . to send out workers into his harvest field.*

For Me to Memorize
The Second Petition
Assigned Bible passages

For Me to Do
Richard's little sister is being baptized. He prays, "Our Father in heaven, thy kingdom come." What is Richard asking of God?

Janet is attending a mission festival service. What may she be asking of God as she prays the Second Petition of the Lord's Prayer?

54. THE WILL OF GOD

THE THIRD PETITION
Thy will be done on earth as it is in heaven.

For Me to Learn
What God's will is

For Me to Remember
What does it mean to "will" something? (A. To want something done)
Parents and teachers want their will done by their children.
God wants His will done on earth. He has given us His Word to read and hear.
What is His will? (A. That we learn His Word and be saved)
1 Timothy 2:3,4. *God our Savior . . . wants all men to be saved and to come to a knowledge of the truth.*

In whom does God want us to believe? (A. In His Son, our Savior)
What does God want to give to all who believe in His Son? (A. Everlasting life)
John 6:40. *My Father's will is that everyone who looks to the Son and believes in him shall have eternal life, and I will raise him up at the last day.*

What, then, is God's will?

GOD'S WILL IS EVERYTHING THAT GOD WANTS TO DO TO SAVE US.

What kind of life does God want us to lead? (A. A holy life)
1 Thessalonians 4:3. *It is God's will that you should be holy.*
A holy life is a sanctified life.
Where has God told us what He wants us to do and to avoid in order to lead holy lives? (A. In His commandments)

What, then, is God's will?

GOD'S WILL IS EVERYTHING THAT GOD WANTS US TO DO AND TO AVOID ACCORDING TO HIS COMMANDMENTS.

We all experience many things during our lifetime. We have joys and sorrows, health and sickness. Whose will is it that we have those experiences? (A. God's will)
They are God's good and gracious will and are meant for our good. Romans 8:28. *We know that in all things God works for the good of those who love him.*

What, then, is God's will?

GOD'S WILL IS EVERYTHING THAT GOD WANTS US TO EXPERIENCE DURING OUR LIFE ON EARTH.

Summary
It is God's will to save us.
It is God's will that we show our love for Him.
It is God's will that we accept His loving guidance in our life.

What, then, is God's will?

GOD'S WILL IS EVERYTHING THAT GOD WANTS FOR OUR GOOD.

What This Means to Me
My loving God wills only that which is good for me. He wants me to hear and believe His Word. He wants to give me faith to believe His Word, so that He can give me everlasting life. He wants me to have the joy of showing my love for Him by leading a God-pleasing life. He wants me to believe that my life is in His hands and that everything that happens in my life is for my good.

For Me to Memorize
Assigned Bible passages

For Me to Prepare for the Next Lesson
Read the Bible story "The Temptation by the Devil" (Genesis 3:1-6).
What did the devil tempt the woman to believe would not happen if she ate of the forbidden fruit?
What lie did he tell her?
What did the devil tempt both the woman and the man to do?
Whom had they obeyed?
Whom had they disobeyed?

55. THE THIRD PETITION

Thy will be done on earth as it is in heaven.

What does this mean?
God's good and gracious will certainly is done without our prayer, but we pray in this petition that it may be done among us also.

How is God's will done?
God's will is done when he breaks and defeats every evil plan and purpose of the devil, the world and our sinful flesh, which try to prevent us from keeping God's name holy and letting his kingdom come. And God's will is done when he strengthens and keeps us firm in his Word and in the faith as long as we live. This is his good and gracious will.

For Me to Learn
What we ask of God when we pray, "Thy will be done on earth as it is in heaven"?

For Me to Remember
Whose enemy is the devil? (A. God's enemy and man's enemy)
What did he tempt Adam and Eve to do? (A. To disobey God, to sin)
What does the devil try to make Christians do ever since he caused Adam and Eve to sin? (A. To sin and to lose their salvation)
1 Peter 5:8. *Be self-controlled and alert. Your enemy the devil prowls around like a roaring lion looking for someone to devour.*
The devil tries to prevent us from hallowing God's name and from letting His kingdom come.

How does the wicked world try to make us sin? (A. By tempting us to love sinful things in the world)
1 John 2:15. *Do not love the world or anything in the world. If*

anyone loves the world, the love of the Father is not in him.
The wicked and godless people of the world try to prevent us from hallowing God's name and from letting His kingdom come.

What do our sinful mind and flesh try to make us do? (A. Sin)
What can we not do with our own strength and will? (A. Please God)
Romans 8:7. *The sinful mind is hostile to God. It does not submit to God's law, nor can it do so.*
Our sinful mind and flesh try to prevent us from hallowing God's name and from letting His kingdom come.
Who overcame the devil? (A. Jesus Christ)
1 John 3:8. *The reason the Son of God appeared was to destroy the devil's work.*
Who can defeat the evil will and plans of the devil, the wicked world, and our sinful flesh? (A. God)

What, then, do we ask of God when we pray, "Thy will be done on earth as it is in heaven"?

WE ASK GOD TO PREVENT THE ENEMIES OF OUR SOULS FROM HARMING US.

Why was Stephen able to remain steadfast in his faith to the end? (A. God kept him faithful.)
What is only God able to do for us to the end of our lives? (A. Keep us in faith)
1 Peter 1:5. *Through faith [you] are shielded by God's power until the coming of the salvation.*
It is God's good and gracious will that we remain in the faith and have eternal salvation.

What, then, do we ask of God when we pray, "Thy will be done on earth as it is in heaven"?

WE ASK GOD TO KEEP US IN THE TRUE FAITH TO THE END.

Summary

We have three enemies who try to prevent us from keeping God's name holy and from letting His kingdom come.
We cannot overcome these enemies with our own strength.
We pray God to hinder the enemies of our souls from carrying out their evil will and plans.
We pray God to keep us steadfast in the faith to the end.

What, then, do we ask of God when we pray, "Thy will be done on earth as it is in heaven"?

WE ASK GOD TO HINDER THE ENEMIES OF OUR SOUL AND TO KEEP US IN THE TRUE FAITH.

What This Means to Me
God wants me and all people to hear and believe His holy Word, so that we will have everlasting life. That is His good and gracious will. The devil, the world, and my sinful flesh try very hard to keep me from hearing, learning, and believing God's Word and from inheriting everlasting life in heaven. When I pray, "Our Father in heaven, thy will be done on earth as it is in heaven," I ask God to defeat the evil plans and purposes of my enemies and to keep me in the true faith to the end.

For Me to Memorize
Assigned Bible passages
The Third Petition

For Me to Do
Mary has just been confirmed. She thinks very seriously about the vow she made to remain faithful to her Lord and Savior. She prays, "Our Father who art in heaven, thy will be done." What is she asking of God in her prayer?

John heard that his synod would like to do mission work in a certain country in Asia, but the state authorities who are not Christians are making it very difficult for his synod to establish mission stations there. John prays, "Our Father in heaven, thy will be done." What is he asking of God in his prayer?

For Me to Prepare for the Next Lesson
Use the Review and Study Guide (Number 56) to prepare for the next lesson. Write the answers on a sheet of paper and study them.

56. REVIEW AND STUDY GUIDE

(Lessons 46 - 55)

I. Complete
Complete these sentences.

1. Prayer is an act of ....
2. We .... to God when we pray to Him.
3. A prayer for help is called a ....
4. In our prayers of .... and .... we tell God that we are thankful for His goodness and mercy.
5. God has .... us to pray to Him.
6. God has .... to hear our prayers.
7. We should pray to God for all our ....
8. We should also .... Him for hearing our prayers.
9. God is our Father through faith in ....
10. We should pray to God .... and ....

II. Answer
Answer these questions.

1. When can we pray to God?
2. Where can we pray to God?
3. What is God eager and willing to do?
4. In whose name should we pray?
5. What do we call the prayer that Jesus gave us to pray?
6. How many petitions are in the Lord's Prayer?
7. To whom do we speak in the Lord's Prayer?
8. Who made us children of God?
9. What did Jesus do to make God our loving Father?
10. Who only can pray the Lord's Prayer and be heard by God?

III. *Choose*
Complete these sentences with words you choose from the list at the right.

1. The .... gives God many names.
2. The name of God means everything that God .... us about Himself
3. The name of God means every name that .... for God.
4. Two names that stand for God are .... and ....
5. To hallow means to make ....
6. We hallow God's name when we lead a .... life.
7. We hallow God's name when we teach His ....
8. The kingdom of God includes all people who .... in Jesus as their Savior.
9. God's kingdom of Glory is ....
10. God's will is .... and ....

tells
holy
godly
stands
Bible
Word
Lord
good
Christ
heaven
gracious
believe

IV. *Choose*
In which petition do we ask our Father in heaven

1. to keep us in the true faith to the end?
2. to grant that we teach His Word in truth and purity?
3. to overcome our enemies, the devil, the world, and our sinful flesh?
4. to give us His Holy Spirit, so that we believe His holy Word?
5. to give us strength to lead a godly life?

For Me to Prepare for the Next Lesson
Read the Bible story "Jacob's Vow" (Genesis 28:10-22).
  What did God promise Jacob?
  What did Jacob promise God?

Read the Bible story "Jacob in Laban's Employ" (Genesis 29:15 - 31:16) in your Bible history book.
  How had God blessed Jacob while he was away from home?

57. OUR DAILY BREAD

THE FOURTH PETITION
Give us this day our daily bread.

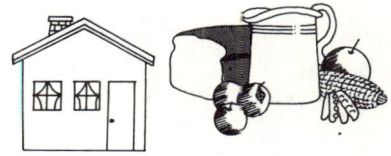

For Me to Learn
   What is meant by daily bread?

For Me to Remember
   For what did Jacob depend on God after he left home? (A. Food, shelter, clothing)
   What word in the Lord's Prayer means food, shelter, and clothing? (A. Bread)
   Psalm 37:25. *I was young and now I am old, yet I have never seen the righteous forsaken or their children begging bread.*
   Food, clothing, and shelter are important bodily needs. We need them every day.

What, then, is meant with daily bread?

DAILY BREAD IS EVERYTHING THAT WE NEED FOR OUR BODY.

What did God provide for Jacob while he was away from home? (A. A home and work)
How did God bless his works? (A. He gave him a family, cattle, servants)
To whom did Jacob give credit for all he had received? (A. God)
Genesis 32:10. *I am unworthy of all the kindness and faithfulness you have shown your servant.*
The work and cattle that God provided were means by which Jacob and his family were able to make a living. They were needed for their life. The explanation of the word "bread" in this petition mentions many things that God gives us for our life.

What, then, is meant with daily bread?

DAILY BREAD IS EVERYTHING THAT WE NEED FOR OUR LIFE.

Summary

Daily bread is food, clothing, and shelter that we need every day for our bodies.

Daily bread is everything that we need for our life.

What, then, is meant with daily bread?

DAILY BREAD IS EVERYTHING WE NEED FOR OUR BODY AND LIFE.

What This Means to Me

Romans 8:32. *He who did not spare his own Son, but gave him up for us all — how will he not also, along with him, graciously give us all things?*

My Father in heaven is good and gracious. Through His Son He saved me and gives me eternal salvation. Daily He gives me what I need for this life.

Matthew 6:34. *Do not worry about tomorrow, for tomorrow will worry about itself. Each day has enough trouble of its own.*

I will plan and diligently do my work at home and in school, but I never have reason to worry, because my loving Father in heaven has promised to take care of me and to give me what is best for me. I should be satisfied with what He gives me, even if it isn't as much as others have. That is why I pray, "Give us *this day* our *daily* bread."

For Me to Memorize

Assigned Bible passages

Prayers before meals, "To Ask a Blessing"

Prayers after meals, "To say Grace"

For Me to Do

Are prayers spoken at mealtime in your home? If not, urge your parents that it be done. Use the prayers you have memorized. See also Hymns 659; 36:1; 575:1 (TLH).

For Me to Prepare for the Next Lesson

Read the Bible story "Jacob's Return" (Genesis 31:17 - 35:29) in your Bible history book.

What had God given Jacob during the twenty years he was in Mesopotamia? To whom did he give credit for all his possessions?

Read the Bible story "The Ten Lepers" (Luke 17:11-19).

How many lepers did Jesus heal?

How many thanked Jesus for His goodness?

58. THE FOURTH PETITION

Give us this day our daily bread.

What does this mean?
God surely gives daily bread without our asking, even to all the wicked, but we pray in this petition that he would lead us to realize this and to receive our daily bread with thanksgiving.

What then is meant by daily bread?
Daily bread includes everything that we need for our bodily welfare, such as food and drink, clothing and shoes, house and home, fields and flocks, money and goods, a godly family, good workers, good government, honest leaders, good citizens, good weather, peace and order, health, a good name, loyal friends and good neighbors.

For Me to Learn
What do we ask of God when we pray, "Give us this day our daily bread"?

For Me to Remember
Jacob returned to Canaan with many possessions. Whom did Jacob give credit for all that he had received?
How did he show his appreciation to God? (A. He said that it was due only to God's goodness that he had any possessions.)
From whom do we receive everything we have?
James 1:17. Every good and perfect gift is from above, coming down from the Father of the heavenly lights.
What will we do when we believe that God gives us everything we have? (A. We will appreciate our possessions as gifts from God.)
Psalm 34:8. Taste and see that the Lord is good.

What do we ask of God when we pray, "Give us this day our daily bread"?

WE ASK GOD TO LEAD US TO RECOGNIZE AND APPRECIATE HIS BLESSINGS.

What did one leper do to show his appreciation to Jesus for healing him? (A. He thanked Jesus.)
What will we do when we recognize and appreciate God's blessings? Psalm 106:1. *Give thanks to the Lord, for he is good; his love endures forever.*
Whose help do we need to lead us to thank God for His goodness and mercy?

What, then, do we ask of God when we pray, "Give us this day our daily bread"?

WE ASK GOD TO LEAD US TO THANK HIM FOR HIS BLESSINGS.

Summary

Daily bread in the Fourth Petition means all the earthly and bodily blessings we receive from God.
When we pray God to give us daily bread, we ask Him to lead us to appreciate His many blessings.
When we pray God to give us daily bread, we ask Him to lead us to thank Him for His many blessings.

What, then, do we ask of God when we pray, "Give us this day our daily bread"?

WE ASK GOD TO LEAD US TO APPRECIATE AND RECEIVE WITH THANKSGIVING HIS MANY BLESSINGS.

What This Means to Me

When I pray, "Give us this day our daily bread," I ask God to provide me and all people with necessary food, clothing, and shelter. Also I ask God to lead me to appreciate and to be satisfied with the blessings He gives me. I also pray God to lead me to thank Him for everything He gives me.

For Me to Memorize

The Fourth Petition
Assigned Bible passages

For Me to Do

Jason's father is a farmer. As Jason and his father sow wheat on their farm, Jason thinks of all the people in the world who are in need of food. He prays, "Give us this day our daily bread." What may Jason be asking of God in his prayer?

The times are hard. Many people are without work. Lora's father still has work in a furniture factory, but he does not know how long he will be able to work there. Lora prays, "Give us this day our daily bread." What may she be asking of God in her prayer?

59. OUR TRESPASSES

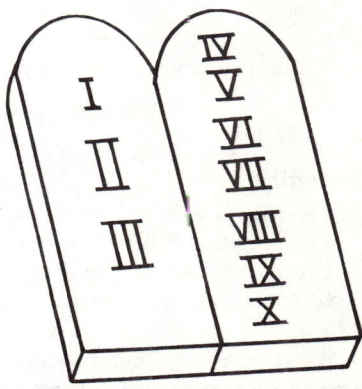

THE FIFTH PETITION
And forgive us our trespasses as we forgive those who trespass against us.

For Me to Learn
What are trespasses?

For Me to Remember
What is another name for trespasses? (A. Sins)
What trespasses come from our hearts? (A. Evil thoughts)
Matthew 15:19. *Out of the heart come evil thoughts.*
What does God forbid? (A. Evil or sinful thoughts)
Matthew 9:4. *Knowing their thoughts, Jesus said, "Why do you entertain evil thoughts in your hearts?"*
Against what do we trespass when we have sinful thoughts? (A. God's Law)

What, then, are trespasses?

TRESPASSES ARE SINFUL THOUGHTS.

What kind of speaking does God forbid? (A. Evil or sinful speaking)
Against what do we trespass when we use sinful words and talk? (A. God's Law)
1 Peter 3:10. *Whoever would love life and see good days must keep his tongue from evil and his lips from deceitful speech.*
Against what do we trespass when we use sinful talk and words? (A. God Law)

What, then, are trespasses?

TRESPASSES ARE SINFUL WORDS.

313

Even though we are children of God, we still have sinful hearts.
What may come out of our sinful hearts?
Matthew 15:19. *Out of the heart come evil thoughts, murder, adultery, sexual immorality, theft, false testimony, slander.*
What may our sinful hearts make us do? (A. Think sinful thoughts and commit sinful acts)
Against what do we trespass when we commit sinful acts? (A. God's Law)

What, then, are trespasses?

TRESPASSES ARE SINFUL ACTS.

Summary
Trespasses are sinful thoughts.
Trespasses are sinful words.
Trespasses are sinful deeds.
Sinful thoughts, words, and deeds are transgressions of God's Law.

What, then, is meant with trespasses?

TRESPASSES ARE TRANSGRESSIONS OF GOD'S LAW.

What This Means to Me

I know that I have not kept the Ten Commandments. I have sinned many times by having sinful thoughts, by speaking evil, and by doing sinful things. My trespasses or sins are many and great. I deserve God's anger and punishment. I cannot save myself from God's punishment, but God in His great love sent His Son Jesus to earth to endure the punishment for my trespasses. I will always want to thank God for saving me and will want to show my love for Him by obeying His Law.

For Me to Memorize

Assigned Bible passages

For Me to Prepare for the Next Lesson

Read the Bible story "The Unmerciful Servant" (Matthew 18:21-35).
  Why did the servant beg for mercy?
  What did the king then do?
  Why did the king later punish the servant?

60. THE FIFTH PETITION

And forgive us our trespasses as we forgive those who trespass against us.

What does this mean?

We pray in this petition that our Father in heaven would not look upon our sins or because of them deny our prayers; for we are worthy of none of the things for which we ask, neither have we deserved them, but we ask that he would give them all to us by grace; for we daily sin much and surely deserve nothing but punishment.

So we too will forgive from the heart and gladly do good to those who sin against us.

For Me to Learn

What do we ask of God when we pray, "Forgive us our trespasses as we forgive those who trespass against us"?

For Me to Remember

How are we and all people by nature? (A. Sinful)
Romans 7:18. *I know that nothing good lives in me, that is, in my sinful nature.*
We do not deserve the things for which we pray.
What do we deserve from God? (A. Punishment)
On what must we depend to free us from our sins? (A. God's mercy)
Luke 18:13. *God, have mercy on me, a sinner.*
For whose sake is God merciful to us? (A. For Jesus' sake)

What do we ask of God when we pray, "Forgive us our trespasses"?

WE ASK GOD TO FORGIVE OUR SINS.

What can we not earn with our good works? (A. Forgiveness of sins)
Neither can we earn forgiveness from God by first forgiving our neighbor's wrongs or sins.
Who receives forgiveness from God? (A. All who have faith in Jesus as their Savior)
How will that faith show itself when a neighbor wrongs us? (A. We will forgive the neighbor's sins.)
Matthew 6:14,15. *If you forgive men when they sin against you, your heavenly Father will also forgive you. But if you do not forgive men their sins, your Father will not forgive your sins.*

What may try to keep us from forgiving our neighbor's sins? (A. Our sinful heart and the devil)
Who only can move us to forgive our neighbor and to do good to him? (A. God)

What do we ask of God when we pray, "Forgive us our trespasses as we forgive those who trespass against us"?

WE ASK GOD TO MOVE US TO FORGIVE OUR NEIGHBOR AS GOD HAS FORGIVEN US.

Summary
God is merciful to us sinners for Jesus' sake.
We ask God to forgive us our sins for Jesus' sake.
We ask God to move us to forgive our neighbor when he sins against us.

What, then, do we ask of God when we pray, "Forgive us our trespasses as we forgive those who trespass against us"?

WE ASK GOD TO FORGIVE OUR SINS AND TO MOVE US TO FORGIVE OUR NEIGHBOR.

What This Means to Me
I am a sinner and do not deserve any of the things for which I pray. When I pray this petition, I ask God not to look upon my sins and not to deny my prayers because of my sins. I ask God to be gracious to me and to forgive me all my sins for Jesus' sake. I also ask God to give me a forgiving heart, especially when my neighbor sins against me.

For Me to Memorize
The Fifth Petition
Assigned Bible passages

For Me to Do
James knows that he is a sinner and that he has sinned against God's commandments many times. He does not know all the times he has trespassed God's Law. He prays, "Dear Father in heaven, forgive me my trespasses." What is he asking of God?

Susan and Alice quarreled on the way home from school. Both girls became very angry at each other. That evening Susan thought very seriously about the quarrel and what had been said. She realized that she and Alice had sinned, and she was sorry for her sin. She prayed,

"Our Father in heaven, forgive us our trespasses as we forgive those who trespass against us." What did Susan ask of God in her prayers? How will Susan show her faith in the forgiveness she received from God?

For Me to Prepare for the Next Lesson

Read the Bible story "The Temptation of Adam and Eve" (Genesis 3:1-6).
What had God forbidden Adam and Eve to do?
What lie did the devil tell Eve?
What did the devil tempt Eve to do?

Read the Bible story "Joseph Tempted by Potiphar's Wife" (Genesis 39:1-20).
Who blessed Joseph in Egypt?
Who wanted to make Joseph sin?
What did Joseph do when she tempted him to commit adultery?

61. OUR TEMPTATIONS

THE SIXTH PETITION
And lead us not into temptation.

For Me to Learn

What is meant with temptations?

For Me to Remember

What did the devil try to make Eve do? (A. To disobey God, to sin)
What was he able to do by his efforts? (A. He made Eve sin.)
1 Peter 5:8,9. *Be self-controlled and alert. Your enemy the devil prowls around like a roaring lion looking for someone to devour. Resist him, standing firm in the faith.*

What are temptations?

TEMPTATIONS ARE EFFORTS OF THE DEVIL TO MAKE CHRISTIANS SIN AND TO LEAD THEM AWAY FROM GOD.

What did Potiphar's wife try to do? (A. She tried to make Joseph sin.)
What kind of a woman was she? (A. A wicked woman of the world)
What do the people of the world try to make us do? (A. To make us sin and lead us away from God)
Proverbs 1:10. *My son, if sinners entice you, do not give in to them.*

What are temptations?

TEMPTATIONS ARE EFFORTS OF THE WORLD TO MAKE US SIN AND TO LEAD US AWAY FROM GOD.

What do our sinful lusts or desires try to do? (A. Tempt us to sin and to draw us away from God)
James 1:14. *Each one is tempted when, by his own evil desire, he is dragged away and enticed.*
What comes out of our sinful hearts? (A. Evil or sinful thoughts and deeds)
Matthew 15:19. *Out of the heart come evil thoughts, murder, adultery, sexual immorality, theft, false testimony, slander.*
What does our sinful nature tempt us to do? (A. To disobey God)
Galatians 5:17. *The sinful nature desires what is contrary to the Spirit.*

What are temptations?

TEMPTATIONS ARE EFFORTS OF OUR SINFUL FLESH TO MAKE US SIN AND TO LEAD US AWAY FROM GOD.

Summary

The devil tempts us when he tries to make us sin and to lead us away from God.
The wicked world tempts us when it tries to make us sin and to lead us away from God.
Our sinful flesh tempts us when it tries to make us sin and to lead us away from God.

What, then, is meant with temptations?

TEMPTATIONS ARE EFFORTS OF THE DEVIL, THE WORLD, AND OUR FLESH TO MAKE US SIN AND TO LEAD US AWAY FROM GOD.

What This Means to Me

God made me his child through Baptism. He wants me to remain in faith and to go to heaven when I die. The devil is God's enemy. He wants to take me away from God and to make me suffer in hell. He does that by trying to make me disobey God's commandments. He has some strong helpers that also try to tempt me to sin. They are the wicked people of the world and my sinful heart. All three are powerful enemies, and they are constantly tempting me. I need God's help to overcome them. That is why Jesus taught us to pray, "Father . . . lead us not into temptation."

For Me to Memorize
Assigned Bible passages

62. THE SIXTH PETITION

And lead us not into temptation.

What does this mean?
God surely tempts no one to sin, but we pray in this petition that God would guard and keep us, so that the devil, the world and our flesh may not deceive us or lead us into false belief, despair and other great and shameful sins; and though we are tempted by them, we pray that we may overcome and win the victory.

For Me to Learn
What do we ask of God when we pray, "And lead us not into temptation"?

For Me to Remember
What does God not tempt us to do? (A. Evil)
1 Peter 5:8. *Be self-controlled and alert. Your enemy the devil prowls around like a roaring lion looking for someone to devour.*
To what can the devil be compared? (A. To a vicious lion)
How does he devour people? (A. By making them sin)
What can we not do of ourselves? (A. Keep the devil from tempting us)
What can God do so that we are not tempted to sin? (A. He can keep temptations away from us.)
2 Thessalonians 3:3. *The Lord is faithful, and he will strengthen and protect you from the evil one.*

What do we ask of God when we pray, "And lead us not into temptation"?

WE ASK GOD TO KEEP TEMPTATIONS AWAY FROM US.

How does God help us when we are tempted? (A. He gives us a way to escape or overcome temptations.)

1 Corinthians 10:13. *God is faithful; he will not let you be tempted beyond what you can bear. But when you are tempted, he will also provide a way out so that you can stand up under it.*

What is the armor or protection that God has given us to defend ourselves against temptations? (A. His Word)
Ephesians 6:13. *Put on the full armor of God, so that when the day of evil comes, you may be able to stand your ground.*
What is the weapon that God has given us to overcome temptations and to gain the victory? (A. His Word)
Ephesians 6:17. *Take the helmet of salvation and the sword of the Spirit, which is the word of God.*

What do we ask of God when we pray, "And lead us not into temptation"?

WE ASK GOD TO GIVE US VICTORY OVER OUR ENEMIES.

Summary

Our enemies are the devil, the world, and our sinful flesh. They tempt us when they try to deceive us and try to lead us into false belief, despair over sins, and other great and shameful sins. Without God's help we are powerless against the temptations of our enemies.
We pray God to keep temptations away from us.
We pray God to give us victory over our enemies whenever they tempt us.

What, then, do we ask of God when we pray, "And lead us not into temptation"?

WE ASK GOD TO KEEP TEMPTATIONS AWAY FROM US AND TO GIVE US VICTORY OVER OUR ENEMIES.

What This Means to Me

I am God's child through faith in Christ Jesus, but the devil, the wicked world, and my sinful flesh want to take me away from God. They try to do that by tempting me to sin. The devil tempts me when he puts sinful thoughts into my mind. The wicked world tempts me when evil-minded people try to make me sin. My sinful flesh tempts me by putting sinful desires into my mind and urging me to say or do sinful things.

God is stronger than my enemies who want me to sin. God has given me His Word to overcome temptations. When I hear and read God's Word, my faith is made strong, so that with the help of God I can resist temptations. I pray, "Increase my faith, dear Father in heaven."

For Me to Memorize
   The Sixth Petition
   Assigned Bible passages

For Me to Do
   June is writing a history test. She does not know the answers to several questions. The information she needs is on a paper in her desk. She is tempted to glance at the paper when the teacher is not looking her way. She prays, "Dear Father in heaven, lead me not into temptation." What is she asking of God in her prayer?

   Kenneth will spend a week at a boys' camp. There he will take part in many planned activities. The boys will also have some free time when they are on their own. Kenneth knows that the devil will be at camp also. Kenneth prays, "Dear Father in heaven, lead us not into temptation." What is Kenneth asking of God in his prayer?

63. EVILS OF THE WORLD

THE SEVENTH PETITION
But deliver us from evil.

For Me to Learn
What is meant with evil?

For Me to Remember
   How was everything that God made when He created the world? Genesis 1:31. *God saw all that he had made, and it was very good.*

   How did evil come into the world? (A. Adam and Eve sinned.)
   How is the world now? (A. Wicked)
   1 John 5:19. *The whole world is under the control of the evil one.*
   Sin is the cause of all that is evil in the world.
   Name some evils that our bodies may have to endure. (Sickness, pain, hunger, thirst, blindness)
   These and other ailments are harmful to the body.

   What is meant with evil?

AN EVIL IS SOMETHING THAT IS HARMFUL TO OUR BODY.

   Name some evils that our soul may have to endure. (A. Sin, despair over sin, false belief, unbelief, grief, fear)
   These and other evils are harmful to the soul.

What is meant with evil?

AN EVIL IS SOMETHING THAT IS HARMFUL TO OUR SOUL.

Name some evils that may come to our property. (A. Robbery, theft, fraud, fire, storms, riots)
These and other evils are harmful to our property.

What is meant with evil?

AN EVIL IS SOMETHING THAT IS HARMFUL TO OUR PROPERTY.

Name some evils that may affect our reputation or good name. (A. Lying, slandering, defaming, betraying)
These and other evils are harmful to our reputation.

What is meant with evil?

AN EVIL IS SOMETHING THAT IS HARMFUL TO OUR REPUTATION.

Summary
Sin is the cause of all evil in the world.
Evil is harmful to our body, soul, property, and reputation.

What, then, is meant with evil?

EVIL MEANS EVERYTHING THAT IS HARMFUL TO OUR BODY, SOUL, PROPERTY, AND REPUTATION.

What This Means to Me

Sin brought evil into God's perfect and beautiful world. I cannot help seeing the results of sin. The newspaper, radio, and TV report many evils that people must endure, such as deaths, wars, famines, fires, storms, accidents. I hear and read how the devil has tempted people to commit crimes and how he has led people into false belief and unbelief. Fear comes to my heart when I think about all the evil in the world, for I know that I may also have to endure some evils. I pray God to keep evils away from me and to help me endure them when He permits them to come to me.

For Me to Memorize
Assigned Bible passages

For Me to Prepare for the Next Lesson
>Read the Bible story "Joseph in Prison" (Genesis 39).
>>What lie did Potiphar's wife tell about Joseph?
>>What did Potiphar do to Joseph?
>>How did God bless Joseph in prison?
>
>Read the Bible story "The Ten Lepers" (Luke 17:11-19).
>>What evil came to the ten people?
>>How did Jesus deliver them of that evil?

64. THE SEVENTH PETITION

But deliver us from evil.

What does this mean?
In conclusion we pray in this petition that our Father in heaven would deliver us from every evil that threatens body and soul, property and reputation, and finally when our last hour comes, grant us a blessed end and graciously take us from this world of sorrow to himself in heaven.

For Me to Learn
>What do we ask of God when we pray, "Deliver us from evil"?

For Me to Remember
>How did God deliver the Children of Israel from the plagues in Egypt? (A. He spared them or kept the plaques away from them.)
>How does God deliver us from many evils? (A. By keeping evils away from us)
>Psalm 91:10. *No harm will befall you, no disaster will come near your tent.*
>
>It is not God's will that we are spared from all evil. What will we have to endure before we enter the kingdom of God in heaven? (A. Tribulations or evils)
>Acts 14:22. *We must go through many hardships to enter the kingdom of God.*
>
>God delivers His children from evil by giving them strength to endure the evils. What purposes are these evils to serve? (A. To benefit the

believer by making him turn to the Lord for help)
Romans 8:28. *We know that in all things God works for the good of those who love him.*
How did God deliver the ten lepers from evil? (A. He cured them of their sickness.)
God often delivers us from evil by taking the evil away.

What do we ask of God when we pray, "But deliver us from evil"?

WE ASK GOD TO DELIVER US FROM ALL EVIL IN THIS WORLD.

From what will we never be free in this world? (A. Evil)
How will God deliver the believers from all evil forever? (A. When they die He will take them to heaven)
2 Timothy 4:18. *The Lord will rescue me from every evil attack and will bring me safely to his heavenly kingdom.*
What kind of an end will death be for the believers in the Savior? (A. A blessed end)
What will no longer trouble them in heaven? (A. Evils)
Revelation 21:4. *He will wipe every tear from their eyes. There will be no more death or mourning or crying or pain, for the old order of things has passed away.*

What do we ask of God when we pray, "But deliver us from evil"?

WE ASK GOD TO GIVE US A BLESSED END AND TO TAKE US TO HEAVEN.

Summary

In this petition we pray God to deliver us from evils while we are living in this world. We ask Him to do that by keeping evil away from us, by helping us to endure evil that comes to us, by turning evil to our good, or by taking evil away from us.
We especially ask God to deliver us from all evil when we die and to take us to heaven.

What, then, do we ask of God when we pray, "But deliver us from evil"?

WE PRAY GOD TO DELIVER US FROM EVERY EVIL IN THIS WORLD AND TO TAKE US TO HEAVEN WHEN WE DIE.

What This Means to Me

This world is filled with many kinds of evil. Some of those evils may come to me and my loved ones, but I know that Jesus is always near to help and strengthen His children when they have troubles. When I am fearful or troubled by any evil, I will pray, "Dear Jesus, deliver me from this evil." I know and believe that He will answer my prayer in the way that is best for me. I also believe that He will give me and all believers a blessed end and take us to heaven where there is no evil.

For Me to Memorize
The Seventh Petition
Assigned Bible passages

For Me to Do
John and his parents live on a farm that borders on a river. Several days of heavy rain have caused the water to rise to flood stage. John prays, "Dear Father in heaven, deliver us from evil." What is John asking of God in his prayer?

A serious sickness has been spreading through the city where Kathy lives. Many people are sick and some have died. Kathy prays, "Dear Father in heaven, deliver us from evil." What is she asking of God in her prayer?

65. THE DOXOLOGY

For thine is the kingdom and the power and the glory forever and ever. Amen.

What does this mean?
We can be sure that these petitions are acceptable to our Father in heaven and are heard by him, for he himself has commanded us so to pray and has promised to hear us. Therefore we say, "Amen," yes, it shall be so.

For Me to Learn
Why we can be certain that God can and will help us when we pray to Him

For Me to Remember
Over what is God king? (A. Heaven and earth)

What is included in His kingdom? (A. Everybody and everything)
What does God our King control and govern? (A. All things and all people)
What can we do when we need help? (A. Go to God our King in prayer)
Psalm 46:7. *The Lord Almighty is with us; the God of Jacob is our fortress.*

Why can we be certain that God can and will help us when we pray to Him?

GOD IS OUR KING WHO RULES HEAVEN AND EARTH.

What is God therefore able to do? (A. Anything)
What can He certainly do when we pray to Him?

Why can we be certain that God can and will help us when we pray to Him?

GOD IS ALL-POWERFUL.

God helps us not just because we pray to Him. We do not deserve anything from God.
For whose sake does He hear our prayers? (A. For Jesus' sake)
To whom does all glory belong for the answering of our petitions? (A. To God)
Psalm 79:9. *Help us, O God our Savior, for the glory of your name.*

ALL GLORY BELONGS TO GOD FOR GRANTING OUR PETITIONS.

Summary

Jesus taught me to pray the Lord's Prayer. I can pray to God because Jesus made God my heavenly Father by suffering and dying for my sins. When I pray to God, I do not just wish and hope that God will hear my prayer and help me. I believe that He will hear me and help me because He is my almighty King. And He has commanded me to pray and promised to hear me. God hears my prayers and helps me out of mercy for Jesus' sake. To God belongs all glory.

For Me to Memorize

The last four petitions and the Doxology (conclusion)
Assigned Bible passages

For Me to Prepare for the Next Lesson
Use the Review and Study Guide (Number 66) to prepare for the next lesson. Write the answers on a sheet of paper and study them.

66. REVIEW AND STUDY GUIDE

(Lessons 57 - 65)

I. *Answer*

Answer these questions.

1. In which petition do we ask God to forgive us our sins?
2. In which petition do we ask God to give us what we need for our body?
3. In which petition do we ask God to free us from the troubles of the world?
4. In which petition do we ask God to make us willing to forgive our neighbor?
5. In which petition do we ask God to give us victory over the devil, the world, and our sinful flesh?

II. *Complete*

Complete these sentences.

1. Trespasses are sinful ...., ..., ...
2. Trespasses are sins committed against God's ....
3. In the Fourth Petition "daily bread" means everything we need for our .... and ....
4. In the Fourth Petition we ask God to lead us to appreciate His ....
5. We are tempted by the ...., the .... and our ....
6. In the Sixth Petition we ask God to keep us from ....
7. In the Sixth Petition we ask God to give us .... over our enemies, the devil, the world, and our sinful flesh.
8. .... is the cause of all evil in the world.
9. Evil is harmful to our ...., ..., ..., and ....
10. In the Seventh Petition we ask God to deliver us from all .... and to take us to .... when we die.

III. *Choose*

Complete these sentences with words you choose from the list at the right.

1. God gives us the things we need for our body without our ....
2. God wants us to receive our bodily blessings with ....
3. We are to remember that .... takes care of all our bodily needs.
4. Another word for trespass is ....
5. We trespass God's Law when we have sinful ....
6. We ask God to be merciful to us and to forgive our sins for .... sake.
7. All who have .... in Jesus as their Savior receive forgiveness of sins.
8. Those who have faith in Jesus will forgive the sins their .... does against them.
9. We are always in danger of being .... to sin by our enemies.
10. We pray God to give us .... over the devil, the world, and our flesh.
11. We must endure many .... in this world.
12. We pray God to give us a .... end when we die.
13. In .... there will be no evils.
14. We can be certain that God will hear our prayers and help us because He is the almighty .... of heaven and earth.
15. .... means, "Yes, I believe that God hears my prayers and will answer them for Jesus' sake."

thanksgiving
Jesus'
sin
prayers
victory
thoughts
tempted
God
Amen
deeds
faith
words
neighbor
evils
blessed
King
heaven

SYMBOLS OF THE CHURCH

A symbol represents or stands for something. Church symbols are used to help us understand and recall teachings from God's Word.

The Triangle Symbol
The triangle is a symbol of the Triune (three-in-one) God. The equilateral triangle has three sides of the same length. The three sides represent or stand for the three persons in the Trinity or Triune God — the Father, the Son Jesus Christ, and the Holy Spirit. There are three distinct lines of equal length that form one triangle. Likewise there are three distinct and equal persons in the one true God.

The X P Symbol
The two Greek letters X P (Ki — ro) in this symbol are an abbreviation of the Greek name for Christ (X P I C T O C = Christos). The first two letters of the Greek word X P are the same as the first letters of the English word CHR (ist). The X P is a symbol for the promised Savior.

The Lamb of God Symbol
The lamb is a symbol of Jesus Christ: "the Lamb of God, who takes away the sin of the world" (John 1:29). The banner on the cross in a symbol of Christ's victory over death.

The Cup and Wafer Symbol
This is a symbol of Holy Communion. The circle with the cross stands for the body of Christ that is received in, with, and under the bread (wafer); the cup stands for the blood of Christ that is received in, with, and under the wine in Holy Communion.

The Shield of Faith Symbol
The shield with the cross is a symbol of the Christian faith in the crucified Savior. Jesus is the Christian's shield against the temptations of the devil, the world, and his sinful flesh.

The Hand of God Symbol
Many passages in the Bible speak about the hand of God. Psalm 139:10: "Your right hand will hold me fast." Isaiah 49:2: "In the shadow of his hand he hid me." The hand, then, is a symbol of God's power, help, and protection. This symbol can have other meanings also.

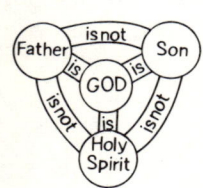

The Shield of the Trinity
The smaller circles represent the Father, the Son, and the Holy Spirit. On each of the curving bands are the words *is not* and on the short bands is the word *is*. The proper reading is, "The Father is God, the Son is God, and the Holy Spirit is God. But the Father is not the Son, the Son is not the Holy Spirit, and the Holy Spirit is not the Father."

The Lamp and Bible Symbol
The lamp on the open Bible is a symbol of the light of God's Word which guides us and shows us the way to eternal salvation. "Your Word is a lamp to my feet and a light for my path" (Psalm 119:105).

The Dove Symbol
The descending dove is a symbol of the Holy Spirit. At the Baptism of Jesus the Holy Spirit descended in the form of a dove and lighted on Jesus.

The Alpha and Omega Symbol
The letters alpha and omega are the first and last letters of the Greek alphabet. We use them in the church to signify that Jesus Christ is eternal. He is the beginning and end of all things. Christ says, "I am the Alpha and the Omega, the First and the Last, the Beginning and the End" (Revelation 22:13). When this symbol is used with the crown, it stands for the eternalness of the kingly office of Christ.

The Cross and Crown Symbol
The cross with the crown is a symbol of everlasting life through faith in Christ Jesus. The cross stands for the suffering and death that Christ endured to earn everlasting life for us. The crown stands for the reward of grace that Christ our King will give to all who remain faithful to Him. (Revelation 2:10)

The Butterfly Symbol
The butterfly is a symbol of the resurrection from death. The butterfly passes through several seemingly lifeless stages before it comes forth as a beautiful creature. On the Last Day Jesus will raise the lifeless bodies of the Christians from the grave and give them glorified bodies.

The Scallop Shell Symbol
The shell with the three drops is a symbol of the Baptism of Jesus and also of the Sacrament of Holy Baptism. The three drops of water stand for the three persons in the Holy Trinity, Father, Son, and Holy Spirit.

MARTIN LUTHER
1483 — 1546

Luther translating the New Testament

Luther is one of the great men in the history of the world. He was not a great ruler or great explorer or great scientist. But what Luther did is of greater importance than what was accomplished by many other famous people. Through Luther God again gave the world the complete and pure teachings of the Bible.

Martin Luther lived about 450 years ago. He was born on November 10, 1483, is Eisleben, Germany. At that time almost all people in Europe belonged to the Roman Catholic Church which was ruled by the Pope in Rome. Many of its teachings were not in agreement with what God says in His Word. The Roman Catholic Church taught the people that they must do many good works and say many prayers to the saints to be saved. They were told not to read the Bible, but to listen to the Pope and the priests explain the Bible for them and to obey the many rules of the Roman Catholic Church.

Martin Luther's parents were strict Catholics; so young Martin was also taught and brought up in the religion of the Roman Catholic Church. In the schools that he attended in Germany he did not learn to know Jesus as the loving Savior, but as a strict, stern judge.

After graduation from high school, Luther entered the University of Erfurt to study law in order to become a lawyer. Luther was a good student, but he was troubled because he thought that he was not doing enough praying and good works to satisfy Jesus. He feared that if he would die, he would be eternally damned. Therefore he entered the Augustinian Monastery in Erfurt. In the monastery he faithfully obeyed all rules and regulations. He prayed to the saints many hours every day; he went without food for days; he tortured himself with the hope of turning God's anger away from him. But he found no peace for his soul. Soon after he became a priest, he was asked to come to the University of Wittenberg to teach philosophy. Later he was appointed to teach the Scriptures to the students. This gave him great joy. He now spent more and more time studying the teachings of the Bible. It was during his studies of the Bible that God led Luther to see that man is not and cannot be saved by his own efforts, but that man is saved by faith in Jesus Christ as his only Savior.

In 1517 an incident took place in Wittenberg that marked the beginning of the Reformation and the return of the Word of God in its truth and purity to the people. A monk by the name of John Tetzel had been sent to the Wittenberg area to sell indulgences. Indulgences were papers that promised the buyers forgiveness and release from suffering in purgatory. Luther had spoken against the selling of indulgences several times, but this time he prepared 95 printed statements called theses and nailed them to the door of the Castle Church. That was on October

31, 1517, which we now call Reformation Day. In those theses Luther stated that forgiveness cannot be obtained from God by purchasing indulgences. Only sinners who repent of their sins and trust in Jesus Christ as their Savior are forgiven.

Luther wanted to discuss the sale of indulgences with learned men in the Roman Catholic Church, but the unexpected happened. His theses were copied and printed and then distributed all over Germany. Copies also reached Rome, the capital of the Roman Catholic Church. Many of the common people and most students at Wittenberg were pleased with Luther's statements, but the Pope and other leaders in the church were not. The Pope ordered Luther to be silent and not write anything more on the subject of indulgences. Several debates were arranged between Luther and important Catholic churchmen. It was during these debates that Luther came to realize that there were not just some differences of opinion between him and the leaders in the church, but that many of the teachings of the church were not Scriptural. They were man-made. They were false teachings. Luther, therefore, openly attacked the false teachings and practices of the Roman Catholic Church.

The Pope then excommunicated Luther. He was told to take back all he had said and written. If he would not obey, he would be subject to arrest and trial. Luther not only ignored the Pope's orders, but in the presence of townspeople and students he burned the letter of excommunication and many Catholic books.

In 1520 Luther was ordered to appear before the Emperor Charles V in the city of Worms. He again was asked to take back all he had said and written against the Pope and the Roman Catholic Church. It was there that Luther stated: "Unless I am convinced on the basis of what the Bible says, I cannot and will not take back what I have said or written." The emperor then outlawed Luther. That meant that he was to be considered an outlaw of the empire, subject to arrest and death.

Luther's friends feared for his safety, so with the help of the Elector of Saxony Luther was kept in hiding for ten months in the Wartburg Castle in Saxony. At the Wartburg Luther had much time for studying and writing. Here he began translating the Bible into the German language so that the common people could read and understand it.

After returning to Wittenberg, he did much teaching, preaching, and writing. His writings fill over 50 large volumes. He also wrote many songs, some of which are found in our hymn book. In 1529 he published a very important little book that we still use in our church and schools today — the Small Catechism. It is a summary of the main teachings of the Bible.

God blessed Martin Luther and his wife Katie with six children, one of whom died as a baby. Their home was a model Christian home. Even the students and visitors at the Luther home were expected to take part in prayer, Bible reading, Catechism study, and hymn singing.

Martin Luther worked hard to the end of his life. Besides writing, he taught religion in the university and preached several times a week. On February 18, 1546, he died at the age of 62 years, in Eisleben, Germany, the town where he was born. He was buried in the Castle Church in Wittenberg, where he had posted his 95 theses and where he had preached many times. He died believing that only through faith in Jesus Christ as the Savior can anyone be justified before God. Salvation is a gift of God's grace!